Network Security

NETWORK SECURITY

Pinkesh Anand

CENTRUM PRESS
NEW DELHI-110002 (INDIA)

CENTRUM PRESS
H.O.: 4360/4, Ansari Road, Daryaganj,
New Delhi-110002 (India)
Tel: 23278000, 23261597, 23255577, 23286875
B.O.: No. 1015, Ist Main Road, BSK IIIrd Stage,
IIIrd Phase, IIIrd Block, Bangalore-560085 (INDIA)
Tel: 080-41723429
Email: centrumpress@gmail.com
Visit us at: www.centrumpress.com

Network Security

First Edition, 2011

PRINTED IN INDIA

Printed at Tarun Offset Printers, Delhi-110053

Contents

Preface

Network security is becoming more and more important as people spend more and more time connected. Compromising network security is often much easier than compromising physical or local security, and is much more common. There are a number of good tools to assist with network security, and more and more of them are shipping with Linux distributions.

Just a few short years ago, Wireless Equivalent Privacy (WEP) was the de facto standard for securing your wireless network. WEP was thought to be super strong and uncrackable at the time, however, just a few short years later, WEP encryption was cracked and deemed obsolete. After the demise of WEP, word didn't really get out to everyone that it was time to upgrade to the new standard. Some people thought that even outdated WEP was better than no security at all.

Author

1

Networking

INTRODUCTION

The interconnection is done through a communication link also known as the physical layer of the network and this link is such that it is totally transparent to the users of the network. The transparency of the communication link is brought about by the interfacing software known as protocols which enables a user in one location to freely access a computer system/database/process/software in another location. For such an extensive and involved subject, which includes so many different technologies, hardware devices and protocols, the definition of networking is actually quite simple. A network is simply a collection of computers or other hardware devices that are connected together, either physically or logically, using special hardware and software to allow them to exchange information and cooperate. Networking is the term that describes the processes involved in designing, implementing, upgrading, managing and otherwise working with networks and network technologies.

Networks are used for an incredible array of different purposes. In fact, the definitions above are so simple for the specific reason that networks can be used so broadly, and can allow such a wide variety of tasks to be accomplished. While most people learning about networking focus on the interconnection of PCs and other "true" computers, you use various types of networks every day. Each time you pick up a phone, use a credit card at a store, get cash from an ATM machine, or even plug in an electrical appliance, you are using some type of network. In fact, the definition can even be expanded beyond the world of technology altogether: I'm sure you've heard the term "networking" used to describe the process of finding an employer or employee by talking to friends and associates. In this case too, the idea is that independent units are connected together to share information and cooperate. Before computers were small and personal, they were large and centralized machines that were shared by many users operating remote terminals. While having all of the computer power in one place had many disadvantages, one benefit was that all users were connected because they shared the central computer.

Individualized PCs took away that advantage, in favour of the benefits of independence. Networking attempts to move computing into the middle ground, providing PC users with the best of both worlds: the independence and flexibility of personal computers, and the connectivity and resource sharing of mainframes. in fact, networking is today considered so vital that it's hard to conceive of an organization with two or more computers that would not want to connect them together!

MODES OF NETWORKING

It conjures up one of three images: calling everyone in your address book to see whether anyone knows anyone who may know anyone who may give you an informational interview, attending club meetings with other job hunters or having your friends come up with ideas and contacts instead of advising you to get out there and network. But there is no need to fear because there are many different types of networking techniques you can use to help with your job search and references.

LOCAL AREA NETWORK

LAN is normally transmit data in a digital form with typical transmission speeds of up to several megabytes per second. These speeds can be achieved using parallel transmission where a cable with multiple core is used, or serial transmission, making use of high frequency carriers, using coaxial cables, fibre optics or even a simple pair of wires because distances are short. Modems are not normally required although some mechanism for converting from parallel to serial transmission and back again may be needed. The former is a special computer which provides a form of auxiliary storage which can be used by any other computer on the network and the latter is a special computer which can receive data from other computers on the network and print it.

There is also an external communication server on the LAN, which enables communication between equipment on the network and system elsewhere. Local Area Network link computers in the same area for the purpose of sharing information and hardware. Usually the computers are within 300 meters of each other, because they must be connected by a cable hookup, which can be expensive. People at the work stations in a LAN gain more capabilities in work processing, data processing, information retrieval and communication without duplication of equipment, databases and activities. LAN has become popular. Many businesses are installing LAN in order to improve the efficiency of office functions and to facilitate office automation. The configuration of the LAN can be a star or a ring topology or simply devises attached along a length of cable.

LAN or Local Area Network is the most common kind of network set up. There are two ways to connect a LAN network. The simplest and easiest way is the peer-to-peer connection network. This is when two or more computers are directly connected to each other. For example if there were four computers in the network, computer 1 would be connected to computer 2, computer 2 would be connected to computer 3 and computer 3 would be connected to computer 4. This means each computer is dependent on the other. And if there were a network problem with any one computer, all of them would be affected. The other type if the client server connection. A local area network, or LAN, is a network of connected computers in a room, building, or set of buildings.

Local area networks have been around since the beginning of computer use. A LAN is defined as a user network whereby data is sent at high rates between people located relatively close to each other. LANs do not usually make use of leased communication lines, but only means of communication that are provided by the installer of the network.

The Internet is a wide area network, or WAN, which is distinct from a LAN. In contrast to the term *Internet,* local area networks are often called *intranets,* though sometimes this term refers to a cluster of LANs associated with a particular company or organization but not connected to the larger Internet. A local area network uses a hub or router to connect computers together. Perhaps the most frequently employed use of a LAN is to connect users to the Internet with only one connected router. In modern times, we use broadband cable or DSL modems to connect to the Internet, and it would be clumsy to have a modem associated with every computer, so we simply plug the modem into a router and link the router to computers with Ethernet cables.

WIDE AREA NETWORK

The term Wide Area Network (WAN) usually refers to a network which covers a large geographical area, and use communications circuits to connect the intermediate nodes. A major factor impacting WAN design and performance is a requirement that they lease communications circuits from telephone companies or other communications carriers. Transmission rates are typically 2 Mbps, 34 Mbps, 45 Mbps, 155 Mbps, 625 Mbps (or sometimes considerably more).

Numerous WANs have been constructed, including public packet networks, large corporate networks, military networks, banking networks, stock brokerage networks, and airline reservation networks. Some WANs are very extensive, spanning the globe, but most do not provide true global coverage. Organizations supporting WANs using the Internet Protocol are known as Network Service Providers (NSPs). These form the core of the Internet. Wide Area Networks, or WANs, connect a geographically diverse group of computers within a state, country, or even across several states or countries. WANs typically are connected by telephone lines, other types of communication lines, or radio waves. Quite often, smaller local area networks (LANs) are linked together to form a WAN. This is accomplished via dedicated private lines, leased from telecommunications firms like Sprint and AT&T, or by Switched Multi-Megabit Data Services (SMDS) technology, developed in 1995 to eliminate the need for a leased line.

WAN technology has been refined over a period of several decades. It first emerged in the mid-twentieth century with the advent of networks like ARPAnet. Developed in 1969 by the Department of Defence, ARPAnet and several other networks eventually evolved into the Internet, the largest WAN in the world. The packet switching technology most commonly used with WANs surfaced in the 1960s, and standard packet switching protocol, known as X.25, was developed in 1976. WANs are used for a variety of purposes. A corporation with offices in several locations may use a WAN to form an intranet.

Quite often, the individual offices will use their own LANs for things like internal messaging, data processing functions, and hardware and software sharing. When these LANs are joined together to form a WAN, similar data sharing and messaging capabilities become possible across a much broader geographic area. Businesses wanting to link up with their suppliers or distributors may create a WAN as a means of establishing an extranet. For example, an extranet could provide a sales representative with electronic access to information in about the time it might take to deliver a product, or the availability of a product. Some WANs bring together various types of communications, such as data, video, and voice. Some organizations, including companies, universities, research centers, hospitals, and libraries, use WANs to connect to the Internet.

The characteristics of the transmission facilities lead to an emphasis on efficiency of communications techniques in the design of WANs. Controlling the volume of traffic and avoiding excessive delays is important. Since the topologies of WANs are likely to be more complex than those of LANs, routing algorithms also receive more emphasis. Many WANs also implement sophisticated monitoring procedures to account for which users consume the network resources.

METROPOLITAN AREA NETWORKS (MAN)

As implied by their names, Metropolitan and Wide area networks have wider geographical reaches than Local area networks. While MAN usually spans over a city, the reach of a WAN extends over one or more computers and possibly the whole world. Despite the differences in their geographical reach, MAN??s and WAN??s of today generally use the same technology. For example if the computers of an Insurance Company spread all over the country are connected together and information/ data travels from operating offices to controlling office and vice versa then we can say that WAN is implemented in the company.

ACTIVITIES

Service-related activities in networks take place on a wide range of time scales. However, resource allocation decisions are typically limited, e.g. per-packet scheduling inside the network combined with a transport protocol executing on the endpoint. Responsive application-aware networking will require coordinated resource allocation at many time scales. Coordination can take the form of exchanging information regarding status and present and future requirements, coordination of resource allocation activities, and the specification (using a language or programme) of actions to be taken under certain conditions. These interactions will pay off in several areas. Examples include application- and service-specific dynamic sharing of resources between streams under changing network conditions; the implementation of services models that sit in between best effort and guaranteed services, for example using application provided hints; application- and service-specific flow control; and the extension of the time horizon of schedulers, for example by considering application frame boundaries during scheduling. Critical to the implementation of this network model is the ability to safely inject application and service state and code into the network. This enables application and service specific actions on switching points without the need for expensive and time consuming interactions with endpoints.

Interactions between switching points and the application running on the endpoints will of course still be required, but they can be done in a service-specific instead of a generic fashion. The application and service "presence" in the network can range from simple parameters, through specifications using more complex languages, to actual code. The full spectrum of mechanisms will be needed in a fully application-oriented network. What mechanism will be used for a specific action will not only depend on what degree of flexibility is needed, but also on practical considerations. For example, including service code for cell-level switching is impractical.

The resource allocation policy of a communication link is represented by a directed acyclic graph with a single root representing the link and leaf nodes representing individual traffic streams. Intermediate nodes represent organizational entities. Each node gets resources from its parents and specifies how its resources are distributed to its children. Examples of policies include fair-sharing at different granularities, reservation, and strict priority. This graph is a language that can be used by different entities to specify how traffic streams or collections of traffic streams should share bandwidth. By combining subgraphs, the resource management policies set by different entities (link, service providers, applications) can be represented simultaneously. Tools are used to translate a graph into a schedule that can be used by switch nodes, and incremental changes in the graph translate into incremental changes in the schedule.

SECURITY

Our approach lends itself naturally to dealing with failure recovery in an integrated fashion throughout the resource allocation process. One of the "changes" that can be considered during the creation of the virtual mesh is the failure of nodes and links, and both the topology of the virtual application mesh and the instructions to switching points can implicitly and explicitly prepare for a quick response to failures. The degree of robustness can be application and service specific. The issue of security shows up in a number of areas. First, the network has to verify that application input (parameters, specification and programmes) can be acted upon safely since incorrect input can endanger the operation of the network. This requires a combination of language, compilation and runtime techniques, and we plan to use mostly existing technology for this security aspect. Second, the network has to guarantee that only authorized entities can modify the network state. We plan to address this using existing authentication methods. Note that the virtual application mesh can form the basis for providing security. As part of the creation of the mesh, relationships of trust can be established between the nodes in the mesh.

STRUCTURE

REFERENCE MODEL

The importance of having standardised networking protocols have led to the evolution of several networking reference models. The Open System Interconnection (OSI) and the TCP/IP models will be looked at. These models allow us to more easily study the structure of networks.

The OSI model is based on a proposal by the International Standards Organisation. The OSI reference model has a layered architecture, whereby each layer encapsulates a function of the overall complex task. The proposed model has 7 layers. The key idea is that although data is transmitted vertically, each layer is programmed horizontally. Each layer ignores the complications of the lower layers and assumes that the information it passes out is immediately seen by destination host. At each layer, appropriate headers are appended onto the data when sending, and are removed as the data is decoded.

The underpinnings of the Internet are formed by the global interconnection of hundreds of thousands of otherwise independent computers, communications entities and information systems. What makes this interconnection possible is the use of a set of communication standards, procedures and formats in common among the networks and the various devices and computational facilities connected to them. The procedures by which computers communicate with each other are called "protocols." While this infrastructure is steadily evolving to include new capabilities, the protocols initially used by the Internet are called the "TCP/IP" protocols, named after the two protocols that formed the principal basis for Internet operation.

On top of this infrastructure is an emerging set of architectural concepts and data structures for heterogeneous information systems that renders the Internet a truly global information system. In essence, the Internet is an architecture, although many people confuse it with its implementation. When the Internet is looked at as an architecture, it manifests two different abstractions. One abstraction deals with communications connectivity, packet delivery and a variety of end-end communication services. The other abstraction deals with the Internet as an information system, independent of its underlying communications infrastructure, which allows creation, storage and access to a wide range of information resources, including digital objects and related services at various levels of abstraction.

Interconnecting computers is an inherently digital problem. Computers process and exchange digital information, meaning that they use a discrete mathematical "binary" or "two-valued" language of 1s and 0s. For communication purposes, such information is mapped into continuous electrical or optical waveforms. The use of digital signaling allows accurate regeneration and reliable recovery of the underlying bits. We use the terms "computer," "computer resources" and "computation" to mean not only traditional computers, but also devices that can be controlled digitally over a network, information resources such as mobile programmes and other computational capabilities. The telephone network started out with operators who manually connected telephones to each other through "patch panels" that accepted patch cords from each telephone line and electrically connected them to one another through the panel, which operated, in effect, like a switch. The result was called circuit switching, since at its conclusion, an electrical circuit was made between the calling telephone and the called telephone. Conventional circuit switching, which was developed to handle telephone calls, is inappropriate for connecting computers because it makes limited use of the telecommunication facilities and takes too long to set up connections. Although reliable enough for voice communication, the circuit-switched voice network had difficulty delivering digital information without errors.

For digital communications, packet switching is a better choice, because it is far better suited to the typically "burst" communication style of computers. Computers that communicate typically send out brief but intense bursts of data, then remain silent for a while before sending out the next burst. These bursts are communicated as packets, which are very much like electronic postcards.

The postcards, in reality packets, are relayed from computer to computer until they reach their destination. The special computers that perform this forwarding function are called variously "packet switches" or "routers" and form the equivalent of many bucket brigades spanning continents and oceans, moving buckets of electronic postcards from one computer to another. Together these routers and the communication links between them form the underpinnings of the Internet.

Without packet switching, the Internet would not exist, as we now know it. Going back to the postcard analogy, postcards can get lost. They can be delivered out of order, and they can be delayed by varying amounts. The same is true of Internet packets, which, on the Internet, can even be duplicated. The Internet Protocol is the postcard layer of the Internet. The next higher layer of protocol, TCP, takes care of re-sending the "postcards" to recover packets that might have been lost, and putting packets back in order if they have become disordered in transit. Thus, the evolution of the Internet was based on two technologies and a research dream. The technologies were packet switching and computer technology, which, in turn, drew upon the underlying technologies of digital communications and semiconductors. The research dream was to share information and computational resources. But that is simply the technical side of the story. Equally important in many ways were the other dimensions that enabled the Internet to come into existence and flourish. This aspect of the story starts with cooperation and far-sightedness in the U.S. Government, which is often derided for lack of foresight but is a real hero in this story.

It leads on to the enthusiasm of private sector interests to build upon the government funded developments to expand the Internet and make it available to the general public. Perhaps most important, it is fueled by the development of the personal computer industry and significant changes in the telecommunications industry in the 1980s, not the least of which was the decision to open the long distance market to competition. The role of workstations, the Unix operating system and local area networking (especially the Ethernet) are themes contributing to the spread of Internet technology in the 1980s into the research and academic community from which the Internet industry eventually emerged.

Many individuals have been involved in the development and evolution of the Internet covering a span of almost four decades if one goes back to the early writings on the subject of computer networking by Kleinrock, Licklider, Baran, Roberts, and Davies. The ARPANET, described below, was the first wide-area computer network. The NSFNET, which followed more than a decade later under the leadership of Erich Bloch, Gordon Bell, Bill Wulf and Steve Wolff, brought computer networking into the mainstream of the research and education communities. It is not our intent here to attempt to attribute credit to all those whose contributions were central to this story, although we mention a few of the key players

REFERENCE MODEL

In the late 1970s, two projects began independently, with the same goal: to define a unifying standard for the architecture of networking systems. One was administered by the *International Organization for Standardization (ISO),* while the other was undertaken by the *International Telegraph and Telephone Consultative Committee,* or *CCITT* (the abbreviation is from the French version of the name). These two international standards bodies each developed a document that defined similar networking models.

In 1983, these two documents were merged together to form a standard called *The Basic Reference Model for Open Systems Interconnection*. That's a mouthful, so the standard is usually referred to as the *Open Systems Interconnection Reference Model,* the *OSI Reference Model,* or even just the *OSI Model*. It was published in 1984 by both the ISO, as standard ISO 7498, and the renamed CCITT (now called the *Telecommunications Standardization Sector of the International Telecommunication Union* or *ITU-T*) as standard X.200. (Incidentally, isn't the new name for the CCITT *much* catchier than the old one? Just rolls off the old tongue, doesn't it. J) One interesting aspect of the history of the OSI Reference Model is that the original objective was *not* to create a model primarily for educational purposes—even though many people today think that this was the case. The OSI Reference Model was intended to serve as the foundation for the establishment of a widely-adopted suite of protocols that would be used by international internetworks—basically, what the Internet became. This was called, unsurprisingly, the OSI Protocol Suite.

The OSI model itself, however, found a home as a device for explaining the operation of not just the OSI protocols, but networking in general terms. It was used widely as an educational tool—much as I use it myself in this Guide—and also to help describe interactions between the components of other protocol suites and even hardware devices. While most technologies were not designed specifically to meet the dictates of the OSI model, many are described in terms of how they fit into its layers.

The OSI reference model specifies standards for describing "Open Systems Interconnection" with the term 'open' chosen to emphasise the fact that by using these international standards, a system may be defined which is open to all other systems obeying the same standards throughout the world. OSI (Open Systems Interconnection) is a standard description or "reference model" for how messages should be transmitted between any two points in a telecommuni-cation network. Its purpose is to guide product implementors so that their products will consistently work with other products. The reference model defines seven layers of functions that take place at each end of a communication. Although OSI is not always strictly adhered to in terms of keeping related functions together in a well-defined layer, many if not most products involved in telecommunication make an attempt to describe themselves in relation to the OSI model. It is also valuable as a single reference view of communication that furnishes everyone a common ground for education and discussion.

The main idea in OSI is that the process of communication between two end points in a telecommunication network can be divided into layers, with each layer adding its own set of special, related functions. Each communicating user or programme is at a computer equipped with these seven layers of function. So, in a given message between users, there will be a flow of data through each layer at one end down through the layers in that computer and, at the other end, when the message arrives, another flow of data up through the layers in the receiving computer and ultimately to the end user or programme.

WEB SERVICES

Web Services are a set of protocols based on XML (Extensible Markup Language). Many readers will be familiar with the following base protocols that formed the initial specification for Web Services.

- *Simple Object Access Protocol (SOAP)*: defines the runtime message that contains the service request and response. SOAP is independent of any particular transport and implementation technology.

- *Web Services Description Language (WSDL)*: describes a Web Service and the SOAP Message. It provides a programmatic way to describe what a service does, paving the way for automation.
- *Universal Discovery, Description, Integration (UDDI)*: UDDI is a cross industry initiative to create a standard for service discovery together with a registry facility that facilitates the publishing and discovery processes.

These base protocols have enabled many companies to put straightforward Web Services into production. However, to improve the security and reliability of Web Services and to address more complex business scenarios, a wide range of additional protocols have since been proposed. Some of these have since been merged with others or morphed into new proposals. The additional protocols have been proposed within the context of a modular framework that would allow,

- Developers to only use the modules needed for their Web Services. Each module can be lightweight and not overburdened with irrelevant syntax.
- Each module to evolve in isolation

There is no standard definition of the Web Services Protocol stack though the W3C Web Services Architecture Working Group did publish a Web Services Architecture document which provides an excellent context for the various protocols. Vendors often draw their own, but similar architecture.

CBDI ASSESSMENT

Alternative Proposals

The degree of industry consensus on Web Service protocols has been significant. Though alternative proposals have been made in some areas, the formation of an appropriate working group in either W3C or OASIS has usually seen the subsequent convergence of all interested parties. There are currently some areas where alternative proposals remain, namely in the areas of Reliable Messaging, Orchestration, and Transaction Coordination. These alternatives have generally reflected an IBM/Microsoft led initiative on one side, and one led by Sun/Oracle on the other.

There has also been some overlap between Web Services and the ebXML initiative. ebXML uses SOAP at the transport level, but has its own registry and orchestration. Though ebXML is an approved, robust standard, its applicability is far narrower than Web Services. As an evolution of EDI, it primarily addresses the B2B domain only. As such we believe the Web Service protocols that are designed to address multiple requirements and usage scenarios will prove more valuable in time and that ebXML will probably evolve to adopt additional Web Service protocols as they mature and are approved. Part of the work of the OASIS ebSOA TC is to evolve the ebXML architecture and address the transition to the adoption of more Web Service protocols.

NETWORK TOPOLOGY

COMPUTER NETWORK TOPOLOGY

Network topology is one of the very important topics to learn when it comes to build up computer network. There are many Network Topologies on which network administrator decide to build the network on. Topology is basically defined as layout or design of network, and computers are connected using the design of the topology. These topologies can be either physical or logical design. Physical topology refers to physical design of network which includes devices, cables, location and installation of network where as in logical topology it is the amount of data to be transferred with in the network as apposed in its design.

There are five different Networking Topologies:

1. Bus
2. Star
3. Ring
4. Mesh
5. Tree.

When networks are design using multiple topologies it is called Hybrid Networks, this concept is usually utilized in complex networks were larger number of computer clients are required.

DELAY ANALYSIS

TECHNIQUES

The as-planned versus as-built method of analysis can be carried out without the need for complex computer project management software, although such software is usually used for its presentation. This method is described by a number of English and American commentators as well as being referred to in SCL Delay and Disruption Protocol.

The method merely compares the durations of the planned activities with the as-built durations, and attributes the variance between the planned construction period and the as-built construction period as an entitlement to an extension of time. The approach is illustrated in the programme chart above right. It therefore assumes that the as-built situation arises by reason of variations or other reasons for which the contractor is entitled to an extension of time and not due to its own culpability.

Selection Criteria

This method is well suited for relatively simple projects where it is easy to identify where the main delays arose. Clearly it requires the planned programme and as-built information in sufficient detail to compare as-built activities with the same planned activities. This method is useful to identify the difference between the planned and actual durations and sequence of events in order to focus the further investigation on areas which appear to have gone particularly wrong and which appear to have been critical.

Issues

This is obviously a very simplistic method of analysis. Indeed it is questionable whether this can really be called a method of analysis in the way that it is described by commentators. It is unlikely that it can credibly be concluded that the difference between the planned and as-built programmes gives rise to an extension of time. To do so assumes that the planned programme was realistic and achievable, the work was appropriately resourced to enable that plan to be achieved and that the only reason for the delay was because of an event for which the contractor is entitled to an extension of time. What is needed is a careful consideration of the facts from which one should seek to determine an actual period of delay, which either will or will not sufficiently explain the difference between the planned and as-built programmes.

For example, if one looks at the programme above, it may be that the planned duration for Activity 1 was an under-estimate and there was no event affecting it, that the same applies to Activity 2, and Activity 3 was an overestimate, but was subject to a delay of four days, thus explaining four of the seven days of delay to completion. None of this would be apparent from the simple comparison shown in the chart, but would become apparent from an investigation of the facts.

Further, the planned programme may well not be in sufficient detail to enable a credible conclusion that the difference between the planned and actual activity durations is explainable by the events relied upon. This method of analysis is generally the cheapest and simplest to perform, although assuming a planned programme exists, it still requires the production of an as-built programme. This approach can be useful in relation to events that are clearly on the critical path.

It has been observed that the fact that this is not a CPM-based method means that it is impossible to demonstrate with any precision the effects of concurrency or parallel delays; unproductive working; the effects of secondary or consequential delay; acceleration; resequencing or mitigation.

DART NETWORK

The purpose of the backbone is to connect regional distribution networks and, in some instances, to provide connectivity to other peer networks. A national infrastructure usually forms a significant part of the operational cost of the network. Given its position at the top of the network hierarchy, two requirements of the backbone topology are clear: it must be reliable and it must scale.

RELIABILITY

Reliability can be acquired by employing two methods. First, you can create more reliable routers through the use of "carrier-class" characteristics, such as multiple CPUs, power supplies, and generators; and even redundant routers. Ultimately, however, any backbone will include WAN links that rely on a great deal of equipment and environmental stability for their operation, which represents a real risk of ultimate failure.

BACKBONE TOPOLOGY

Because you have a basic need for resilience in the backbone, a good starting point for the backbone topology is a ring connecting all distribution networks. This ring could represent the minimum cost of WAN circuits, compromised by an initial estimate of major traffic flows, and possibly some very particular delay requirements (although this is rare, with notable exceptions being high-performance networks).

Backbone routing protocols, such as IBGP, properly coupled with OSPF, IS-IS, and Enhanced IGRP, can rapidly circumvent failures by simple link-costing mechanisms. However, the bandwidth allocations with the core topology should consider failure modes. What happens when the ring is broken due to WAN or node failure? Is the re-routed path sufficient to carry the additional traffic load? Although TCP performs extremely well in congested environments compared with other protocols, it is still possible to render the network useless for most practical applications.

Traditionally, the use of a ring topology made it difficult to estimate the traffic levels between individual distribution networks. SNMP statistics, for example, provided only input and output byte counts for WAN interfaces, making it difficult to determine the appropriate sizing for new direct links between distribution networks.

Typically, this had to be accomplished using a cumbersome approach, such as "sniffers" on WAN links, or through accounting capabilities within routers that scaled rather poorly. However, IP accounting facilities, such as Netflow, now provide a scalable way for network managers to collect and analyse traffic flows, based on source and destination addresses, as well as many other flow parameters. This significantly eases traffic engineering and accounting activities.

LOCAL ACCESS NETWORK

DATA COMMUNICATION

Ethernet is by far the most commonly used LAN technology. Token Ring technology is still used by some companies. FDDI is sometimes used as a backbone LAN interconnecting Ethernet or Token Ring LANs. WLAN using IEEE 802.11 technologies is rapidly becoming the new leading LAN technology for its mobility and easy to use features.

Local Area Network could be interconnected using Wide Area Network (WAN) or Metropolitan Area Network (MAN) technologies. The common WAN technologies include TCP/IP, ATM, Frame Relay etc. The common MAN technologies include SMDS and 10 Gigabit Ethernet.

LANs are traditionally used to connect a group of people who are in the same local area. However, the working group are becoming more geographically distributed in today's working environment. There, virtual LAN (VLAN) technologies are defined for people in different places to share the same networking resource.

SOFTWARE

Edraw Network Diagram is ideal for network engineers and network designers who need to draw wan diagrams. It had defined some common used WAN symbols in drawing WAN diagrams. Just drag and drop pre-drawn shapes representing computers and network devices. Double click and set equipment data.

WIDE AREA NETWORK TECHNOLOGIES

A Wide Area Network (WAN) is a computer network covering multiple distance areas, which may spread across the entire world. WANs often connect multiple smaller networks, such as local area networks (LANs) or metro area networks (MANs). The world's most popular WAN is the Internet. Some segments of the Internet are also WANs in themselves. The key difference between WAN and LAN technologies is scalability C WAN must be able to grow as needed to cover multiple cities, even countries and continents.

A set of switches and routers are interconnected to form a Wide Area Network. The switches can be connected in different topologies such as full mesh and half mesh. A wide area network may be privately owned or rented from a service provider, but the term usually connotes the inclusion of public (shared user) networks.

Both packet switching and circuit switching technologies are used in the WAN. Packet switching allows users to share common carrier resources so that the carrier can make more efficient use of its infrastructure. In a packet switching setup, networks have connections into the carrier's network, and many customers share the carrier's network. The carrier can then create virtual circuits between customers' sites by which packets of data are delivered from one to the other through the network. Circuit Switching allows data connections to be established when needed and then terminated when communication is complete. This works like a normal telephone line works for voice communication. Integrated Services Digital Network (ISDN) is a good example of circuit switching.

WAN Diagram Software

Edraw Network Diagram is ideal for network engineers and network designers who need to draw wan diagrams. It had defined some common used WAN symbols in drawing WAN diagrams. Just drag and drop pre-drawn shapes representing computers and network devices. Double click and set equipment data.

DATA LINK LAYER

ENCODING

The data link layer is responsible for encoding *bits* into *packets* prior to transmission and then decoding the packets back into bits at the destination. Bits are the most basic unit of information in computing and communications. Packets are the fundamental unit of information transport in all modern computer networks, and increasingly in other communications networks as well. The data link layer is also responsible for logical link control, media access control, hardware addressing, error detection and handling and defining physical layer standards. It provides reliable data transfer by transmitting packets with the necessary synchronization, error control and flow control.

The data link layer is divided into two sublayers: the *media access control* (MAC) layer and the *logical link control* (LLC) layer. The former controls how computers on the network gain access to the data and obtain permission to transmit it; the latter controls packet synchronization, flow control and error checking. The data link layer is where most LAN (local area network) and wireless LAN technologies are defined. Among the most popular technologies and protocols generally associated with this layer are Ethernet, Token Ring, FDDI (fibre distributed data interface), ATM (asynchronous transfer mode), SLIP (serial line Internet protocol), PPP (point-to-point protocol), HDLC (high level data link control) and ADCCP (advanced data communication control procedures).

The data link layer is often implemented in software as a driver for a network interface card (NIC). Because the data link and physical layers are so closely related, many types of hardware are also associated with the data link layer. For example, NICs typically implement a specific data link layer technology, so they are often called *Ethernet cards, Token Ring cards*, etc. There are also several types of network interconnection devices that are said to operate at the data link layer in whole or in part, because they make decisions about what to do with data they receive by looking at data link layer packets. These devices include most bridges and switches, although switches also encompass functions performed by the network layer.

The second-lowest layer (layer 2) in the OSI Reference Model stack is the *data link layer,* often abbreviated "DLL" (though that abbreviation has other meanings as well in the computer world). The data link layer, also sometimes just called the *link layer,* is where many wired and wireless local area networking (LAN) technologies primarily function. For example, Ethernet, Token Ring, FDDI and 802.11 ("wireless Ethernet" or "Wi-Fi') are all sometimes called "data link layer technologies". The set of devices connected at the data link layer is what is commonly considered a simple "network", as opposed to an internetwork.

SUB LAYERS

The data link layer is often conceptually divided into two sublayers: *logical link control (LLC)* and *media access control (MAC).* This split is based on the architecture used in the IEEE 802 Project, which is the IEEE working group responsible for creating the standards that define many networking technologies (including all of the ones I mentioned above except FDDI). By separating LLC and MAC functions, interoperability of different network technologies is made easier, as explained in our earlier discussion of networking model concepts.

FUNCTIONS

The following are the key tasks performed at the data link layer:

Media Access Control (MAC)

This refers to the procedures used by devices to control access to the network medium. Since many networks use a shared medium (such as a single network cable, or a series of cables that are electrically connected into a single virtual medium) it is necessary to have rules for managing the medium to avoid conflicts. For example. Ethernet uses the

CSMA/CD method of media access control, while Token Ring uses token passing.

Data Framing

The data link layer is responsible for the final encapsulation of higher-level messages into *frames* that are sent over the network at the physical layer.

Addressing

The data link layer is the lowest layer in the OSI model that is concerned with addressing: labeling information with a particular destination location. Each device on a network has a unique number, usually called a *hardware address* or *MAC address,* that is used by the data link layer protocol to ensure that data intended for a specific machine gets to it properly.

Error Detection and Handling

The data link layer handles errors that occur at the lower levels of the network stack. For example, a cyclic redundancy check (CRC) field is often employed to allow the station receiving data to detect if it was received correctly.

ELEMENTARY DATA

TYPES

What are the different kinds of data types that are available for use in programming? Data types fall under several categories and can be divided into the elementary data type, the structured data type, or the abstract data type. The elementary data types are the most basic of all. The structured data types are a composition of the elementary data types and a little more. The abstract data types basically have traits from both the elementary and the structured data types.

Elementary data types are the basic data types. Basic numeric data like integers and floating point real numbers are considered to be elementary data types. The integer data type that you have been using is one of the many elementary data types in Visual Basic. Boolean or Logical data types are also of the elementary category. A Boolean value is either True or False, 1 or 0, respectively. Characters are elementary data types too. A character is a letter, a digit, or a special symbol used to represent a data element. Characters are usually strung together to form names.

Enumerations are considered to be an elementary data type. An enumeration is a set of values which can be represented by the set of positive integers. For example, you can make the type "BoxColor" which could take on the values of blue, green, red, orange, or yellow. The colours represent the integers from one to five. The programmer is the one who defines the values and the associated integers for it. A subrange is an elementary data type that has programmer specified ranges too. These subranges are restricted within a parent range. A subrange results in better type checking.

COMMON DATA LINK PROTOCOLS

The most common data link level protocols are listed here with a short description. Note that most of these data link protocol are used for WAN and Modem Connections. LLC is a LAN data link protocol.

SDLC (Synchronous Data Link Protocol): This protocol was originally developed by IBM as part of IBM's SNA (Systems Network Architecture). It was used to connect remote devices to mainframe computers at central locations in either point-to-point (one-to-one) or point-to-multipoint (one-to-many) connections.

HDLC (High-level Data Link Control): This protocol is based on SDLC and provides both a best-effort unreliable service and a reliable service. It is used with various serial interface protocols defined in the physical layer, such as EIA/TIA-232, V.24, V.35, and others.

SLIP (Serial Line Interface Protocol): SLIP is a data link control facility for transmitting IP packets, usually between an ISP (Internet service provider) and a home user over a dial-up link. SLIP has some limitations, including a lack of any error-detection and correction mechanisms. It is up to higher-layer protocols to perform these checks. Used over much of the same serial interfaces as HDLC.

PPP (Point-to-Point Protocol): PPP provides the same functionality as SLIP (*i.e.,* it is commonly used for Internet connections over dial-up lines); but it is a more robust protocol that can transport not only IP, but also other types of packets. Frames contain a field that identifies the type of protocol being carried (IP, IPX, and so on). It is used over much of the same serial interfaces as HDLC.

LAN DATA LINK CONTROL

The IEEE (Institute of Electrical and Electronics Engineers) has defined a number of LAN technologies in the data link layer, including Ethernet, Fast Ethernet, Gigabit Ethernet, and token ring. The actual data link layer is split into two sub layers, called the MAC (Medium Access Control) sub layer and the LLC (Logical Link Control) sub layer, as shown in Figure. The lower MAC layer defines the media access method, which can be CSMA/CD (carrier sense multiple access/collision detection), token ring, or other IEEE physical interface. The LLC sublayer provides a way for the network layer to communicate with one of these protocols.

Data link layer devices include bridges and switches. Refer to "Bridges and Bridging" and "Switching and Switched Networks" for more information. Frame relay is a high-speed data link protocol. It uses LAPF (Link Access Procedure for Frame-Mode Bearer Services). See "Frame Relay" for more information. ATM (Asynchronous Transfer Mode) is a cell-based data link-level service. See "ATM (Asynchronous Transfer Mode)" for more information.

PROTOCOLS

DEFINITION

The most obvious improvement in IPv6 over IPv4 is that IP addresses are lengthened from 32 bits to 128 bits. This extension anticipates considerable future growth of the Internet and provides relief for what was perceived as an impending shortage of network addresses. IPv6 also supports auto-configuration to help correct most of the shortcomings in version 4, and it has integrated security and mobility features.

features include:

- Supports source and destination addresses that are 128 bits (16 bytes) long.
- Requires IPSec support.
- Uses Flow Label field to identify packet flow for QoS handling by router.
- Allows the host to send fragments packets but not routers.
- Doesn't include a checksum in the header.
- Uses a link-local scope all-nodes multicast address.
- Does not require manual configuration or DHCP.
- Uses host address (AAAA) resource records in DNS to map host names to IPv6 addresses.
- Uses pointer (PTR) resource records in the IP6.ARPA DNS domain to map IPv6 addresses to host names.
- Supports a 1280-byte packet size (without fragmentation).

The Internet Protocol (IP) is the most widely used communications protocol. Because it is the most pervasive communication technology, it is the focus of hundreds of thousands of IT professionals like you. Because so many people rely on the protocol, the safety of communications is top of mind. The security research that is performed on IP is conducted by both benevolent and malevolent people. All the security research has caused many patches and adjustments to IP, as it has been deployed internationally. In hindsight, it would have been better if deeper consideration were given to the security of the protocol before it was extensively deployed. This book provides you with insight into the security ramifications of a new version of IP and provides guidance to avoid issues prior to deployment. A review of the current risks and industry knowledge of the vulnerabilities is provided, as well as the common ways that IPv6 can be secured. The Internet Engineering Task Force (IETF) is the organization that is responsible for defining the Internet Protocol standards. When the IETF developed IPv4, the global expansion of the Internet and the current Internet security issues were not anticipated. In IPv4's original design, network security was only given minor consideration. In the 1980s, when IPv4 was developing, the "Internet" was constructed by a set of cooperative organizations. As IPv4 was developed and the Internet explosion took place in the 1990s, Internet threats became prolific. If the current environment of Internet threats could have been predicted when IPv4 was being developed, the protocol would have had more security measures incorporated into its design.

In the early 1990s, the IETF realised that a new version of IP would be needed, and the Task Force started by drafting the new protocol's requirements. IP Next Generation (IPng) was created, which then became IPv6 (RFC 1883). IPv6 is the second network layer standard protocol that follows IPv4 for computer communications across the Internet and other computer networks. IPv6 offers several compelling functions and is really the next step in the evolution of the Internet Protocol. These improvements came in the form of increased address size, a streamlined header format, extensible headers, and the ability to preserve the confidentiality and integrity of communications. The IPv6 protocol was then fully standardized at the end of 1998 in RFC 2460, which defines the header structure. IPv6 is now ready to overcome many of the deficiencies in the current IPv4 protocol and to create new ways of communicating that IPv4 cannot support.

IPv6 provides several improvements over its predecessor. The advantages of IPv6 are detailed in many other books on IPv6. However, the following list summarizes the characteristics of IPv6 and the improvements it can deliver:

- *Larger address space:* Increased address size from 32 bits to 128 bits
- *Streamlined protocol header*: Improves packet-forwarding efficiency
- *Stateless autoconfiguration*: The ability for nodes to determine their own address

- *Multicast*: Increased use of efficient one-to-many communications
- *Jumbograms*: The ability to have very large packet payloads for greater efficiency
- *Network layer security*: Encryption and authentication of communications
- *Quality of service (QoS) capabilities*: QoS markings of packets and flow labels that help identify priority traffic
- *Anycast*: Redundant services using nonunique addresses
- *Mobility*: Simpler handling of mobile or roaming nodes

Note: Remember the following IPv6 terminology:

- A *node* is any system (computer, router, and so on) that communicates IPv6.
- A *router* is any Layer 3 device capable of routing and forwarding IPv6 packets.
- A *host* is a node that is a computer or any other access device that is not a router.
- A *packet* is the Layer 3 message sourced from an IPv6 node destined for an IPv6 address.

During the development of IPv6, one of the requirements was that this new protocol must have flexible transition mechanisms. It should be easy to transition to this new protocol gradually, over many years. Because it was evident that IPv6 would become very popular, the transition would need to be slow and methodical.

Running both IPv4 and IPv6 at the same time, called *dual stack*, is one of the primary transition strategies. This concept describes the scenario in which a router supports two or more different routed protocols and forwards each type of traffic, independent of the behaviour of the other routed protocol. Seasoned network engineers will recall the concept of "ships-in-the-night routing." This term refers to the fact that packets from either protocol can pass by each other without affecting each other or having anything to do with each other. Because "dual stacking" can be a dominant migration strategy, running a network with both protocols can open that network to attacks on both protocols. Attacks can also evolve that leverage a combination of vulnerabilities in IPv4 and IPv6.

In addition to dual stack, the transition to IPv6 involves various types of tunneling approaches where IPv6 is carried over IPv4 networks that have yet to migrate to IPv6. There will likely be attacks on the transition mechanisms themselves to gain access to either the IPv4 or IPv6 portions of a network. The security of IPv6 systems must be assessed before IPv6 is permitted to be enabled on current and future networks and systems.Because IPv6 and IPv4 are both network layer protocols, many of the network layer vulnerabilities are therefore similar. However, because the protocol layers above and below the IP layer remain the same for either IP version, many of those attacks will not change. Because the two protocols are related, the similarities between the protocols can create similar attack patterns. IPv6 could improve security in some areas, but in other areas, it could also open new threats.

IPv6 has continued to evolve since December 1998, when the IETF published RFC 2460. As the number of available IPv4 public addresses has reduced, IPv6 has become more attractive. In fact, IPv6 is the only viable solution to this IP address depletion problem. Many of the problems in current IPv4 networks relate to address conservation. For example, perpetuating the use of Network Address Translation (NAT) and double-NAT is not a realistic long-term strategy for Internet expansion.

Today, the identity of users on the Internet is often unknown, and this has created an environment where attackers can easily operate. The use of anonymizer tools such as Tor and open proxies and the use of NAT allow users to hide their source IP addresses and allow hackers to operate without their targets knowing much about the source of the messages. NAT is often misunderstood as a security protection measure because it hides the internal addresses and thus obfuscates the internal network topology. Many network administrators feel a false sense of security and put too much faith in NAT. NAT breaks the use of the full end-to-end communication model that IP Security (IPsec) needs to be fully effective. The firewalls that perform the NAT function have difficulty maintaining the NAT state during failover. Troubleshooting application traffic that flows through a NAT is often difficult. When using IPv6, the use of NAT is not necessary because of the large amount of addresses available. Each node has its own unique address, and it can use that address for internal and external communications.

After the core, distribution, and access layers are dual-stack enabled, the computer systems themselves can be IPv6 enabled. After this takes place, the system administrators can start to enable IPsec tunnels between IPv6-enabled nodes to provide confidentiality and the integrity of the communications between systems. This provides a greater level of security over current unencrypted IPv4 implementations. IPsec deployments utilizing both authentication and encryption are rarely used today for computer-to-computer communication. Today the common method of using IPsec only encrypts the payload in tunnel mode because the NATs that are in place prevent authenticating the header. However, communications between critical systems can optionally be secured with IPv6 IPsec, using both authentication and encryption.

IPv6 Update

IPv6 is becoming a reality. The many years of early protocol research have paid dividends with products that easily interoperate. Several early IPv6 research groups have disbanded because the protocol is starting to move into the transition phase. The 6BONE (phased out with RFC 3701) and the KAME IPv6 research and development projects have wound down and given way to more IPv6 products from a wide variety of vendors. Deployment of IPv6 is not a question of if but when. IPv6 is an eventuality.

The transition to IPv6 continues to take place around the world. The protocol is gaining popularity and is being integrated into more products. There are many IPv6-capable operating systems on the market today. Linux, BSD, Solaris, Microsoft

Vista, and Microsoft Server 2008 operating systems all have their IPv6 stacks enabled by default, and IPv6 operates as the preferred protocol stack. Of course, Cisco equipment fully supports dual-stack configuration, and the number of IPv6 features within IOS devices continues to grow. However, the production use of IPv6 is still in the domain of the early adopters.

The rate of IPv6 adoption is growing but is also unpredictable. The timeline for the deployment of IPv6 is long and difficult to measure. Generally speaking, the transition to IPv6 has thus far been based on geography and politics. The Asian and European regions that did not have as many allocated IPv4 addresses have felt the pressure to transition to IPv6. While organizations in North America have more IPv4 addresses, the address-depletion effects are making the migration to IPv6 more urgent. The market segments that are focused on IPv6 are few and far between. There are few IPv6-specific applications that appeal to enterprises, service providers, and consumers that make them want to transition sooner. Some vertical markets such as government and defence, public sector, education, video distribution, and high tech are starting to see the benefits of IPv6 and are working on their transition plans.

There are still many areas of IPv6 where issues remain to be resolved. One of the remaining challenges for IPv6 is that few IPv6 service providers exist. Currently, Internet IPv6 traffic is still light compared to IPv4, but it continues to grow. This can be attributed to the lack of last-mile IPv6 access and customer premises equipment (CPE) that does not support IPv6. Multihoming, which is the concept of connecting to multiple service providers for redundancy, is an issue that will take some time to resolve, but it is doubtful that it is significantly holding back organizations from deploying IPv6. Hardware acceleration for IPv6 is not universal, and many applications lack IPv6 support. Just like the deployment of other networking technologies, network management and security are left to the end. The goal of this book is to raise awareness of the security issues related to IPv6 and to provide methods to secure the protocol before deployment.

IPv6 Vulnerabilities

IPv6 will eventually be just as popular as IPv4, if not more so. Over the next decade as IPv6 is deployed, the number of systems it is deployed on will surpass those on IPv4. While early adopters can help flesh out the bugs, there are still many issues to resolve. IPv6 implementations are relatively new to the market, and the software that has created these systems has not been field tested as thoroughly as their IPv4 counterparts. There is likely to be a period of time where defects will be found, and vendors will need to respond quickly to patching their bugs. Many groups are performing extensive testing of IPv6, so they hopefully can find many of the issues before it is time to deploy IPv6. However, all the major vendors of IT equipment and software have published vulnerabilities in their IPv6 implementations. Microsoft, Juniper, Linux, Sun, BSD, and even Cisco all have published vulnerabilities in their software. As IPv6 has been noticed, it is evident that these major vendors have drawn the attention of the hackers.

The early adopters of IPv6 technology are encouraged to tread lightly and make sure that security is part of their transition plans. There are distinct threats of running IPv6 on a network without any security protection measures. Some operating systems can run both protocols at the same time without the user's intervention. These operating systems might also try to connect to the IPv6 Internet without explicit configuration by the user. If users are not aware of this fact and there is no security policy or IPv6 security protections implemented, they are running the risk of attack. IPv6 can be used as a "backdoor protocol" because many security systems only secure IPv4 and ignore IPv6 packets. For these reasons, it is important to secure IPv6 before it is widely deployed.

When you consider the ways that an IPv4 or IPv6 network can be compromised, there are many similarities. Attacks against networks typically fall within one of the following common attack vectors:

- Internet (DMZ, fragmentation, web pages, pop-ups)
- IP spoofing, protocol fuzzing, header manipulation, session hijacking, man-in-the-middle, sniffing

- Buffer overflows, SQL injection, cross-site scripting
- E-mail (attachments, phishing, hoaxes)
- Worms, viruses, distributed denial of service (DDoS)
- Macros, Trojan horses, spyware, malware, key loggers
- VPN, business-to-business (B2B)
- Chat, peer-to-peer (P2P)
- Malicious insider, physical security, rogue devices, dumpster diving

In 2007, The Computer Security Institute (CSI) 12th Annual Computer Crime and Security Survey stated that 59 per cent of all survey respondents suffered from insider abuse of network access. This percentage historically has been lower in the mid- to late 1990s and has risen steadily each year. So the percentage of internal attack sources is likely to be even higher today. Those internal sources of attacks could either be a legitimate hacker or an unknowing end user. The key issue is that most organizations do not spend 50 per cent of their security budget on mitigating inside threats. Therefore, external as well as internal devices must be hardened equally well but not necessarily against the same types of attacks.

One disadvantage of both IP versions is the fact that the signaling of network reachability information takes place in the same medium as the user traffic. Routing protocols perform their communication in-band, and that increases the risks to infrastructure destabilization attacks. The threat mentioned here is that user traffic can affect the protocol-signaling information to destabilize the network. Protections against these types of attacks involve securing the signaling communications between network devices. IPv6 routing protocols can use encryption and authentication to secure the signaling information, even if it is transported inside the data path. Domain Name System (DNS) is another key infrastructure component that provides important signaling functions for IPv4 and IPv6. As seen over the past ten years, there is an increase in the number of attacks that target the infrastructure and DNS of the Internet and private networks. The attacks aim to create a denial of service (DoS), which affects the usability of the entire network. Attacks against network elements typically come from the Internet for perimeter-based devices, while attacks on intranet devices originate from malicious insiders. Most internal routers have simple protection mechanisms like simple passwords and Simple Network Management Protocol (SNMP) community strings. Ease of management typically outweighs security in most enterprise networks. Internet routers do not enjoy this friendly environment, and they are constantly susceptible to many different forms of attack.

Routers are not usually capable of running traditional server software or other applications that can have vulnerabilities. However, they can be the target of a buffer overflow, where the attacker attempts to send information to the router to overrun an internal memory buffer. The side effects can be anything from erratic behaviour to a software crash or gaining remote access. Any software that the router runs could be vulnerable, and any protocol supported and implemented within that software for communications to other devices is at risk for potential exploitation. Routers communicate over many different protocols, and each of those protocols is a potential target.

Hacker Experience

As mentioned before, there is a lack of IPv6 deployment experience in the industry. There is also a lack of experience in securing an IPv6 network. That is why it is important to understand the issues with IPv6 and prepare your defences. This should be done before IPv6 networks become a larger target for hackers. Not many IPv6 attacks exist or are publicly known, and there are few best practices for IPv6 security or reference security architectures for IPv6. However, a select few sophisticated hackers already use IPv6 for Internet Relay Chat (IRC) channels and back doors for their tools. Some DoS attacks are available and one IPv6 worm already exists, but there is little information available on new IPv6 attacks. It is fair to say that the current IPv6 Internet is not a big target for hackers. This is likely to change as the number of IPv6-

connected organizations grows. As IPv6 becomes more popular, it will continue to grow as a target of attacks, just as Microsoft software became more popular it became a larger target. Internet Explorer is a dominant web browser and experiences many attacks. As the Firefox web browser increased in popularity, so did the number of people working to find flaws in it. IPv6 will follow the same course as the number of deployments increases and it becomes a focus of new security research. The process of finding and correcting vulnerabilities will only make IPv6 stronger. However, because IPv6 has had so long to develop prior to mass adoption, the hope is that many of the early vulnerabilities have already been corrected.

The underground hacker community has started exploring IPv6. IPv6 is beginning to be well understood by these groups, and they are constructing tools that leverage weaknesses in the protocol and IPv6 stack implementations. Back doors that utilize IPv6 or IPv6 within IPv4 to obscure attacks and bypass firewalls are part of their repertoire. In fact, IPv6 capabilities have started to be added to several popular hacker tools.

Many of these IPv6 attack tools are already available and relatively easy to install and operate. Tools such as Scapy6 and The Hacker's Choice IPv6 Toolkit come to mind.

NOTE - Throughout this book, you will see the terms *attacker, hacker,* and *miscreant* used interchangeably to refer to malevolent forces that try to take advantage of IPv6 vulnerabilities. Attacks can be initiated by an outsider such as a *malicious user* or some *malicious host* that has been compromised and is being remotely controlled. However, attacks also can be carried out by unknowing insiders who are not aware that they have just caused a problem.

IPv6 Security Mitigation Techniques

IPv6 security architectures are not substantially different from those for IPv4. Organizations can still have the same network topologies when they transition to IPv6 as they have today. The network can still support the organization's mission, and the network can still have data centers, remote sites, and Internet connectivity, regardless of what IP version is being used.

With IPv6, the perimeter design has the same relevance as for IPv4, and most organizations can continue to have the "hard, crunchy" exterior and the "soft, squishy" interior networks. The problem is that most organizations put most of their effort into securing the perimeter, and they overlook the internal security of their environments. If these organizations considered the malicious insider threat, they might rethink the perimeter model and move to a model that has an even layer of security spread throughout. Many of these classic security paradigms still apply to IPv6 networks. When it comes to securing IPv6 networks, the following areas of an IT environment needs to be protected:

- Perimeter protections from the Internet and external entities
- Secure remote-site connectivity with Virtual Private Network (VPN) technologies
- Infrastructure protection measures to ensure a secure network foundation
- Server security to protect the critical IT assets and data
- Client security measures to mitigate the insider threat

Over time, there will be changes in the way systems communicate with IPv6. Traffic patterns can change from being primarily client/server to being more peer-to-peer in nature. The use of anycast communications can add redundancy to communications but also make them less deterministic. Mobile IPv6 and tunnels can change the perimeter concept because there needs to be trusted nodes outside the perimeter. This can transform the perimeter into a more fuzzy and nebulous concept. Greater use of end-to-end encryption is needed to secure the different communication flows. Therefore, over time, the security architectures for IPv6 networks will transform to keep up with the way people communicate. Standard IT security principles still apply when thinking about the security of IPv6 networks.

Organizations should utilize multiple defensive strategies that support each other. Organizations should also have diversity in their defences so that different types of protections help protect against multiple types of threats. Your defensive mechanisms are only as strong as the weakest link, so all parts of the protections should be fortified like a castle. A good example of this concept is to have a security architecture that has a perimeter and internal controls to not only mitigate the Internet threats but also the insider threats. Having both defence in depth and diversity of defence is like having "both a belt and suspenders" to prevent you from getting caught with your pants down. If you do not consider both for IPv6, you will have a network that is embarrassingly exposed to the elements.

The Cisco Self Defending Network (SDN) can also be a guide for protecting IPv6 networks. The SDN philosophies apply to IPv4 and IPv6 networks alike. The concepts of integration, collaboration, and adaptability are core capabilities of the self-defending network. Integrated security is the idea that security for networks should be inherent in the design and not added after the fact. This is very much the case with IPv6, where many devices have IPsec built in right from the start.

Collaboration between many diverse security solutions makes the security of the entire system more robust. IPv6 allows this form of collaboration because every node can have its own address and can easily communicate seamlessly across boundaries. Adaptability allows the security systems to respond dynamically to the situation at hand. IPv6 can provide the ability to communicate in new ways that can adapt to the needs of the users while providing security awareness. IPv6 can be the secure network platform that is the fundamental foundation of the Cisco Self Defending Network architecture.

The ways to protect IPv6 networks are much the same as those methods used to protect IPv4 networks. Concepts such as network perimeters, LAN security, remote-site communications and VPNs, infrastructure protection, server farm protection, and host/client security are all areas of focus for IPv6. The building blocks of a Self Defending Network include the following components:

- Endpoint protection
- Admission control
- Infection containment
- Intelligent correlation and incident response
- Inline Intrusion Prevention Systems (IPS) and anomaly detection
- Application security and anti-X defence

While not all of these technologies work seamlessly for IPv4 and IPv6, these are the types of components required for securing either IP version).

Few best practices exist for IPv6 deployment. As the Internet community continues to evolve IPv6 solutions, there will be solutions to the problems discovered through testing and trial deployments. IPv6 mailing lists, collaboration groups, the IETF v6ops working group, and interoperability testing organizations are deeply involved with gathering information on IPv6 deployment experiences. These organizations are experimenting with the early IPv6 solutions and documenting the best ways to implement IPv6. However, there are no current IETF Best Current Practices (BCP) for IPv6 security. As more is known about how IPv6 operates in live networks and more ways are found to secure it, the BCPs will develop.

Security risks can be mitigated through adequate training of the IT staff and the security administrators. Network professionals must understand the risks related to IPv6 and ensure that they are installing the correct protection mechanisms. Security policies need to be drafted or updated with the new security issues that IPv6 brings, and end users need security awareness training to help avoid unknowingly becoming insider threats.

Virtually all organizations rely heavily on their staff and their network security devices to protect their critical computer systems. Most organizations use firewalls, host-based and network-based intrusion prevention systems (IPS), antivirus software, and Security Information Management Systems (SIMS) to help monitor security events in this locked-down environment. Companies have spent a lot of money trying to secure their computer network infrastructure from invasion. This is primarily because there are weaknesses in the protocols and defects in applications used on computer networks that can be subverted by malicious individuals. While malicious individuals exploit weaknesses in protocols, unknowing individuals help propagate the threats by ignoring corporate security policy, guidelines, and standards.

IPv6 security devices need to be purchased when they are available and kept up to date so that when new IPv6 vulnerabilities are discovered, the computer systems are protected. Organizations are going to need IPv6-capable security products ahead of the deployment of IPv6. Firewalls are pervasive in today's networks, and there are several firewall solutions available for IPv6. However, in 2008, many IPSs and VPN concentrators do not support IPv6. The planning for the migration to IPv6 has been taking place for several years, but for now, much of the needed functionality does not exist. It can take a couple of years for there to be feature parity between IPv4 and IPv6 security products. Therefore, organizations should plan to upgrade their current security systems to achieve IPv6 functionality.

Instead of focusing on the theoretical security implications of IPv6, you should aim to implement the practical practices of securing a network based on the information that is available today. No one can yet claim extensive experience deploying all the IPv6 security mitigation techniques. For now, we can only discuss what is known to be true, based on limited deployment experiences. However, there is some certainty that the techniques shown in this book are effective based on the current knowledge of IPv6, testing, and experience securing computer networks.

Summary

Effective security involves finding that perfect balance between protecting an asset and the handling the extra burden security adds to doing business. The implementation of security should match the value of your assets and the acceptable level of risk. You should craft a security strategy that matches your level of risk. When it comes to IPv6, this means adjusting the security measures to fit the changes related to using a new network layer protocol. First you must understand the differences between IPv4 and IPv6 and know how those deltas have security implications. Next you must understand what vulnerabilities in IPv6 you must address. The final step is to implement security mitigation techniques to provide adequate coverage for your environment.

Even though the guidelines in this book are based on sound principles, they are not necessarily considered time-tested best practices. Just as IPv6 is in its early stages, the methods of securing IPv6 are rapidly changing. Because few IPv6 attacks exist, not all the future attacks are fully understood. Therefore, the guidelines in this book need to be customised to meet your organization's needs. Please do not just implement every command listed in this book. Rather, you should read the book, understand the threats, and then embark on using the correct techniques to secure your own IPv6 network.

2

Mobility

An application ending unit performs the ending processing of the ending application selected by the ending-application selecting unit and deletes the selected ending application from the list of started applications. A mobile communication terminal for starting and simultaneously using a plurality of applications, comprising: Application start determining means which compares the number of started applications with a preset numerical value that is a maximum number of simultaneously used applications, determines that the application can start when the number of started applications is less than the numerical value, and determines that the application cannot start when the number of started applications reaches the numerical value; ending-priority list creating means which calculates values indicating the using situation of the started applications in response to the determination of the application start determining means that the application cannot start and creates a list of ending priority indicating the order of applications with low influence in the case of ending the application; ending-application selecting means which selects the ending application based on the list of ending priority in response to the determination of the application start determining means that the application cannot start and clears the list of ending priority; application ending means which performs the ending processing of the ending application selected by the ending-application selecting means; application starting means which starts the application instructed by a user in response to the determination of the application start determining means that the application starts; and wherein the ending-priority list creating means collects data on evaluation items indicating the using situations including the total time displayed after starting the application, the number of switching times for display operation, and the last display time, obtains the order of started applications every evaluated item, multiplies the order by a weighting coefficient preset every evaluated item and every type of application, adds the multiplied result every application, calculates the values indicating the using situations, sorts the applications in order of the larger values, and creates the list of ending priority.

An application starting control method of a mobile communication terminal for starting and simultaneously using a plurality of applications, comprising the steps of: presetting a numerical value that is a maximum number of simultaneously used applications; selecting, from started applications, an ending application to be ended based on a priority when the number of simultaneously used applications will exceed the numerical value; newly allowing to start an application after ending the selected ending application; and collecting data for the started applications, including a total time displayed after starting the application, the number of switching times for display operation, and the last display time, determining an order of the respective data for each of the started applications, multiplying each determined order by respective weighting coefficients for each of the started applications, adding the multiplied results for each of the started applications, and creating the priority by sorting the applications based on the added results.

A mobile communication terminal for starting and simultaneously using a plurality of applications, comprising: application start determining means which compares the number of started applications with a preset numerical value that is a maximum number of simultaneously used applications, determines that the application can start when the number of started applications is less than the numerical value, and determines that the application cannot start when the number of started applications reaches the numerical value; selecting means which selects an ending application to be ended on the basis of low priority from the started applications, in response to the determination of the application start determining means that the application cannot start; application ending means which performs ending processing of the ending application selected by the ending application selecting means; application starting means which starts the application instructed by a user in response to the determination of the application start determining means that the application can start; and ending-priority list creating means for collecting data on evaluation items indicating the using situations including the total time displayed after starting the application, the number of switching times for display operation, and the last display time, obtaining the order of started applications every evaluated item, multiplying the order by a weighting coefficient preset every evaluated item and every type of application, adding the multiplied result every application, calculating the values indicating the using situations, sorting the applications in order of the larger values, and creating a priority list.

INVENTION

The present invention relates to a mobile communication terminal and an application starting control method thereof. More particularly, the present invention relates to a mobile communication terminal for starting and simultaneously using a plurality of applications and an application starting control method thereof.

Recently, one type of mobile phones is sold to start a plurality of applications and simultaneously use a plurality of functions similarly to a personal computer or the like, under the improvement of CPU processing capacity. Such a mobile phone terminal enables a user to send an e-mail while viewing a site screen on the Internet or to check the schedule by a scheduler while having a call. However, the mobile phone terminal does not have a sufficient memory capacity or power capacity. Therefore, if many applications simultaneously start similarly to the personal computer, a malfunction is caused in the communication function or the started application operation becomes unstable.

An unnecessary application must terminate without continuously staying resident in memory when the number of simultaneously-used applications reaches a predetermined limiting number. Preferably, the unnecessary application automatically ends. As disclosed in the above-mentioned publication, the degree of importance is set to the application so as to use the application with the high degree of importance for a long time when the remaining amount of battery is reduced while a plurality of applications start, and the application with the low degree of importance ends when the remaining amount of battery reduces. However, when the number of applications to be started is over a predetermined number, the application to be ended does not automatically end.

DETAILS

It is an object of the present invention to provide a mobile communication terminal and an application starting control method thereof, for fast starting a desired application and improving the operability by automatically selecting and ending the application to be ended when the number of started applications reaches a predetermined limiting number upon starting the application.

According to the present invention, there is provided an application starting control method of a mobile communication terminal for starting and simultaneously using a plurality of applications, comprising the steps of presetting a limiting number of simultaneously used applications; selecting, from started applications, an ending application to be ended based on the priority when applications over a limiting number are going to be started; and newly allowing to start an application after ending the selected ending application. The priority may be preset or may be determined based on a using situation of the started application.

The selected ending application may be displayed on a screen in response to the selection of the ending application. In this case, the selected ending application is ended in response to the approval operation of a user.

According to the present invention, there is also provided a mobile communication terminal for starting and simultaneously using a plurality of applications, comprising application start determining means which compares the number of started applications with a preset limiting number of simultaneously used applications, determines that the application can start when the number of started applications is less than the limiting number, and determines that the application cannot start when the number of started applications reaches the limiting number; selecting means which selects an ending application to be ended on the basis of low priority from the started applications in response to the determination of the application start determining means that the application cannot start; application ending means which performs ending processing of the ending application selected by the ending application selecting means; and application starting means which starts the application instructed by a user in response to the determination of the application start determining means that the application can start.

The application starting means may start the application instructed by the user in response to the ending processing of the application ending means. The application start determining means may determine whether or not the application starts in response to the instruction to start the application from the user.

The mobile communication terminal may have a list of started applications indicating the started applications. In this case, the application start determining means searches the list of started application to obtain the number of started applications. The application ending means deletes the selected ending application from the list of started applications. The application starting means starts the application determined as the start by the application start determining means and registers the started application to the list of started applications. The mobile communication terminal may further comprises means for receiving the approval of the user before the ending processing of the ending application in response to the selection of the ending application by the ending application selecting means.

According to the present invention, there is also provided a mobile communication terminal for starting and simultaneously using a plurality of applications, comprising application start determining means which compares the number of started applications with a preset limiting number of simultaneously used applications, determines that the application can start when the number of started applications is less than the limiting number, and determines that the application cannot start when the number of started applications reaches the limiting number; ending-priority list creating means which calculates values indicating the using situation of the started applications in response to the determination of the application start determining means that the application cannot start and creates a list of ending priority indicating the order of applications with low influence in the case of ending the application; ending-application selecting means which selects the ending application based on the list of ending priority in response to the determination of the application start determining means that the application cannot start and clears the list of ending priority; application ending means which performs the ending processing of the ending application selected by the ending-application selecting means; and application starting means which starts the application instructed by a user in response to the determination of the application start determining means that the application starts.

The ending-priority list creating means may collect data on evaluation items indicating the using situations including the total time displayed after starting the application, the number of switching times for display operation, and the last display time, place a number to each of started applications in the order of their magnitude every evaluated item, multiply the number by a weighting coefficient preset every evaluated item and every type of application, add the multiplied results every application, calculate the values indicating the using situations, sort the applications in order of the larger values, and create the list of ending priority.

The mobile communication terminal may have a list of started applications indicating the started application. In this case, the application start determining means searches the list of started applications and obtains the number of started applications; the application ending means deletes the selected ending application from the list of started applications, and the application starting means starts the application determined as the start by the application start determining means and registers the started application to the list of started applications.

According to the present invention, the limiting number (maximum number) of applications for simultaneous use is set and when the start of a new application amounts to the number of applications over the limiting number, the application for ending is automatically determined and is ended in accordance with the priority from among the using applications. Thus, in case that the number of applications reaches the limiting number, the new application is started quickly and the operability upon starting the application is improved.

WIRELESS COMMUNICATIONS

Wireless communications is a rapidly growing segment of the communications industry, with the potential to provide high-speed high-quality information exchange between portable devices located anywhere in the world. Potential applications enabled by this technology include multimedia Internet-enabled cell phones, smart homes and appliances, automated highway systems, video teleconferencing and distance learning, and autonomous sensor networks, to name just a few. However, supporting these applications using wireless techniques poses a significant technical challenge.

This course will cover advanced topics in wireless communications for voice, data, and multimedia. We begin with a brief overview of current wireless systems and standards. We then characterize the wireless channel, including path loss for different environments, random log-normal shadowing due to signal attenuation, and the flat and frequency-selective properties of multipath fading. Next we examine the fundamental capacity limits of wireless channels and the characteristics of the capacity-achieving transmission strategies.

These strategies are typically not practical. Thus, our next focus will be on practical digital modulation techniques and their performance under wireless channel impairments, including flat and frequency selective fading. The next part of the course is spent investigating techniques to improve the speed and performance of wireless links. We will investigate the design and performance of adaptive modulation and diversity techniques to compensate for flat-fading. Three techniques to combat frequency-selective fading are then examined: adaptive equalization, multicarrier modulation, and spread spectrum. We will also study the multiple access capabilities of spread spectrum with multiuser detection. The course concludes with a brief overview of wireless networks, including multiple and random access techniques, WLANs, cellular system design, and ad-hoc network design. Applications for these systems, including the evolution of cell phones and PDAs, smart homes and appliances, sensor networks, and automated highways and skyways, will also be discussed.

Presenting comprehensive coverage of this fast moving field, Wireless Communications and Mobile Computing provides the R&D communities working in academia and the telecommunications and networking industries with a forum for sharing research and ideas.

The convergence of wireless communications and mobile computing is bringing together two areas of immense growth and innovation. This is reflected throughout the journal by strongly focusing on new trends, developments, emerging technologies and new industrial standards.

Under the guidance of an international editorial and advisory board drawn from academia and industry, this high quality, peer-reviewed journal, provides leading edge coverage of the opportunities and challenges driving the research and development of mobile communication systems.

All you need to stay ahead:

- High calibre survey papers
  Written by leading experts in the wireless and networking communities.
- Rapid publication times
  Due to electronic review and submission of original research papers
- Special Issues
  Addressing key topics of interest and managed by high profile editors
- An international forum for the sharing of research and ideas
  Key topics presented by leading individuals at the cutting edge of new technologies.

BANDWIDTH

In computer networks, bandwidth is often used as a synonym for data transfer rate-the amount of data that can be carried from one point to another in a given time period (usually a second). This kind of bandwidth is usually expressed in bits (of data) per second (bps). Occasionally, it's expressed as bytes per second (Bps). A modem that works at 57,600 bps hastwice the bandwidth of a modem that works at 28,800 bps. In general, a link with a high bandwidth is one that may be able to carry enough information to sustain the succession of images in a video presentation.

It should be remembered that a real communications path usually consists of a succession of links, each with its own bandwidth. If one of these is much slower than the rest, it is said to be a bandwidth bottleneck.

In electronic communication, bandwidth is the width of the range (orband) of frequencies that an electronic signal uses on a given transmission medium. In this usage, bandwidth is expressed in terms of the difference between the highest-frequency signal component and the lowest-frequency signal component. Since the frequency of a signal is measured in hertz (the number of cycles of change per second), a given bandwidth is the difference in hertz between the highest frequency the signal uses and the lowest frequency it uses. A typical voice signal has a bandwidth of approximately three kilohertz (3 kHz); an analog television (TV) broadcast video signal has a bandwidth of six megahertz (6 MHz) -- some 2,000 times as wide as the voice signal.

MOBILE INTERNET

WML (Wireless Markup Language) is the new web language for making sites on mobile phones. Over the past few months new WAP (Wireless Applications Protocol) phones have become extremely popular and many large websites have created special'mobile' versions of their site. Many people predict that, over the next few years, WAP sites will become even morepopular and e-commerce over mobile phones will be widely available.

USING WML

Although you might not have any plans immediately for creating a WAP version of your site, it is always a good idea to get involved in new technology. All you need to do is make a small site (even one page) which tells people a bit about your website. In the future you can develop the site further with things like e-mail and information for people to get directly off their phones. The main sites which will benefit from WAP are ones providing a service like e-mail, live sports scores or a calendar service etc. but there are many other uses. For example, a site giving music reviews could put their reviews on a WAP site. People could then read the reviews on their mobile phone while browsing through the CDs in a shop.

HAVING WAP PHONE

To create a WAP site you don't need a WAP enabled phone. You can get a WAP simulator for a PC. This is a piece of software which will give you a WAP phone on your desktop. You can then type in the URLs of WAP sites and can view them on your PC. You can get a very good free WAP simulator from YourWAP

COMPARING SITES

WAP sites are not like standard web sites at all. As an example, you are looking at part of the Gowansnet web site. Here is a screenshot of the Gowansnet WAP site (http:// gowansnet.waphosts.net):

BEGINNING WAP SITE

After reading the introduction you should understand about WAP sites, WML and what you can do with them so I will go straight into how to create a site. Note that you should really either have a WAP phone or a WAP simulator so that you can view your site and a knowledge of HTML is useful.

Finding A WML Host

Unfortunately WML cannot be run on all web hosts. For WML content to be run, a web host must make some changes to the configuration of their web server. If your host cannot do this for you, you can try WAPHosts.net. They can provide you with a server which will support WML.

Declaring A WML Document

Cards

Instead of having pages, WAP sites have cards. These are what is displayed on the screen at one time, just like a page. More than one card can be inserted in each WML document. To declare a card, insert the following:

```
<card id="index" title="My WAP Site"
newcontext="true">
```

This will make a card with the ID index (used for linking) and will display the text:

My WAP Site at the top of the screen.

Closing Tags

Unlike with HTML, it is extremely important to close WML tags.

If you do not, a page will certainly not work. You must close both the <card> and <wml> tags:

```
</card>
</wml>
```

ADDING TEXT

In the last part I showed you how to create the basic file which will contain your WAP site. In this part I am going to show you how to insert text and how to format it.

The <p> Tag

Just like in HTML the <p> tag is used to show where a paragraph begins and ends. Unlike HTML, though, all text on a WML page must be inside these tags. You are not allowed to nest these tags either. One important thing to remember about WML is that, unlike HTML where a page will still display even if there is bad code, a WAP phone will just reject a page if there is and code it doesn't understand.

As with HTML you use the tags as follows:

```
<p>
information
</p>
```

Aligning Text

Aligning text in WML is nearly exactly the same as in HTML, except you can't use the center tag. All aligning must be done using the following <p> tags:

Center:

```
<p align="center">
```

Right:

```
<p align="right">
```

The
 Tag

In WML (as mentioned earlier) all tags must be closed. This causes problems when using old HTML tags (like <Br>) which have no closing tag. To get around this, some tags have had a/ put on the end *e.g.*

```
<Br/>
```

This, like in HTML will make a line break.

Text

In WML there is actually no font tag (as you can only display text in the phone's default font in black). To show text all you need to do is put it in between the <p> and </p> tags. Here is an example of a full WML document:

```
<?xml version="1.0"?>
<!DOCTYPE wml PUBLIC"-//WAPFORUM//DTD WML 1.1//EN""http://www.wapforum.org/DTD/wml_1.1.xml">
<wml>
<card id="index" title="My WAP Site" newcontext="true">
<p align="center">
Welcome to my new WAP site. You can view this on your mobile phone anywhere in the world!<Br/>
It is amazing!
</p>
</card>
</wml>
```

HYPERLINKS AND IMAGES

In part 3 I showed you how to create a basic WAP site with one page and some text. This week I will show you how you can make this better by adding extra parts, linking to them (and other sites) and how to add images to your site.

More Cards

As I explained in the second part of this tutorial, WAP sites have cards instead of pages. They are really the same as pages except they can all be written in one file. To add another card, all you need to do is put in another <card> tag with a different ID to the others.

For example:

```
<card title="About Me" id="about">
information
</card>
```

would be added below the first card but before the </wml> tag.

Linking

There are three ways to link to another WAP site, file or card. Just like in HTML these can either be the full path to a file or a relative link.

To link to a WAP site you use the following:

```
<a href="http://gowansnet.waphosts.net/">
```

Gowansnet</a>

in your text. To link to another file on your site you would use:

```
<a href="links.wml">My Links</a>
```

and to link to another card in the same page you use:

```
<a href="#about">About Me</a>
```

Images

Unfortunately, because WAP phones only have monochrome screens, images do not work very well on WML pages. They also use their own image format: WBMP. When you are creating an image to use on your site you will need to make it small (mobile phone screens are about 100x50 pixels).

The easiest way to get an image into the WBMP format is to create it as a GIF or JPG (it can be in colour if you want) and then visit Teraflops.com to convert it into a monochrome (black and white) WBMP image which you can then include on your site.

Images in WML are inserted using the <img> tag, just like in HTML:

```
<img src="logo.wbmp" alt="Logo"/>
```

Again, you can see that a/ has been added at the end as the <img> tag has no closing tag. It is very important that you also include the alt text as it will be displayed while the image is being downloaded.

NETWORK SYSTEM

A network operating system (NOS) is a computer operating system system that is designed primarily to support workstation, personal computer, and, in some instances, older terminal that are connected on a local area network (LAN).

Artisoft's LANtastic, Banyan VINES, Novell's NetWare, and Microsoft's LAN Manager are examples of network operating systems. In addition, some multi-purpose operating systems, such asWindows NT and Digital's OpenVMS come with capabilities that enable them to be described as a network operating system.

A network operating system provides printer sharing, common file system and database sharing, application sharing, and the ability to manage a network name directory, security, and other housekeeping aspects of a network.

A network operating system (NOS) is a software programme that controls other software and hardware that runs on a network. It also allows multiple computers, also known as network computers, to communicate with one main computer and each other, so as to share resources, run applications, and send messages, among other things.

A computer network can consist of a wireless network, local area network (LAN), a wide area network (WAN), or even two or three computer networks. The heart of any of these networks, however, is the network operating system.

There are different types of operating systems. Most individual computer users run client operating systems, like Windows XP®, which run on a single computer. Personal computers that individuals use at home have a client operating system which manages the interactions and processes between the computer and its peripherals such as the keyboard, mouse, external monitor, and printer. In a sense, this is also a network, though it is different in scale than a network operating system which manages the interactions of many computers.

A network usually consists of many network computers that are connected to a central hub or router. The central hub, in turn, is connected to a larger, main computer. The network may also include other devices like printers, a tape-backup system, and a central storage facility. The main network computer runs all the connected computers and devices with the help of the operating system software. A network administrator is the person who installs and manages the network and its operating system. He or she may configure the NOS to recognize a wireless network as well. If a WAN is involved, this would probably require more than one network administrator, as the network would likely be located offsite. A network operating system has a menu-driven administration interface.

From this interface, the network administrator may perform a variety of activities. He or she can use the interface to format hard drives, set up security restrictions, or establish log-in information for each user. The interface of a network operating system can also be used to attach shared printers to the network, or configure the system to automatically back data up on a daily basis.

An important component of a network is the file server. A file server is the device where data is stored for use by network computers. It can be a single computer or it can be a cluster of external hard drives hooked up in series to store data.

A network operating system helps manage the flow of information between that file server and the network computers. Examples of network operating systems include UNIX®, Windows 2000 Server ®, and Netware®. Each operating system runs differently, and as such has to be configured to perform the actions the network requires. A good knowledge of each operating system is necessary to work with them. Network administrators may need to be certified in order to manage particular network operating systems.

UNIX

DESCRIPTION

Is it possible for an Information Technology [IT] product to be both mature and state-of-the-art at the same time? In the case of the UNIX® system, the answer is an unqualified"Yes." The UNIX system has continued to develop over the past twenty-five years. In millions of installations running on nearly every hardware platform made, the UNIX system has earned its reputation for stability and scalability. Over the years, UNIX system suppliers have steadily assimilated new technologies so that UNIX systems today provide more functionality as any other operating system.

Perhaps the key to the continuing growth of the UNIX system is the free-market demands placed upon suppliers who produce and support software built to open standards. The"open systems" approach is in bold contrast to other operating environments that lock in their customers with resultant high switching costs. UNIX system suppliers, on the other hand, must constantly provide the highest quality systems in order to retain their customers. Those who become dissatisfied with one UNIX system implementation retain the ability to easily move to another UNIX system implementation.

The continuing success of the UNIX system should come as no surprise. No other operating environment enjoys the support of every major system supplier. Mention the UNIX system and IT professionals immediately think not only of the operating system itself, but also of the large family of application software that the UNIX system supports. In the IT marketplace, the UNIX system has been the catalyst for sweeping changes that have empowered consumers to seek the best-of-breed without the arbitrary constraints imposed by proprietary environments.

In a nutshell then, the UNIX system is the users' and suppliers' operating environment of choice. The UNIX system represents the best collective efforts of competing suppliers, the most refined standards in the public domain, and the rock-solid stability that comes from years of quality assurance testing, mission-critical use, and refinement. This white paper examines the UNIX system with a special concern for both its extraordinary past and its equally extraordinary prospects for the future.

THE UNIX SYSTEM

The UNIX system has been around for a long time, and

many people may remember it as it existed in the previous decades. Many IT professionals who encountered UNIX systems in the past found it uncompromising. While its power was impressive, its command-line interface required technical competence, its syntax was not intuitive, and its interface was unfriendly. Moreover, in the UNIX system's early days, security was virtually nonexistent. Subsequently, the UNIX system became the first operating system to suffer attacks mounted over the nascent Internet. As the UNIX system matured, however, the organization of security shifted from centralized to distributed authentication and authorization systems.

Now, a single Graphical User Interface is shipped and supported by all major vendors has replaced command-line syntax, and security systems, up to and including B1, provide appropriate controls over access to the UNIX system.

THE VALUE OF STANDARDS

The UNIX system's increasing popularity spawned the development of a number of variations of the UNIX operating system in the 1980s, and the existence of these caused a mid-life crisis. Standardization had progressed slowly and methodically in domains such as telecommunications and third-generation languages; yet no one had addressed standards at the operating system level.

For suppliers, the thought of a uniform operating environment was disconcerting. Consumer lock-in was woven tightly into the fabric of the industry. Individual consumers, particularly those with UNIX system experience, envisioned standardized environments, but had no way to pull the market in their direction.

However, for one category of consumer -governments- the standardization of the UNIX system was both desirable and within reach. Governments have clout and are the largest consumers of information technology products and services in the world. Driven by the need to improve commonality, both US and European governments endorsed a shift to the UNIX system. The Institute of Electrical and Electronic

Engineers POSIX family of standards, along with standards from ISO, ANSI and others, led the way. Consortia such as the X/Open Company (merged with the Open Software Foundation in 1995 to form The Open Group) hammered out draft standards to accelerate the process.

In 1994, the definitive specification of what constitutes a UNIX system was finalized through X/Open Company's consensus process. The Single UNIX Specification was born-not from a theoretical, ivory tower approach, but by analyzing the applications that were in use in businesses across the world.

With the active support of government and commercial buyers alike, vendors began to converge on products that implement the Single UNIX Specification, and now all major vendors have products labeled UNIX 95, which indicates that the vendor guarantees that the product conforms to the Single UNIX Specification.

Vendors continue to add value to the UNIX system, particularly in areas of new technology, however that value will always be built upon a single, consensus standard. Meanwhile, the functionality of the UNIX system was established and the mid-life crisis was resolved. Suppliers today provide UNIX systems that are built upon a single, consensus standard.

It is also important to remember that even when variance among UNIX systems was at its worst, IT professionals agreed that migration among UNIX system variants was far easier than migration among the proprietary alternatives.

Now with UNIX 95 branded products available from all major systems vendors, the buyer can for the first time buy systems from different manufacturers, safe in the knowledge that each one is guaranteed to implement the complete functionality of the Single UNIX Specification and will continue to do so.

UNIX system suppliers can assure customers that they own a standards-based system by registering them to use the Open Brand. Below is a list of suppliers who give users this guarantee.

UNIX AND WINDOWS NT

It is common these days to read analysts' accounts and IS professionals' experiences that compare and contrast the UNIX system with Microsoft Corporation's latest operating system, called Windows NT. Opinions vary, of course, but a number of common themes have emerged. The key differences between these operating environments are as follows: The UNIX system today is more robust, reliable and scalable. Analysts say this observation, which is widely reported from many different viewpoints, makes practical sense. Engineers at Microsoft are retracing the steps that the UNIX system has completed. How else could it be?

In sharp contrast to the open standards that define the UNIX system, Windows NT technology remains fiercely proprietary. Microsoft remains ambivalent to the world of standards. Choosing NT entangles customers with nonstandard utilities, directories, and software tools that do not conform to any de jure or consensus standards.

The UNIX system today is available on a wide spectrum of computer hardware. Particularly when high performance is at issue, hardware suppliers suggest the UNIX system, rather than Windows NT. The primary appeal of NT is for low-end, office-centered, departmental applications.

Unit shipment growth rates for Windows NT exceed the rates for the UNIX system, which is to be expected for a new product. However, revenue growth in UNIX systems sales is much higher than NT. It is reasonable to expect Windows NT to take a share in the operating systems market, along with other more specialized operating systems. There is no evidence today to indicate that NT will be dominant; in fact, most IT professionals predict that it will not.

Windows NT Server 4.0 is still not a full-function server operating system. While it does support multi-user computing via third-party add-on tools, it lacks certain fundamental features that the UNIX system is known for providing, such as directory services for managing user access and peripherals over a distributed enterprise network. The presence of the UNIX system in the marketplace has been good for Windows

NT. The UNIX system established the market for cross-platform client and server operating environments that NT seeks to address. In turn, NT will improve the market for UNIX systems in the future. That is, competition among UNIX system providers will be enhanced by competition with NT. The choice between open and proprietary products will be quite crisp.

TODAY'S UNIX SYSTEM

The key to the continuing growth of the UNIX system is the free-market demands placed upon suppliers who produce and support software built to public standards. The"open systems" approach is in bold contrast to other operating environments that lock in their customers with high switching costs. UNIX system suppliers, on the other hand, must constantly provide the highest quality systems in order to retain their customers. Those who become dissatisfied with one UNIX system implementation retain the ability to easily move to another UNIX system implementation.

The continuing success of the UNIX system should come as no surprise. No other operating environment enjoys the support of every major system supplier. Mention the UNIX system and IT professionals immediately think not only of the operating system itself, but also of the large family of hardware and application software that the UNIX system supports. In the IT marketplace, the UNIX system has been the catalyst for sweeping changes that have empowered consumers to seek the best-of-breed without the arbitrary constraints imposed by proprietary environments.

The market's pull for the UNIX system was amplified by other events as well. The availability of relational database management systems, the shift to the client/server architecture, and the introduction of low-cost UNIX system servers together set the stage for business applications to flourish. For client/server systems, the networking strengths of the UNIX system shine. Standardized relational database engines delivered on low-cost high-performance UNIX system servers offered substantial cost savings over proprietary alternatives.

EXISTENCE

UNIX system suppliers also have a proud tradition of integration with legacy systems as well as innovation to uphold. No other system can ensure that disparate systems-usually proprietary systems-can be integrated, allowing the buyer's investment in data and information to be realised with minimal disruption and reinvestment.

There is every reason to believe that the UNIX system will continue to be the platform of choice for innovative development. In the near term, for example, UNIX system vendors will define the scope of Java and provide the distributed computing environment into which the Network Computer terminal will fit and enable it to thrive and grow.

How will Java and the Network Computer terminal manifest themselves? The exact answer is unknown; however, in open computing, the process for finding that answer is well understood. The UNIX system community has set aside (via consensus standards) the wasteful task of developing arbitrary differences among computing environments. Rather than building proprietary traps, this community is actively seeking ways to add value to the UNIX system with improved scalability, reliability, price/performance, and customer service.

Java and the Network Computer terminal offer several potential advantages for consumers. One key advantage is a smaller, lighter, standards-based client. A second advantage is a specification that is not controlled by one company, but is developed to the benefit of all by an open, consensus process. Thirdly, greater code reuse and a component software market based on Object technology, such as CORBA and Java. All of these options and more are being deployed first by members of the UNIX system community.

INDUSTRIAL STRENGTH UNIX SYSTEM

Today's UNIX system is robust, scalable, and it continues to provide uniform access to a wide variety of computing hardware. For these reasons the UNIX system continues to be the operating system of choice for mission-critical systems.

The UNIX system is the key enabler for enterprises that wish to keep switching costs as low as possible. That is, the UNIX system remains the only open alternative to locking in on a proprietary operating system.

Scalability is here today, enabling application to run on small-scale systems through to the largest servers necessary. The UNIX system is available on hardware ranging from low-cost PC-class servers on through parallel architectures that harness together 60 or more processors. This range is wider and the choices of hardware more cost effective than any other system. The UNIX system is the only option for Massively Parallel Processing (MPP).

A robust operating system is tough enough to perform successfully under a variety of different operating conditions. By virtue of its worldwide deployment by an international community of system vendors, the UNIX system has earned the reputation for robustness.

Uniform operating system services are at the heart of the standardized UNIX system. Many enterprise systems are assembled with hardware from several different sources. Atop these different hardware platforms, the UNIX operating system provides a uniform platform for database management systems and application software.

The market for the UNIX system continues to expand. IDC estimates the market at US$ 39 billion in 1996 and forecasts the market to be US$ 50 billion in the year 2000. In addition, the installed base of the UNIX system has an estimated value of US$ 122 billion. These market estimates lead to several conclusions about the UNIX system, as follows:

An annual market of US$ 39 billion is large enough to remain attractive to many suppliers and to provide sufficient revenue to fund continuing high levels of investment in support and product enhancement.

The UNIX system's growth rates, which appear modest in comparison to the unit shipment growth of newer products, are anchored by an enormous installed base. High unit shipment growth rates are typical of new entries in a marketplace.

In key benchmarks and mission-critical applications, the UNIX system consistently performs better. The UNIX system is the dominant software platform for Relational Database Management Systems. Investment in developing and enhancing UNIX system products is significantly larger than in any other operating environment.

SINGLE UNIX SPECIFICATION

Today, The Open Group's UNIX 95 brand may be applied to any operating system product that is guaranteed to meet the Single UNIX Specification. The Single UNIX Specification is designed to give software developers a single set of APIs to be supported by every UNIX system.

The most significant consequence of the Single UNIX Specification initiative is that it shifts the focus of attention away from incompatible UNIX system product implementations on to compliance with a single, agreed-upon set of APIs. If an operating system meets the specification, and commonly available applications can run on it, then it can reliable viewed as open. So, the future looks as though it will be about a set of sturdy and dependable specifications standing as a firm foundation upon which many competing product implementations will be built.

BENEFITS FOR USERS

The Single UNIX Specification will evolve and develop in response to market needs protecting users investment in existing systems and applications. The availability of the UNIX system from multiple suppliers gives users freedom of choice rather than being locked in to a single supplier. And the wide range of applications-built on the UNIX system's strengths of scalability, availability and reliability-ensure that mission critical business needs can be met.

SUMMARY

When the history of the information age is written, the extraordinary dynamics of the UNIX system marketplace will be seen as playing an important role. The UNIX system was developed at just the right time and place to be the critical enabler for a revolution in information technology. Client/ server architectures, the Internet, object databases, heterogeneous transaction processing, and Web computing all emerged on the shoulders of the UNIX system.

Most importantly, the UNIX system continues to be a driving force for innovation because of its commitment to standards. When proprietary differences are set aside, and with the wide implementation of the Single UNIX Specification they are set aside, suppliers compete by adding value. This fundamental tenet is the reason that the UNIX system has thrived-and will continue to thrive in the years to come.

HISTORY

Unix was originally developed in the 1960s and 1970s by a group of AT&T employees at Bell Labs. Today, Unix systems are split into different branches which have developed over time by AT&T and by commercial vendors and non-profit organizations. Many variations (usually called"flavours") of Unix and Unix-like Operating Systems were released during the dot com boom of the 1990's. The dot com bust caused many of these to consolidate. As a result, of the dozens of commercial variations of Unix that were developed in the 1980s, only Solaris, HP-UX, and AIX are still doing relatively well in the market. Of these, Solaris currently holds the highest market share.

A system is termed UNIX only if it complies fully with (and is certified by) the Single Unix Specification (SUS) standards. Similar systems that do not comply fully or are not certified are termed"Unix-like" operating systems. Examples of popular Unix-like systems include Linux and Xenix.

LINUX

Linux is quite possibly the most important free software achievement since the original Space War, or, more recently, Emacs. It has developed into an operating system for business, education, and personal productivity. Linux is no longer only for UNIX wizards who sit for hours in front of a glowing console (although we assure you that many users fall into this category).

Linux can turn any 80386 or better personal computer into a workstation that puts the full power of UNIX at your fingertips. Businesses install Linux on entire networks of machines, and use the operating system to manage financial and hospital records, distributed computing environments, and telecommunications. Universities worldwide use Linux to teach courses on operating system programming and design. Computing enthusiasts everywhere use Linux at home for programming, productivity, and all-around hacking.

What makes Linux so different is that it is a free implementation of UNIX. It was and still is developed cooperatively by a group of volunteers, primarily on the Internet, who exchange code, report bugs, and fix problems in an open-ended environment. Anyone is welcome to join the Linux development effort. All it takes is interest in hacking a free UNIX clone, and some programming know-how.

HISTORY

UNIX is one of the most popular operating systems worldwide because of its large support base and distribution. It was originally developed at AT&T as a multitasking system for minicomputers and mainframes in the 1970's, but has since grown to become one of the most widely-used operating systems anywhere, despite its sometimes confusing interface and lack of central standardization.

Many hackers feel that UNIX is the Right Thing--the One True Operating System. Hence, the development of Linux by an expanding group of UNIX hackers who want to get their hands dirty with their own system.

Versions of UNIX exist for many systems, from personal computers to supercomputers like the Cray Y-MP. Most versions of UNIX for personal computers are expensive and cumbersome. At the time of this writing, a one-machine version of UNIX System V for the 386 runs about US$1500.

Linux is a free version of UNIX developed primarily by Linus Torvalds at the University of Helsinki in Finland, with the help of many UNIX programmers and wizards across the Internet. Anyone with enough know-how and gumption can develop and change the system. The Linux kernel uses no code from AT&T or any other proprietary source, and much of the software available for Linux was developed by the GNU project of the Free Software Foundation in Cambridge, Massachusetts, U.S.A. However, programmers from all over the world have contributed to the growing pool of Linux software.

Linux was originally developed as a hobby project by Linus Torvalds. It was inspired by Minix, a small UNIX system developed by Andy Tanenbaum. The first discussions about Linux were on the Usenet newsgroup, comp.os.minix. These discussions were concerned mostly with the development of a small, academic UNIX system for Minix users who wanted more.

The very early development of Linux mostly dealt with the task-switching features of the 80386 protected-mode interface, all written in assembly code. Linus writes, ``After that it was plain sailing: hairy coding still, but I had some devices, and debugging was easier. I started using C at this stage, and it certainly speeds up development. This is also when I started to get serious about my megalomaniac ideas to make `a better Minix than Minix.' I was hoping I'd be able to recompile gcc under Linux someday...

``Two months for basic setup, but then only slightly longer until I had a disk driver (seriously buggy, but it happened to work on my machine) and a small file system. That was about when I made 0.01 available (around late August of 1991): it wasn't pretty, it had no floppy driver, and it couldn't do much of anything. I don't think anybody ever compiled that version. But by then I was hooked, and didn't want to stop until I could chuck out Minix." No announcement was ever made for Linux version 0.01. The 0.01 sources weren't even executable. They contained only the bare rudiments of the kernel source and assumed that you had access to a Minix machine to compile and experiment with them. On October 5, 1991, Linus announced the first ``official'' version of Linux, which was version 0.02. At that point, Linus was able to run bash (the GNU Bourne Again Shell) and gcc (the GNU C compiler), but not much else. Again, this was intended as a hacker's system. The primary focus was kernel development--user support, documentation, and distribution had not yet been addressed. Today, the Linux community still seems to treat these issues as secondary to ``real programming''--kernel development.

After version 0.03, Linus bumped up the version number to 0.10, as more people started to work on the system. After several further revisions, Linus increased the version number to 0.95 in March, 1992, to reflect his expectation that the system was ready for an ``official'' release soon. (Generally, software is not assigned the version number 1.0 until it is theoretically complete or bug-free.). Almost a year and a half later, in late December of 1993, the Linux kernel was still at version 0.99.pl14--asymptotically approaching 1.0. At the time of this writing, the current stable kernel version is 2.0 patchlevel 33, and version 2.1 is under development.

Most of the major, free UNIX software packages have been ported to Linux, and commercial software is also available. More hardware is supported than in the original kernel versions. Many people have executed benchmarks on 80486 Linux systems and found them comparable with mid-range workstations from Sun Microsystems and Digital Equipment Corporation. Who would have ever guessed that this ``little'' UNIX clone would have grown up to take on the entire world of personal computing?

SYSTEM FEATURES

Linux supports features found in other implementations of UNIX, and many which aren't found elsewhere. In this section, we'll take a nickel tour of the features of the Linux kernel. Linux is a complete multitasking, multiuser operating system, as are all other versions of UNIX. This means that many users can log into and run programmes on the same machine simultaneously. The Linux system is mostly compatible with several UNIX standards (inasmuch as UNIX has standards) at the source level, including IEEE POSIX.1, UNIX System V, and Berkely System Distribution UNIX. Linux was developed with source code portability in mind, and it's easy to find commonly used features that are shared by more than one platform. Much of the free UNIX software available on the Internet and elsewhere compiles under Linux ``right out of the box." In addition, all of the source code for the Linux system, including the kernel, device drivers, libraries, user programmes, and development tools, is freely distributable.

Other specific internal features of Linux include POSIX job control (used by shells like csh and bash), pseudoterminals (pty devices), and support for dynamically loadable national or customised keyboard drivers. Linux supports virtual consoles that let you switch between login sessions on the same system console. Users of the screen programme will find the Linux virtual console implementation familiar.

The kernel can emulate 387-FPU instructions, and systems without a math coprocessor can run programmes that require floating-point math capability. Linux supports various file systems for storing data, like the ext2 file system, which was developed specifically for Linux. The Xenix and UNIX System V file systems are also supported, as well as the Microsoft MS-DOS and Windows 95 VFAT file systems on a hard drive or floppy. The ISO 9660 CD-ROM file system is also supported.

Linux provides a complete implementation of TCP/IP networking software. This includes device drivers for many popular Ethernet cards, SLIP (Serial Line Internet Protocol) and PPP (Point-to-Point Protocol), which provide access to a TCP/IP network via a serial connection, PLIP (Parallel Line Internet Protocol), and NFS (Network File System).

The Linux kernel is developed to use protected-mode features of Intel 80386 and better processors. In particular, Linux uses the protected-mode, descriptor based, memory-management paradigm, and other advanced features. Anyone familiar with 80386 protected-mode programming knows that this chip was designed for multitasking systems like UNIX. Linux exploits this functionality.

The kernel supports demand-paged, loaded executables. Only those segments of a programme which are actually in use are read into memory from disk. Also, copy-on-write pages are shared among executables. If several instances of a programme are running at once, they share physical memory, which reduces overall usage. When the system requires more physical memory, it swaps inactive pages to disk, letting you run larger applications and support more users. However, swapping data to disk is no substitute for physical RAM, which is much faster.

The Linux kernel also implements a unified memory pool for user programmes and disk cache. All free memory is used by the cache, which is reduced when running large programmes.

Executables use dynamically linked, shared libraries: code from a single library on disk. This is not unlike the SunOS shared library mechanism. Executable files occupy less disk space, especially those which use many library functions. There are also statically linked libraries for object debugging and maintaining ``complete" binary files when shared libraries are not installed. The libraries are dynamically linked at run time, and the programmer can use his or her own routines in place of the standard library routines.

To facilitate debugging, the kernel generates core dumps for post-mortem analysis. A core dump and an executable linked with debugging support allows a developer to determine what caused a programme to crash.

SOFTWARE FEATURES

Virtually every utility one would expect of a standard UNIX implementation has been ported to Linux, including basic commands like ls, awk, tr, sed, bc, and more. The familiar working environment of other UNIX systems is duplicated on Linux. All standard commands and utilities are included. (Novice UNIX or Linux users should introduction to basic UNIX commands.) Many text editors are available, including vi, ex, pico, jove, and GNU emacs, and variants like Lucid emacs, which incorporates extensions of the X Window System, and joe. The text editor you're accustomed to using has more than likely been ported to Linux.

The choice of a text editor is an interesting one. Many UNIX users prefer ``simple'' editors like vi. (The original author wrote this book with vi.) But vi has many limitations due to its age, and modern editors like emacs have gained popularity. emacs supports a complete, Lisp based macro language and interpreter, powerful command syntax, and other extensions. There are emacs macro packages which let you read electronic mail and news, edit directory contents, and even engage in artificially intelligent psychotherapy sessions (indispensible for stressed-out Linux hackers).

3

Security in IT

INTRODUCTION

MISUSE OF COMPUTER SYSTEMS

As we store more and more information in computer data bases, and as these data bases become more closely linked in networks, more people have broader access to more information than ever before. Computer technology has magnified many times the ability of a careless or disaffected employee to cause severe damage. Owing to the magnitude of problems that can be caused by misuse of computer systems, Misuse of Technical Information Systems is now one of the 13 criteria used in adjudicating approval and revocation of security clearances for access to classified information. Adjudicative Guidelines for Determining Access to Classified Information

Many aspects of computer use are governed by your organization's policy rather than by federal government regulation. Many government agencies and defence contractors specify the security procedures and prohibited or inappropriate activities discussed below.

SECURITY RULES

The following are basic rules for secure use of the computer:

- Do not enter into any computer system without authorization. Unauthorized entry into a protected or compartmented computer file is a serious security violation and is probably illegal. It can be a basis for revocation of your security clearance. Whether motivated by the challenge of penetrating the system or by simple curiosity to see what is there, unauthorized entry is a deliberate disregard for rules and regulations. It can cause you to be suspected of espionage. At a minimum, it violates the need-to-know principle and in some cases is an invasion of privacy.

- Do not store or process classified information on any system not explicitly approved for classified processing.
- Do not attempt to circumvent or defeat security or auditing systems without prior authorization from the system administrator, other than as part of a system test or security research authorized in advance.
- Do not install any software on your computer without the approval of your system administrator.
- Do not use another individual's userid, password, or identity.
- Do not permit an unauthorized individual (including spouse, relative or friend) access to any sensitive computer network.
- Do not reveal your password to *anyone* — not even your computer system administrator.
- Do not respond to any telephone call from anyone whom you do not personally know who asks questions about your computer, how you use your computer, or about your userid or password.
- If you are the inadvertent recipient of classified material sent via e-mail or become aware of classified material on an open bulletin board or web site, you must report this to the security office.
- Do not modify or alter the operating system or configuration of any system without first obtaining permission from the owner or administrator of that system.
- Do not use your office computer system to gain unauthorized access to any other computer system.

TYPICAL USAGE

Many offices permit some, minimal personal use of office equipment when such personal use involves minimal expense to the organization, is performed on your personal non-work time, does not interfere with the office's mission, and does not violate standards of ethical conduct.

The following activities are considered to be misuse of office equipment:

- The creation, download, viewing, storage, copying, or transmission of sexually explicit or sexually oriented materials can cause you to be fired from your job. See discussion under E-Mail.
- Annoying or harassing another individual, for example through uninvited e-mail of a personal nature or using lewd or offensive language can cause you to be fired from your job. See discussion under E-Mail.
- Using the computer for commercial purposes or in support of "for-profit" activities or in support of other outside employment, business activity (*e.g.*, consulting for pay, sales or administration of business transactions, sale of goods or services), or gambling.
- Engaging in any outside fund-raising activity, endorsing any product or service, participating in any lobbying activity, or engaging in any prohibited partisan political activity.
- The creation, copying, transmission, or retransmission of chain letters or other unauthorized mass mailings.
- Any activities that are illegal, inappropriate, or offensive to fellow employees or the public. Such activities include hate speech or material that ridicules others on the basis of race, creed, religion, colour, sex, disability, national origin, or sexual orientation.
- Use for posting office information to any external newsgroup, chat room, bulletin board, or other public forum without prior approval.

- Any personal use that could cause congestion, delay, or disruption of service to any office equipment. This includes sending pictures, video, or sound files or other large file attachments that can degrade computer network performance.
- The unauthorized acquisition, use, reproduction, transmission, or distribution of any controlled information. This includes copyrighted computer software; other copyrighted or trademarked material or material with intellectual property rights (beyond fair use); privacy information; and proprietary data or export-controlled data or software.

SECURITY RISKS

As a result of the Internet and e-mail, there has been a sharp increase in security incidents involving the accidental disclosure of classified and other sensitive information. One common problem occurs when individuals download a seemingly unclassified file from a classified system, and then fail to carefully review this file before sending it as an attachment to an e-mail message. Too often, the seemingly unclassified file actually has some classified material or classification markings that are not readily apparent when the file is viewed on line. Sending such material by e-mail is a security violation even if the recipient has an appropriate security clearance, as e-mail can easily be monitored by unauthorized persons.

More important, even if the downloaded file really is unclassified, the electronic version of that file may have recoverable traces of classified information. This happens because data is stored in "blocks." If a file does not take up an entire block, the remainder of that block may have recoverable traces of data from other files. Your system administrator must follow an approved technical procedure for removing these traces before the file is treated as unclassified.

Some organizations have found it necessary to lock their computer drives to prevent any downloading of files from the classified system. If an individual wishes to download and retransmit an unclassified file from a classified system, the file must be downloaded and processed by the system administrator to remove electronic traces of other files before it is retransmitted.

INAPPROPRIATE MATERIALS

Sending e-mail is like sending a postcard through the mail. Just as the mailman and others have an opportunity to read a postcard, network eavesdroppers can read your e-mail as it passes through the Internet from computer to computer. E-mail is not like a telephone call, where your privacy rights are protected by law.

The courts have repeatedly sided with employers who monitor their employees' e-mail or Internet use. In an American Management Association poll, 47% of major companies reported that they store and review their employees' e-mail. Organizations do this to protect themselves against lawsuits, because the organization can be held liable for abusive, harassing, or otherwise inappropriate messages sent over its computer network. In the same poll, 25% of companies reported that they have fired employees for misuse of the Internet or office e-mail.

In the past couple years, *The New York Times* fired 23 employees for exchanging off-colour e-mail. Xerox fired 40 people for inappropriate Internet use. Dow Chemical fired 24 employees and disciplined another 230 for sending or storing pornographic or violent material by e-mail. Several years ago, Chevron Corp. had to pay $2.2 million to plaintiffs who successfully brought a suit of sexual harassment, in part because an employee sent an e-mail to coworkers listing the reasons why beer is better than women.

SECURITY OF TOOLS

Secrets in the computer require the same protection as secrets on paper. This is because information can be recovered from a computer hard drive even after the file has been deleted or erased by the computer user. It is estimated that about a third of the average hard drive contains information that has been "deleted" but is still recoverable.

Computers on which classified information is prepared must be kept in facilities that meet specified physical security requirements for processing classified information. If necessary to prepare classified information on a computer in a non-secure environment, use a removable hard drive or laptop that is secured in an approved safe when not in use. Alternatively, use a typewriter. Check with your security office concerning rules for traveling with a laptop on which classified or other sensitive information has been prepared. Laptop computers are a particular concern owing to their vulnerability to theft.

COMPUTER PASSWORDS

Passwords are used to authenticate an individual's right to have access to certain information. Your password is for your use only. Lending it to someone else is a security violation and may result in disciplinary action against both parties. Never disclose your password to anyone. Memorize it – do not put it in writing. If you leave your terminal unattended for any reason, log off or use a screen lock. Otherwise, someone else could use your computer to access information they are not authorized to have. You will be held responsible if someone else uses your password in connection with a system transaction.

Do change your password regularly. Use a password with at least six and preferably eight characters and consisting of a mix of upper and lower case letters, numbers, and special characters such as punctuation marks This mix of various types of characters makes it more difficult for a hacker to use an automated tool called a "password cracker" to discover your password. Cracking passwords is a common means by which hackers gain unauthorized access to protected systems.

SOCIAL ENGINEERING

"Social engineering" is hacker-speak for conning legitimate computer users into providing useful information that helps the hacker gain unauthorized access to their computer system. The hacker using social engineering usually poses as a legitimate person in the organization (maintenance technician, security officer, inexperienced computer user, VIP, etc.) and employs a plausible cover story to trick computer users into giving useful information. This is usually done by telephone, but it may also be done by forged e-mail messages or even in-person visits. Most people have an incorrect impression of computer break-ins. They think they are purely technical, the result of technical flaws in computer systems which the intruders are able to exploit.

The truth is, however, that social engineering often plays a big part in helping an attacker slip through security barriers. Lack of security awareness or gullibility of computer users often provides an easy stepping stone into the protected system if the attacker has no authorized access to the system at all.

COMPUTER APPLICATIONS IN BUSINESS

Computer Applications in Business provides an overview of the integrated software packages most often used in the workplace. By the end of this course, you will have a sound understanding of the basic features and business applications for the word processor, spreadsheet, database, and presentation software in your choice of either Microsoft Works Suite or Microsoft Office Professional packages. This process of completing this course, you will also learn how to problem solve and use the Help function and online tutorial assistance for your software. Finally, as this is an online course, you will learn about using the Internet and e-mail.

DELIVERY METHOD

There is continuous enrolment for this course. Delivery is self-paced, allowing you the flexibility to proceed through the course according to your own schedule.

PREREQUISITES

None. Students will need access to a PC with full internet

access and MS Office Professional (XP preferred) including Access database software or MS Works (the 2002 or newer Works 'Suite' with Word included is preferred). This course is not ideal for those using the MS Office 2007 version.

EXCLUSIONS

Students with credit for CMPT 109, 150 or a similar course may not take CMPT 119 for further credit.

OBJECTIVES

- Answer questions regarding your computer's hardware, software, and basic operations.
- Set up your computer for World Wide Web connection.
- Use e-mail to send messages and file attachments.
- Participate in on-line discussion groups.
- Describe the types of documents created with a word processing programme.
- List the principal features of a word processing programme.
- Create and format a business letter.
- Create and format a schedule containing a table.
- Design either a textual or a visual message for a public audience.
- Select and use style features to create new documents.
- Use the Help system to answer questions and troubleshoot problems.
- Describe the purposes of a spreadsheet and define its vocabulary.
- Set up and analyse itemized lists of numbers, such as the various types of budgets or financial statements.
- Perform and manipulate the calculations to achieve meaningful information.
- Present the numerical data in the spreadsheet in a graphical format.
- Conduct "what if" simulations of the numerical statements.

- Import spreadsheet reports and charts into word processing and/or database documents.
- Define the purpose of a database programme.
- Describe the components of a database.
- Plan a simple two-table database.
- Use wizards to enter and to search data, and to create a report.
- Enter data in a form.
- Merge data with a document.
- Create mailing labels.
- Analyse data in a database.
- Privacy issues related to databases.
- Plan a presentation.
- Apply good design principles to a presentation.
- Examine examples of a presentation.
- Describe the purpose of presentation software.
- Describe the components of a presentation.
- Create a presentation outline.
- Apply and modify a design template.
- Add clip art and charts to a presentation.
- Run a slide show.

Small, rural high schools are constantly trying to determine what type of computer training should be provided to students to meet the needs of business in the surrounding area. Many students in high schools today are not college bound and attempt to find local employment after graduation. Leaders in the community are also interested in retaining as many young people as possible in the area by helping them find local jobs through adequate high school training.

CHANGING FACE OF BUSINESS

Reports of shipments of personal computers to small businesses and home offices are growing at a 16% annual rate.(1) The power of the computer, the fax machine and voice mail allow a small company to do almost anything a larger corporation does. New technology has streamlined every part of our business lives. The challenge for small firms is to apply these technologies appropriately. After investing in a computer, for example, most discover other peripherals they want to incorporate into their office systems. The bottom line is that even small businesses can, and do, utilize computers and related technologies in their day-to-day operations. This means that even a high school graduate who does not plan to further his or her formal education should have some knowledge of computers.

In addition, it is important to bridge the gap between basic theory and computer applications.2 There is a strong correlation between high anxiety and reduced computer competence. Experience with computers in school tends to reduce anxiety on the job and leads to more productive workers. A good computer course also shows students how the computer can be utilized in many diverse fields.

IDENTIFYING SKILLS

Businesses must be periodically surveyed for information on the type of skills needed by their workers. In today's evolving world of work, required skills change as fast as the available technologies.

In Nebraska, for example, the Manpower company surveyed offices from Lincoln west to the Colorado border by sending a questionnaire on office automation topics to over 2,500 businesses. The results indicated that word processing was the number one activity, using a spreadsheet was number two, and manipulating a database was number three. Lotus 1-23 was the most widely installed software. WordPerfect was the most popular word processing package, capturing 40% of those responding to their survey. Service companies were the largest number of respondents, with government second and retail/wholesale businesses third.

Previous to its decisions on what type of computers to purchase and which software packages to teach, Auburn High School needed to know similar information. They wanted to provide their students specific experience with the computers and applications being utilized by business and industry in the local geographic area. This would reassure their students that they would be employable after graduation. It would also assist the local communities by keeping young people in the area and not have them travel to find jobs elsewhere. Upon the suggestion of Auburn's computer programming teacher, Claudette Stevens, a comprehensive survey of local area businesses was conducted in southeast Nebraska in two rural counties, Richardson and Nemaha. All of both counties' businesses were identified from the telephone book and local Chamber of Commerces, totalling 627. A random sample of 150 (approximately 25%) of these firms were contacted by telephone. All companies that were contacted agreed to answer the questions on the survey. Table 1 contains the exact numbers and results of the survey.

EXAMINING THE SURVEY RESULTS

Almost half of the small, rural businesses contacted (46%) are still not using computers. Of those using computers, over 68% said they purchased them mainly for accounting. However, most companies indicated they use computers for a variety of functions. Surveyed companies reported using a total of 38 different software packages. The most common type of programme used was for accounting, the second most common was word processing, and the third most common software produced customer receipts.

The questionnaire also dealt with the amount of knowledge new employees were expected to possess. Only one employer expected to hire a person with a bachelor's degree in computer science, and that job also required a four month period of intense training. A majority of companies expected to hire employees with basic knowledge on how to use the type of computer the firm owned. Some companies wanted potential employees to have an amount of keyboarding skills; other firms wanted general computer ability.

USING COMPUTER

LARGE-SCALE APPLICATIONS

Government use of computer applications need to be flexible enough to cope with holding a lot of data about the entire population of the country. Examples of government use of computer applications are public records systems, revenue collection and electronic voting.

Public Records

- The Office of National Statistics holds census information on every person and household in England and Wales.
- Similarly, the General Register Office for Scotland holds census information for Scotland and the Northern Ireland Statistics and Research Agency holds census information for Northern Ireland.
- The Driver and Vehicle Licensing Agency holds records of all registered drivers and vehicles in England, Wales and Scotland.

Revenue Collection

- The U.K. Inland Revenue has one of the biggest I.T. systems in use by the U.K. government. It has to be capable of holding many years' worth of tax data for every person and company in the United Kingdom.
- If that wasn't complex enough, it has to be accessible in real time-that is, whenever needed-to every Tax Office in the United Kingdom at the same time.

Electronic Voting (E-Voting)

- Electronic voting or e-voting is being tested, or is in use, in many countries and jurisdictions around the world.
- In the U.K., the Office of the Deputy Prime Minister hope to introducing electronic voting for general elections by about 2010, enabling citizens to vote from any polling station across the country rather than just their designated one.
- This would mean that every local authority's electoral register would have to be stored in a secure database, and on polling days every electronic polling booth would need to connect to the relevant electoral

register, verify voter details and record who has voted in real time.

COMPUTER LANGUAGE

PROBLEM

To obtain information linking clinical actions to the costs of health care, clinicians and health enterprise managers require very specific tools: the computerized patient record (CPR) chief among them. But the CPR alone is insufficient, because standard methods of representing and communicating health data are missing.

The complexity of the English language, which is formidable indeed, pales in comparison to the eclectic, ambiguous, redundant idiom of clinicians. The down side of the 'uncontrolled' parlance of medicine has been sharply accentuated by the computer age, because without standard vocabulary the ability to acquire knowledge about healing professions through information technology is painfully limited. The clinical applications available today have restricted utility because they cannot 'understand' each other. Today's information technology tools fail without 'controlled medical terminology' (CMT). Christopher Chute of the Mayo clinic pointed out with elegant simplicity that for "clinical information systems to be broadly useful... comparable information...is needed.' Central to obtaining 'comparable information' is standardized language. Over the past two decades academicians have grappled with issues surrounding clinical terminology.

We have learned from these efforts that there are several areas of our medical language and codes that must be integrated and managed if we are to leverage our health system information technology to benefit our profession and the health status of American society.

SCENARIO

Despite the wide availability and acceptance of computer applications in some niches of medicine—such as lab systems that print clear reports and ICU monitors that check for irregular heart beats—the majority of these systems "know" very little about medicine. Critical knowledge, such as what should be done about a cardiac arrhythmia or unexpected lab results, still exists in the minds of practitioners and in the notes they write in patient charts. To date, healthcare IT has failed to get the knowledge into the machine.

The irony is that many of the mundane, repetitive tasks involved in caring for people can be more efficiently and securely handled by computers. Computers can do things more reliably than humans: they rarely make mistakes when they are given precise, correct instructions, and they never forget. And when they are given improved instructions they totally forget the old, inadequate methods of doing things (which we humans call habits) and move ahead. As recently highlighted by the Institute of Medicine of the National Academy of Sciences, human error and the lack of basic information are harming many people who seek aid in our healthcare system.

A strong recommendation for greater reliance on technology arose from these findings. Physicians are the consummate users of medical information and health technology, so why do we fail to effectively harness the power of computers? One reason is that despite a firm understanding of how to gather clinical information and care for patients, we have used computers almost exclusively to deal with illogical rules on how to submit bills, order lab tests or document treatments in compliance with governmental or payor mandates.

Each of these practical tasks revolves around separate systems with their own codes or languages, none of which actually enhance the delivery of care nor communicate with each other. Although physicians are trained to document care and propose proper courses of treatment in 'the chart', we are unprepared to craft clinical notes to match-up with the more than 20,000 idiosyncratic billing codes.

This detraction from pure clinical thinking is but one of many reasons physicians are so unhappy with the changes in medical practice today. Add to this the fear of ungrounded malpractice claims, the barriers to efficient information transfer, the need to re-collect evidence for clinical decision making in an almost ludicrous fashion from encounter to encounter, the often poorly constructed 'report cards' based on utilization patterns rather than clinical effectiveness measurements, and one has just a preliminary grasp of the elements driving physicians to lash out at or leave their profession in droves.

At the same time, we, and the health plans we practice with, remain rightfully wary of the possibility of Medicare fraud charges because of coding errors. And despite all of the data collection and submission efforts we attend to, we still have no reliable way to recover accurate information about our efforts and efficacy because of the inherent faults of billing data sets.

CONTROLLED MEDICAL TERMINOLOGY

The Computer Based Patient Record Institute suggests that clinical terminology is: 'Standardized terms and their synonyms, which [allow one to] record patient findings, circumstances, events and interventions with sufficient detail to support clinical care, decision support, outcomes research and quality improvement; and can be efficiently mapped to broader classifications for administrative, regulatory, oversight and fiscal requirements.' Work with existing terminologies has allowed several important observations: First, simple *'nomenclatures'* (lists) of terms have proven inadequate as CMT schemas because they are difficult to manage and nearly impossible to use for knowledge derivation. Second, *'classifications'*, which are better because they relate terms to each other in various ways, are still less robust than optimal for efficiently managing, updating and tracking term and concept changes. And third, *'knowledge based ontologies*, in which concepts and their terms are strictly defined and related to each other based on their definitions, seem to be best suited to accomplishing the controlled medical terminology task. Ontologies provide a human readable yet machine processable conceptual framework that diverse computer systems may utilize for purposes of interoperability. A seamless bridge is built from our 'words' to the abstract concepts they represent in the computer. Note how closely such an approach approximates the dictum that 'the core utility of any language is to represent concepts by terms or words with meanings that are commonly understood.'

SOFTWARE TOOLS TO MANAGE CMT

Controlled medical terminology is optimally modeled and updated in knowledge-based 'ontologies'. A 'lexical runtime engine', formerly called a vocabulary server (VOSER), then serves up the relevant vocabulary to users of applications in the clinical environment. The ontology, housed in a lexicon *model,* implies the existence of a data structure that supports both the maintenance and use of controlled vocabulary data. The model is accessed via a *modeling environment,* which can be simple or complex. The measure of a modeling environment is simply its ability to convey the information contained within the model to its users.

Some of the core facilities provided by a modeling environment include:

- *Browsing*: A user interface for looking through the lexicon and moving from concept to concept in a logical fashion.
- *Searching*: Finding and navigating directly to a desired spot in the knowledge model without having "know where it is" at the start. A robust search interface allows rapid navigation to needed information.
- *Editing*: Making manual and or/bulk changes to the existing vocabulary for the purposes of local requirements. Editing systems should have some form of security to ensure the integrity of the underlying knowledge model.
- *Configuration Management and version control*: As changes are made to the lexicon, careful tracking of the changes is important.

- *List management*: While the vocabulary must be very rich in content as a whole, the user or application may only need or want a select portion of the 100,000+ concepts at a time. Lists are used to accomplish this task.

Billing Codes

Attempts to cross map, catalogue, and unify medical terminology have occurred historically, resulting in multiple 'right' clinical vocabularies. Medicine ultimately found itself infiltrated by proprietary and diverging sets of 'standard vocabularies', some in the form of nomenclatures and others as classifications. Today there are over 100 vocabulary sets defined internationally for some purpose, and in the United States institutions must deal with from 5-10 of them just to meet reporting or reimbursement requirements!

In 1968, at the behest of the Department of Health and Human Services, the United States adopted ICD as the 'official code set', and realizing it was woefully inadequate, set about creating ICD-CM (Clinical Modifications). Third party insurers followed suit, but stirred in the equally inadequate CPT codes as requirements for clinical service reimbursement.

These chosen schemes, detailed below, lack accuracy, precision and cognitive coherence. But since the actual communication and documentation of care were largely unaffected by the new add-on coding regulations, clinical professionals swallowed hard and closed their eyes to the downstream effects such derisory coding schemes would have on their professional lives.

Progressive healthcare information system developers knew that billing codes were inadequate for electronic clinical documentation and that precise medical words were needed if analysis of information from automated medical records was to improve quality and service in healthcare. Rather than gravitate towards any existing clinical vocabulary standard, they elected to create their own 'dictionaries' or 'vocabulary sets'. Their methods represented an improvement over completely un-encoded or free text documentation (which is still the norm in many computer based patient records), but each vendor, working in isolation, created a terminology which could not be read or understood by other vendor systems. Thus the potential of data exchange and aggregation was impossible. Managing these highly proprietary code sets, and then trying to compare information gathered in one system to data from another proved quite expectedly problematic.

- *Code Set*: Diagnosis coding systems.
  - *Overview*: ICD versions are *classifications*, thus one code typically represents a category into which several diseases may be mapped. There are several consequences of this arrangement: Large numbers of categories are too broad to be clinically useful. A significant amount of clinical detail is lost when a paper-based medical record is coded, and the only way to retrieve the level of detail in the medical record is to review the chart manually (an expensive and time consuming task). ICD contains many ambiguous and redundant catch-all categories. The combination categories make the process of information retrieval using ICD codes extraordinarily complex. *Designing searches in systems with combination categories is a nightmare*
- *Code Set*: Procedure coding systems.
  - *Overview*: There are three procedure-coding systems in use in the United States. They are volume 3 of ICD-9-CM, the American Medical Association's (AMA) Current Procedural Terminology (CPT), and the Health Care Financing Administration's Common Procedure Coding System (HCPCS). These systems have all of the weaknesses of the diagnosis coding systems discussed above.
- *Code Set*: Ambulatory Patient Classification (APC)
- *Overview*: The APC is made up of groups of procedures such that the services within each group

have comparable resource usage and are clinically similar. It is obvious that APC was developed and is best suited for billing. With CPT/HCPCS codes as elements, APC has the same shortcomings as those terminologies have, with the added burden of having been reorganized to fit a particular need, that of being a method for the calculation of payments.

- *Code Set*: UMLS
- *Overview*: The Unified Medical Language System (UMLS) was developed by the National Library of Medicine (NLM) in an attempt to relate disparate medical vocabularies and facilitate the sharing of medical knowledge across information systems. While initial efforts were directed at providing a linguistic framework for integrating clinical knowledge, additions covering more arcane coding systems have complemented its content, and now, the 11th edition of the UMLS Metathesaurus contains more than 60 source vocabularies. The UMLS Metathesaurus is a coding and language support tool, rather than a coding system per se; it was never intended as a common vocabulary for clinical use.
- *Code Set*: SNOMED and SNOMED-RT (Systematized Nomenclature of Medicine, with RT referring to 'Reference Terminology')
- *Overview*: Under development by the College of American Pathology (CAP) for more than 30 years, SNOMED contains the best overall coverage of clinical content. The underlying granularity of SNOMED-RT allows expressiveness, and the organization of these granular terms into hierarchies with logical relationships, provides the basis for computational categorization and management of the vocabulary based on strict concept definitions. The heart of SNOMED-RT is its breadth of terminological coverage, its logical classification system, and its compositional nature based upon medically relevant and granular concept elements.

- *Code Set*: Logical Observation Identifier Names and Codes (LOINC)
- *Overview*: LOINC is an example of how a modern, concept-based terminology can solve system integration problems and thus find widespread acceptance in the healthcare IT community. LOINC provides a set of standard codes for observations made by providers during the process of care. By far, its largest and most important domain is that of laboratory tests, but it also includes such clinical observations such as vital signs, intake and output measurements, temperature, EKG tracing measurements, and echocardiogram measurements.
- *Code Set*: Consumer Terminology
- *Overview*: The need for a consumer-oriented terminology has been debated. When patients are able to access their clinical records online can the problem list, treatment plan and test results be represented in a way that is understandable to them? What happens when patients begin to use online applications that allow them? Will consumers be able to self-report their own health history in a way that is clinically acceptable? Will this information be machine-readable and linked to accepted clinical terminologies? With the new Internet-enabled e-Health environment, patients are realizing the promise of access to health records, access to insurance information, access to credible health content, and greater clinical and billing efficiency. In order to enable greater patient participation, however, the words of the patient must be treated with as much respect as the words of the health care professional.

CLINICAL INFONOMICS

The term *clinical infonomics* implies a new science in which care practices, health informatics and national economics are finally recognized as inseparable. Healthcare delivery is reliant on information technology because clinical decision-making, as well as the reengineering of business and clinical processes, depends on the immediate availability of current accurate information about patients, diseases and populations.

In fact, information technology, along with strong clinical leadership, are key to bringing about a badly needed shift in the entire care delivery system from one based on *cost*, to one based on *value*. Never before have tools existed that could verify, validate, or debunk treatments, narrow practice variation to a more cost-effective mean, allow discovery and communication of optimal methods of diagnosis or therapy and literally *prove* the value of clinical interventions.

Iatrogenic injury has received a great deal of attention lately. During hospitalization in the US it is estimated that as many as a third of patients suffer from complications related to their care ; between 5% and 13% of hospital admissions result from the adverse effects of diagnosis or treatment , and some 70% of iatrogenic complications affecting more than 1.3 million hospitalized patients annually are preventable!

There are from 44,000 to 180,000 treatment related deaths in hospitals every year and of life threatening/serious adverse drug events, the most common failures relating to these errors are system errors involving drug knowledge dissemination, drug dosing, patient identity checking and patient information availability, suggesting inadequate systems, rather than individual inadequacy, as causes for error.

In a survey of attendees conducted at the 2000 Healthcare Information Management and Systems Society, it was discovered that a startling 98% of respondents believed that controlled medical terminology would be important to mitigation of iatrogenic mishaps.

CMT BENEFITS

Benefits include faster, more accurate billing, more informed patient management, faster, clearer and more precise documentation (the ultimate in 'decision support'), lower malpractice premiums and improved knowledge. We cannot develop nor exercise the ability to move healthcare forward, as clinicians or administrators, without the informatics tools, language and communication standards outlined above. Without technology that "listens to and understands us" we cannot act in accordance with evidence based guidelines and principles, narrow practice variation and improve knowledge of appropriate and cost-effective techniques for managing health.

ACTION

The tools and language content sets exist today to help with this problem, but unless *controlled medical terminology* and the informatics infrastructure suggested above are widely embraced, we cannot possibly make good decisions about whether interventions are in a range of from 'possibly beneficial' to 'highly indicated', determine *physiologic from biologic outcomes* based on measurements, or assess clinician assessment versus patients perceived*health outcomes* (including pain, suffering, disfigurement, disability). Without a common language we cannot improve the quality of healthcare, no matter how many times we say the words, nor even approach evidence based medicine on anything but a microcosmic scale.

To get there, the steps one can take as an individual are relatively simple:

- Insist that clinical computing systems to be purchased for your ambulatory or in-patient environments be based upon a *controlled medical terminology*, (not 'our' standard terminology); and one which meets the requirements of good CMT.
- Seek greater understanding of the clinical systems that are being purchased for use by your group, because they are not going away; they are enormously helpful once you get over the initial fear of using them, and if you insist that they collect good information they will be tools you can use rather than weapons that can be used against you.
- Become familiar with E-mail interactions and the

formalities surrounding them because they will become a norm in the future, and even a billable one at that , but do NOT become comfortable with the fact that these 'un-encoded' communications are sufficient, for all the same reasons un-encoded information in the medical record are insufficient.

- Don't be afraid of the change, in either the technology or the language. Having lived through it, and having helped many clinicians through the transition, we know it can be done to our own great advantage, and to the benefit of healthcare in the United States population in entirety.

Without CMT- enabled health informatics technology we are 'sewing in the dark'; we have no standard methods for evaluating either our work or the preferences of our patients. Controlled medical terminology essentially 'turns on the lights'. Failing to move this direction with our language and information technology dooms us to control by those who have more data, but far less knowledge.

COMPUTER APPLICATIONS IN EDUCATION

A computer helps to manipulate data according to a list of instructions, called a programme. It can save a lot of data and produce the same, instantly. It is also called a universal information-processing machine. It is a common operating system used in corporate businesses, educational organizations and many research programmes.

The computer technology has been used proficiently in various educational fields. There are many professional courses that programme their curriculum on computers. It enables the students and teachers to methodically study or conduct classes. Most schools highlight the importance of computer education. They provide computer education to children, at a very young age. It helps them to learn and develop interest in the basics of computers. The main purpose is to make them comfortable using the system, as the future holds a bright promise for the technology. Many students become proficient and plan to pursue careers in the world of computers. Computers are used in running school and college administrations, during the admission procedures, storing of official and student records. They are also used in syllabus planning and decision-making, controlling, assisting instructions and simulation. Computers are helpful in directing aptitude tests and achievement tests, at the time of entrance exams. There is computer software designed to process performances related to teachers and employees promotion avenues. They also process records of salaries, examinations, schemes of examination, printing of papers and question papers, evaluation of answer sheets, mark sheets and certificates.

Computers are used in colleges, by the professors, to conduct special classes and enable their students to adopt a methodical way of study. Students take more interest in the documented programmes, designed on different topics. Internet has provided a favorable means of pursuing courses from renowned universities, across the world. These facilities become available at a click of the mouse. Computer Education provides detailed information on Computer Education, Computer Education Online, Computer Science Education, Computer Education Institute and more. Computer Education is affiliated with Computer Graphic Training. Over the years apprenticeship has undergone a desperate change. Acceptance accept confused from cardboard assignment to computer applications and Internet.

In abounding of the educational institutions, acceptance assignment on apriorism or projects appliance desktop software. They abide these to advisers as e-mail accessories or hard-copy documents. Assorted computer programmes and applications are acclimated for authoritative presentations, projects, research, publication, etc. Nowadays a apprentice learns to address web pages, resumes, cards, newsletters, etc. with the use of computer systems. Various applications and accoutrement accept been alien by the advice technology. They accept revolutionized communication, abundance and accord amid agents and students. For instance, web conferencing, online chat processing, book administration are few such solutions. They accept enabled users to actualize and allotment documents. Coordination from anywhere is additionally possible. It facilitates teaching and learning. Acceptance additionally use assorted accoutrement like, PDF Software. It helps them to catechumen a Power Point, Excel or Chat book to Pdf book or carnality versa.

It is acclimated for presentations, thesis, etc. It is acclimated back absolute argument in one architecture has to be adapted into addition format. In this conversion, layout, style, graphics, images, etc. abide intact. The accoutrement are either chargeless or accept a price. If they appear with a amount they are affordable. Technical barriers are attenuated which helps acceptance and agents to coact with anniversary other. The acceptance additionally go for online learning.

There are assorted online courses, tutorials and examinations. The online acquirements is an accessible to use tool. It has boundless accessibility and able features. The affection of the assignment gets bigger as able-bodied as the akin of cerebral engagement. The educators accommodate in abyss revisions and comments. With the use of chat processing the affection of apprentice autograph has improved. It is because acceptance tend to address added and get authentic end notes.

They can absorb cartoon into their work. For instance, with the use of Microsoft Chat it is possible. They gradually apprentice to be professional. It sharpens their minds for the business world. In an Excel, the acceptance do calculations accurately. Power Point appliance enables them to accomplish a presentation in a added adapted manner. Hence, assorted computer Chat to PDF accoutrement an.

HOME COMPUTING

DEFINITION

Home computers were a class of personal computers entering the market in 1977, and becoming increasingly common during the 1980s. They were marketed to consumers as accessible personal computers, more capable than video game consoles. These computers typically cost much less than business, scientific or engineering-oriented desktop personal computers of the time, and were generally less powerful in terms of memory and expandability.

However, a home computer often had better graphics and sound than contemporary business personal computers. Usually they were purchased for education, game play, and personal productivity use such as word processing. Advertisements for early home computers were rife with possibilities for their use in the home, from cataloging recipes to personal finance to home automation, but these were seldom realised in practice. If no packaged software was available for a particular application, the home computer user was required to learn computer programming; a significant time commitment many weren't willing to make. Still, for many the home computer offered the first opportunity to learn to programme.

SECURITY

Your home computer is a popular target for *intruders*. Why? Because intruders want what you've stored there. They look for credit card numbers, bank account information, and anything else they can find. By stealing that information, intruders can use your money to buy themselves goods and services.

But it's not just money-related information they're after. Intruders also want your computer's resources, meaning your*hard disk* space, your fast *processor*, and your Internet connection. They use these resources to *attack* other computers on the *Internet*. In fact, the more computers an intruder uses, the harder it is for law enforcement to figure out where the attack is really coming from. If intruders can't be found, they can't be stopped, and they can't be prosecuted.

Why are intruders paying attention to home computers? Home computers are typically not very secure and are easy to break into. When combined with high-speed Internet connections that are always turned on, intruders can quickly find and then attack home computers. While intruders also attack home computers connected to the Internet through dial-in connections, high-speed connections (*cable modems* and *DSL modems*) are a favourite target.

No matter how a home computer is connected to the Internet, intruders' attacks are often successful. Many home computer owners don't realise that they need to pay attention to computer security. In the same way that you are responsible for having insurance when you drive a car, you need to also be responsible for your home computer's security. This document explains how some parts of the Internet work and then describes tasks you can do to improve the security of your home computer system. The goal is to keep intruders and their programmes off your computer.

How do intruders break into your computer? In some cases, they send you *e-mail* with a *virus*. Reading that e-mail activates the virus, creating an opening that intruders use to enter or access your computer. In other cases, they take advantage of a flaw or weakness in one of your computer's programmes – a *vulnerability* – to gain access.

Once they're on your computer, they often install new *programmes* that let them continue to use your computer – even after you plug the holes they used to get onto your computer in the first place. These *backdoors* are usually cleverly disguised so that they blend in with the other programmes running on your computer.

The next section discusses concepts you need to know, especially trust. The main part of this document explains the specific issues that need your attention. There are examples of how to do some of these tasks to secure a Microsoft Windows 2000-based computer. We also provide checklists you can use to record information about the steps you have taken to secure your computer. Finally, a glossary defines many of the technical terms used in this document. Unless otherwise stated in the glossary, the definitions come from the *Webopedia Online Dictionary for Computer and Internet Terms*

Whether your computer runs Microsoft® Windows®, Apple's Mac OS, LINUX, or something else, the issues are the same and will remain so as new versions of your system are released. The key is to understand the security-related problems that you need to think about and solve.

SECURING YOUR HOME COMPUTER

Before diving into the tasks you need to do to secure your home computer, let's first think about the problem by relating it to something you already know how to do. In this way, you can apply your experience to this new area.

So, think of your computer as you would your house, your apartment, or your condo. What do you know about how that living space works, what do you routinely do to keep it secure, and what have you installed to improve its security? (We'll use this "computer-is-like-a-house-and-the-things-in-it" analogy throughout, departing only a few times to make a point.)

For example, you know that if you have a loud conversation, folks outside your space can probably hear you. You also routinely lock the doors and close the windows when you leave, and you don't give the keys to just anyone. Some of you may install a security system to complement your practices. All of these are part of living in your home.

Let's now apply similar thinking to your home computer. E-mail, *instant messaging,* and most web traffic go across the Internet *in the clear*; that is, anyone who can capture that information can read it. These are *things you ought to know.* You should always select and use strong passwords and exercise due care when reading all e-mail, especially the unsolicited variety. *These are things you ought to do.* Finally, you can add a *firewall,* an anti-virus programme, *patches,* and file encryption to improve the level of security on your home computer, and we'll call these *things you ought to install.*

One starting point for solving home computer security problems is being aware of how the Internet and some of its technologies work. If you know how they work, you can evaluate solutions to the problems that come up. You can also use the Internet more safely and responsibly. In this section, we'll talk about two topics: trust and information in the clear as it crosses the Internet.

Trust

Human beings are trusting by nature. We trust much of what we hear on the radio, see on television, and read in the newspaper. We trust the labels on packages. We trust the mail we receive. We trust our parents, our partner or spouse, and our children. We trust our co-workers. In fact, those who don't trust much are thought to be cynical. Their opinions may be all too quickly ignored or dismissed.

The Internet was built on trust.[1] Back in the mid 1960s, computers were very expensive and slow by today's standards, but still quite useful. To share the expensive and scarce computers installed around the country, the U.S. government funded a research project to connect these computers together so that other researchers could use them remotely. This project was called the *Arpanet*, named after the government research agency – ARPA, the Advanced Research Projects Agency – that funded and managed the project.

Key to the ARPAnet was the level of trust placed in its users; there was little thought given to malicious activity. Computers communicated using a straightforward scheme that relied on everybody playing by the rules. The idea was to make sharing ideas and resources easy and as efficient as the technology of the day provided. This philosophy of trust colours many of the practices, procedures, and technologies that are still in place today.

Only within the last few years, when Internet commerce (known as *e-commerce*) began to spread, it has become inadequate to rely principally on trust. Since the days of the ARPAnet, we've changed the way we use computer networks while others have changed the underlying technologies, all in an attempt to improve the security of the Internet and the trust we place on it.

Let's dig deeper into two examples of what we trust in our daily lives. When you receive mail through the post office, many envelopes and the letters in them contain the sender's address. Have you ever wondered if those addresses were valid; that is, do they match the address of the person or persons who really sent them? While you could check to see that those addresses are valid and refer to the person they name, it's not an easy task.

How would you go about it? Would you call the phone number provided with the letter? That number could also be invalid, and the person that answers the phone could be as misleading as the original address. Perhaps you could call directory assistance or the police department that has jurisdiction over the town where the letter was supposedly from. They might be helpful, but that is likely to take lots of time. Most people wouldn't bother.

And it's not just return addresses either. How about advertisements, news stories, or the information printed on groceries? Suppose you were on a low-fat diet. You'd want to buy foods low in fat. To select the right foods, you'd read the product label at the grocery store. How do you know that the label information is valid? What's to say it's not forged? And how would you know? The Internet has many of the same issues, and e-mail is one of the best examples. In an e-mail message, an intruder can easily fabricate where the came from. But this information forging–called *spoofing* by intruders and security professionals – is not limited to just e-mail. In fact, the basic unit of information transferred on the Internet – called a *packet* – can also be easily forged or spoofed.

What does this mean and why should you care? It means that any information you receive from some other computer on the Internet should not be trusted automatically and unconditionally. When you trust an e-mail message that turns out to have a harmful virus attached to it, your computer can be infected, your *files* destroyed, and your work lost. And that's why you should care. This is how the Internet works. It was built on trust. Over time, there have been technological changes that are worthy of a higher level of our trust than before. Nonetheless, a true sense of insecurity is better than a false sense of security. So, think about the information you trust. Be critical and cautious.

Information in the Clear

When you have a conversation with someone in your

living space, everybody within earshot can hear the words and probably understand them. If your conversation is especially loud and your windows open, even passersby can hear. If you want privacy, you and your conversation partner need to go to another room and close the doors and windows.

The Internet works much the same way, except the room is much, much bigger. When you send e-mail, browse a web site, or chat online with someone, the conversation between you and that person does not go directly from your computer to his or her computer. Instead, it goes from your computer to another computer to still another computer and so on, eventually reaching his or her computer. Think of all of these computers as an Internet "room."

Anyone, or, more accurately, any programme, in that Internet room that can hear that conversation can also probably understand it. Why? Because just like the conversation at home, most Internet conversations are in the clear, meaning that the information exchanged between computer systems is not concealed or hidden in any way.

Again, this is how the Internet works. You need to know that the information sent across the Internet may be at *risk* of others listening in, capturing what you send, and using it for their own benefit. Later, we'll talk about encryption as a way to address this problem. Encryption uses mathematics to conceal information. There are many programmes you can install to encrypt the information you send across the Internet.

PLAN

Securing your home computer is not a trivial task. There are many topics to consider and many steps to follow. They take time to learn and do. If you can, read this entire document before you begin to secure your computer. You'll have a better understanding of the effort and all its facets. This ought to help you when you begin to tackle the tasks described here.

In the next part of this document, we describe two types of activities. Some you can do using the programmes that came with your computer: working with *passwords* and e-mail attachments, running programmes, and *backing up* your work. For other activities, you might need to obtain some specialized programmes: applying patches, and running anti-virus, firewall, and file encryption programmes. Though some vendors' products provide these features, we'll assume your computer doesn't have any of them so you'll need to add all of them.

Here then is the list of tasks you need to do to secure your home computer. Their order is based on how intruders attack computers, beginning with the most-often used attack methods. By starting with the lower numbered tasks, you address the biggest problems you face in securing your home computer. Remember that most sections end with a reference to a web site that you can use to find an example of how to do the task on a Microsoft Windows 2000 computer.

INSTALL AND USE ANTI-VIRUS PROGRAMMES

If someone rang your doorbell and wanted to come into your living space to sell you something or to use your telephone, you'd need to make a decision whether or not to let them in. If they were a neighbour or someone you knew, you'd probably let them in. If you didn't know them but believed their story and found them to be otherwise acceptable, say they were neat and clean and not threatening, you'd probably also let them in, but you'd watch them closely while they were in your space.

What are you doing here? You are profiling this person and then deciding what to do based on that profile. It's your responsibility to be concerned about who enters your living space. Further, if you have children, you've probably also taught them how to deal with strangers who come to your door.

Anti-virus programmes work much the same way. These programmes look at the contents of each file, searching for specific patterns that match a profile – called a *virus signature* – of something known to be harmful. For each file that matches a signature, the anti-virus programme typically provides several options on how to respond, such as removing the offending patterns or destroying the file. To understand how anti-virus programmes work, think about scam artists – people who visit your home to try to get you to buy a phony product or service, or to let them in. Once inside, they may try to steal your valuables or try to harm you in some way.

There are a variety of ways you might find out about a specific scam artist lurking in your neighborhood. Perhaps you see a television report or read a newspaper article about them. They might include pictures and excerpts of the story the scam artist uses to scam their victims. The news report gives you a profile of someone you need to be on the lookout for. You watch for that person until either the story fades away or you hear that they've been caught.

Anti-virus programmes work much the same way. When the anti-virus programme vendors learn about a new virus, they provide an updated set of virus signatures that include that new one. Through features provided by the updated anti-virus programme, your home computer also automatically learns of this new virus and begins checking each file for it, along with checking for all the older viruses. However, unlike scam artists, viruses never completely fade away. Their signatures remain part of the master version of all virus signatures.

Suppose a scam artist was at your front door. What would you do? Perhaps you'd not encourage them to come in nor buy their product but, at the same time, you'd try not to upset them. You'd politely listen to their story and then send them on their way. After you closed the door, you may call the police or the telephone number given in the report that initially brought them to your attention.

With viruses, you often have the chance to react to them when they've been discovered on your home computer. Depending upon the specific characteristics of the virus, you might be able to clean the infected file. Or you might be forced to destroy the file and load a new copy from your backups or original distribution *media*. Your options depend upon your choice of anti-virus programme and the virus that's been detected. In your living space, you look at those who come to your door and you look at what you receive in the mail. These are two of the ways that items can get into your living space, so you examine them, sometimes closely, sometimes not.

Viruses can reach your computer in many ways, through floppy disks, *CD-ROMs*, e-mail, web sites, and *downloaded* files. All need to be checked for viruses each time you use them. In other words, when you insert a floppy disk into the drive, check it for viruses. When you receive e-mail, check it for viruses (remember to use the KRESV tests described in Task 3 - *Use Care When Reading E-mail with Attachments*). When you download a file from the Internet, check it for viruses before using it. Your anti-virus programme may let you specify all of these as places to check for viruses each time you operate on them. Your anti-virus programme may also do this automatically. All you need to do is to open or run the file to cause it to be checked.

Just as you walk around your living space to see if everything is OK, you also need to "walk" around your home computer to see if there are any viruses lurking about. Most anti-virus programmes let you schedule periodic exams of all files on your home computer on a regular basis, daily for example. If you leave your computer turned on over night, think about scheduling a full-system review during that time.

Some anti-virus programmes have more advanced features that extend their recognition capabilities beyond virus signatures. Sometimes a file won't match any of the known signatures, but it may have some of the characteristics of a virus. This is comparable to getting that "there's something not quite right here, so I'm not going to let them in" feeling as you greet someone at your door. These *heuristic*tests, as they're called, help you to keep up with new viruses that aren't yet defined in your list of virus signatures.

An anti-virus programme is frequently an add-on to your home computer, though your newly purchased computer might include a trial version. At some point, say after 60 days, you must purchase it to continue using it. To decide whether to make that purchase or to look elsewhere, use these steps for evaluating anti-virus programmes:

- *The Demand test*: Can you check a file on demand, for example, when you want to send an attachment as part of the KRESV tests?
- *The Update test:* Can you update the virus signatures automatically? Daily is best.
- The Respond test: What are all the ways that you can respond to an infected file? Can the virus checker clean a file?
- *The Check test*: Can you check every file that gets to your home computer, no matter how it gets there, and can those checks be automated?
- *The Heuristics test*: Does the virus checker do heuristics tests? How are these defined?

These tests – the DURCH tests – help you compare anti-virus programmes. Once you've made your selection, install it and use all of its capabilities all of the time.

Intruders are the most successful in attacking all computers – not just home computers – when they use viruses and *worms*. Installing an anti-virus programme and keeping it up to date is among the best defences for your home computer. If your financial resources are limited, they are better spent purchasing a commercial anti-virus programme than anything else.

- Use a Checklist to help you think anti-virus issues.
- Example: *Operating an Anti-Virus Programme.*

KEEP YOUR SYSTEM PATCHED

If one of your appliances broke, you'd probably try to have it repaired. You'd call a repairperson whom you hope could do the job. You'd get an estimate and then you'd either get it fixed or replace it. Your goal is to somehow restore the functions that the appliance provides.

What do you do when a software "appliance" – a programme – or the *operating system* itself breaks? How do you restore the functions that they provide? Do you know whom to call or even where to look to determine what to do next? Most vendors provide patches that are supposed to fix *bugs* in their products. Frequently these patches do what they're supposed to do. However, sometimes a patch fixes one problem but causes another. For example, did you ever have a repairperson fix an appliance but in the process, they scratched the floor or damaged a countertop during their visit? For a computer, the repair cycle might have to be repeated until a patch completely fixes a problem.

Vendors often provide free patches on their web sites. When you purchase programmes, it's a good idea to see if and how the vendor supplies patches, and if and how they provide a way to ask questions about their products. Just as appliance vendors often sell extended warranties for their products, some software vendors may also sell support for theirs. Have you ever received a recall notice for your car or another product you've purchased? Vendors send these notices to product owners when a safety-related problem has been discovered. Registering your purchase through the warranty card gives the vendor the information they need to contact you if there is a recall.

Programme vendors also provide a recall-like service. You can receive patch notices through e-mail by subscribing to mailing lists operated by the programs' vendors. Through this type of service, you can learn about problems with your computer even before you discover them and, hopefully, before intruders have the chance to exploit them. Consult the vendor's web site to see how to get e-mail notices about patches as soon as they're available.

Some vendors have gone beyond mailing lists. They provide programmes bundled with their systems that automatically contact their web sites looking for patches specifically for your home computer. These automatic updates tell you when patches are available, download them, and even install them. You can tailor the update features to do only want you want, such as just telling you something new is waiting but doing nothing more.

While the patching process is getting easier, even to the point where it can be completely automated, it is not yet foolproof. In some cases, installing a patch can cause another seemingly unrelated programme to break. The challenge is to do as much homework as you can to learn what a patch is supposed to do and what problems it might cause once you've installed it. This is a hard job. Often, the vendors don't tell you about problems their patches can cause. Why? Because it is simply impossible to test all possible programmes with all possible patches to discover unexpected side effects. Imagine doing that job and then continuing to do that for each new programme and patch that comes along. Vendors rely on their customers to tell them when something unexpected happens once a patch is installed. So, if this happens to you, let them know.

Imagine then that you've either found a patch on the vendor's site or you've received notice that a patch is available. What do you do next? Follow the steps below to evaluate a patch before you install it:

- *The Affected test*: Does this patch affect one of the programmes on your computer? If it doesn't affect your computer, you're done. Whew!
- *The Break test*: Can you tell from the vendor's web site or the patch's description if installing it breaks something else that you care about? If installation does break something, then you have to decide how to proceed. Try notifying the vendor of the programme that might break to learn what their strategy is for addressing this problem. Also, use your web browser to learn if anyone else has experienced this problem and what he or she did about it.
- *The Undo test*: Can you undo the patch? That is, can you restore your computer to the way it was before you installed the patch? Currently, vendors are building most patches with an uninstall feature that enables you to remove a patch that has unwanted consequences. In addition, some computers also come with features that help you restore them to a previously known and working state should there be a problem. You need to know what your computer provides so that you can undo a patch if necessary.

Recall from the *Introduction* that intruders exploit vulnerabilities to gain access to home computers. How do intruders find out about these vulnerabilities? In many cases, they read the same vendor mailing lists and use the same automatic notification schemes that you use. This means that you need to evaluate and install patches on your home computer as soon as they're available. The longer a vulnerability is known, the greater the chances are that an intruder will find it on your home computer and exploit it. With the ABU tests, you can quickly evaluate and install patches to keep intruders off your home computer.

One last thing: patches are usually distributed as programmes. This means that you need to use the DCAL steps described in before loading and installing a patch. Intruders often take advantage of vulnerabilities wherever they may be. In many cases, the vulnerabilities they exploit may have patches, but those patches were not installed. For your home computer, make time to keep your programmes patched wherever possible. If you can't patch a programme, shop around for an equivalent programme and use it until the original programme is fixed or you've abandoned it in favour of something more reliable. You can spend money on maintenance where you get patches for programmes, but that's usually not necessary. Since most vendors provide free patches, mailing lists, and automatic updates, keeping your computer patched usually only costs you time.

- Use a Worksheet to record your important patch information.
- *Example*: *Installing Patches.*

CARE WHILE READING E-MAIL

We've all heard stories about people receiving an item in the mail that in some way caused them harm. We've heard of letter bombs and exploding packages, and in 2001, we learned about Anthrax-laden letters. Although their frequency is low, they do make news. These unsolicited items are sent to unsuspecting recipients. They may contain a return address, a provocative envelope, or something else that encourages its receiver to open it. This technique is called *social engineering*. Because we are trusting and curious, social engineering is often effective.

In the case of the Anthrax letters addressed to United States senators, the envelopes contained a school's return address as an inducement to open them. What government official wouldn't want to serve their constituency by reading and responding to a letter supposedly sent by a class at a school, especially an elementary school? By opening the letter and subsequently spreading its lethal contents, the recipient complied with the wishes of the sender, a key foundation of social engineering. In the pre-Anthrax letter days, a mail handler might have given little thought to the contents of the letter or the validity of the return address. Those days are behind us.

You probably receive lots of mail each day, much of it unsolicited and containing unfamiliar but plausible return addresses. Some of this mail uses social engineering to tell you of a contest that you may have won or the details of a product that you might like. The sender is trying to encourage you to open the letter, read its contents, and interact with them in some way that is financially beneficial – to them. Even today, many of us open letters to learn what we've won or what fantastic deal awaits us. Since there are few consequences, there's no harm in opening them. E-mail-borne viruses and worms operate much the same way, except there are consequences, sometimes significant ones. Malicious e-mail often contains a return address of someone we know and often has a provocative Subject line. This is social engineering at its finest – something we want to read from someone we know.

E-mail viruses and worms are fairly common. If you've not received one, chances are you will. Here are steps you can use to help you decide what to do with every e-mail message with an attachment that you receive. You should only read a message that passes all of these tests.

- *The Know test*: Is the e-mail from someone that you know?

- *The Received test*: Have you received e-mail from this sender before?
- *The Expect test*: Were you expecting e-mail with an attachment from this sender?
- The Sense test: Does e-mail from the sender with the contents as described in the Subject line and the name of the attachment(s) make sense? For example, would you expect the sender – let's say your Mother – to send you an e-mail message with the Subject line "Here you have,;o)" that contains a message with attachment – let's say AnnaKournikova.jpg.vbs? A message like that probably doesn't make sense. In fact, it happens to be an instance of the Anna Kournikova worm, and reading it can damage your system.
- *The Virus test:* Does this e-mail contain a virus? To determine this, you need to install and use an anti-virus programme. That task is described in *Install and Use Anti-Virus Programmes.*

You should apply these five tests – KRESV – to every piece of e-mail with an attachment that you receive. If any test fails, toss that e-mail. If they all pass, then you still need to exercise care and watch for unexpected results as you read it. Now, given the KRESV tests, imagine that you want to send e-mail with an attachment to someone with whom you've never corresponded – what should you do? Here's a set of steps to follow to begin an e-mail dialogue with someone.

- Since the recipient doesn't already Know you, you need to send them an introductory e-mail. It must not contain an attachment. Basically, you're introducing yourself and asking their permission to send e-mail with an attachment that they may otherwise be suspicious of. Tell them who you are, what you'd like to do, and ask for permission to continue.
- This introductory e-mail qualifies as the mail Received from you.
- Hopefully, they'll respond; and if they do, honour

their wishes. If they choose not to receive e-mail with an attachment from you, don't send one. If you never hear from them, try your introductory e-mail one more time.

- If they accept your offer to receive e-mail with an attachment, send it off. They will Know you and will have Received e-mail from you before. They will also Expect this e-mail with an attachment, so you've satisfied the first three requirements of the KRESV tests.
- Whatever you send should make Sense to them. Don't use a provocative Subject line or any other social engineering practice to encourage them to read your e-mail.
- Check the attachments for Viruses. This is again based on having virus-checking programmes, and we'll discuss that later.

The KRESV tests help you focus on the most important issues when sending and receiving e-mail with attachments. Use it every time you send e-mail, but be aware that there is no foolproof scheme for working with e-mail, or security in general. You still need to exercise care. While an anti-virus programme alerts you to many viruses that may find their way to your home computer, there will always be a lag between when a virus is discovered and when anti-virus programme vendors provide the new virus signature. This means that you shouldn't rely entirely on your anti-virus programmes. You must continue to exercise care when reading e-mail.

- Use a checklist to help you make decisions about opening e-mail attachments.

USE A FIREWALL PROGRAMME

This section describes a firewall, its importance to your home computer strategy, and a way to think about the job you need to do. We're going to depart from our "computer-is-like-a-house-and-the-things-in-it" analogy to use another that you are probably also familiar with: an office building.

Have you ever visited a business where you first stopped at the reception desk to interact with a security guard? That guard's job is to assess everybody who wishes to enter or leave the building to decide if they should continue on or be stopped. The guard keeps the unwanted out and permits only appropriate people and objects to enter and leave the business's premises.

Let's dig deeper into this analogy. When someone enters a building, the security guard usually greets them. If they have an appropriate identification badge, they show it to the guard or swipe it through a reader. If all is OK, they pass through the guard's checkpoint. However, if something's wrong or if they are a visitor, they must first stop at the guard desk. The guard asks whom they wish to see. The guard may also ask for identification such as a driver's license or their company ID. The guard reviews the list of expected guests to see if this person is approved to visit the party in question. If the guard decides everything is all right, the visitor may pass. The visitor usually signs a logbook with their name, the company they represent, whom they are seeing, and the time of day. On a computer, the firewall acts much like a guard when it looks at network traffic destined for or received from another computer. The firewall determines if that traffic should continue on to its destination or be stopped. The firewall "guard" is important because it keeps the unwanted out and permits only appropriate traffic to enter and leave the computer.

To do this job, the firewall has to look at every piece of information – every packet – that tries to enter or leave a computer. Each packet is labeled with where it came from and where it wants to go. Some packets are allowed to go anywhere (the employee with the ID badge) while others can only go to specific places (visitors for a specific person). If the firewall allows the packet to proceed (being acceptable according to the rules), it moves the packet on its way to the destination. In most cases, the firewall records where the packet came from, where it's going, and when it was seen. For people entering a building, this is similar to the ID card system keeping track of who enters or the visitor signing the visitor's log. The building's guard may do a few more tasks before deciding that the person can pass. If the person is a visitor and is not on the visitors list, the guard calls the employee being visited to announce the visitor's arrival and to ask if they may pass. If the employee accepts the visitor, they may proceed. The guard may also give the visitor a badge that identifies them as a visitor.

That badge may limit where in the building they can go and indicate if they need to be escorted. Finally, no matter whether the person is a visitor or an employee, the guard may inspect their briefcase or computer case before they pass. The firewall can also check whether a given packet should pass, allowing the computer's user to respond to unanticipated network traffic (just as the guard does with the unexpected visitor).

Individual packets can be allowed to pass, or the firewall can be changed to allow all future packets of the same type to pass. Some firewalls have advanced capabilities that make it possible to direct packets to a different destination and perhaps even have their contents concealed inside other packets (similar to the visitor being escorted). Finally, firewalls can filter packets based not only on their point of origin or destination, but also on their content (inspecting the briefcase or computer case before being allowed to pass).

Back to the office building, when employees leave the building, they may also have to swipe their ID card to show that they've left. A visitor signs out and returns their temporary badge. Both may be subject to having their possessions inspected before being allowed to leave.

Firewalls can also recognize and record when a computer-to-computer connection ends. If the connection was temporary (like a visitor), the firewall rules can change to deny future similar connections until the system's user authorizes them (just as visitors must re-identify themselves and be re-approved by an employee). Finally, outgoing connections can also be filtered according to content (again, similar to inspecting possessions at the exit).

What does this all mean? It means that with a firewall, you can control which packets are allowed to enter your home computer and which are allowed to leave. That's the easy part. The hard part is deciding the details about the packets that are allowed to enter and exit your home computer. If your firewall supports content filtering, you also need to learn which content to allow and which not to allow. To help you get a handle on this harder task, let's return to our security guard analogy.

Imagine that you are that security guard and it's your first day on the job. You have to decide who's allowed in, who's allowed out, and what people can bring into and take out of the building. How do you do this? One strategy is to be very conservative: let no one in or out and let no possessions in or out. This is very simple, very easy to achieve, but not particularly helpful to the business if none of its employees or visitors can get in or out. Nor is it helpful if they can't bring anything with them. With this type of strategy, your tenure as a security guard may be short-lived. If you try this, you quickly learn that you need to change your strategy to allow people in and out only if they have acceptable identification and possessions using some agreed-to criteria. Add the requirement that if you don't meet the precise criteria for admittance, you don't get in.

With most firewalls, you can do the same thing. You can programme your firewall to let nothing in and nothing out. Period. This is a *deny-all*firewall strategy and it does work, though it effectively disconnects you from the Internet. It is impractical for most home computers. You can do what the security guard did: review each packet (employee or visitor) to see where it's coming from and where it's going. Some firewall products let you easily review each packet so that you can decide what to do with it.

When you are shopping for a firewall, look for this review feature because it can be quite helpful. Practically speaking, it isn't easy to decide which traffic is all right and which is not all right. Any feature that makes this job easier helps you achieve your goal of securing your home computer. Just like the security guard who learns that anybody with a company photo ID is allowed to pass, you too can create firewall rules that allow traffic to pass without reviewing each packet each time. For example, you may choose to allow your Internet browsers to visit any web site.

This rule would define the source of that traffic to be your browsers (Netscape Navigator and Microsoft Internet Explorer, for example) and the destination location to be any web server. This means that anybody using your home computer could visit any Internet web site, as long as that web server used the well-known standard locations.

Now that you have an idea of what your firewall security guard is trying to do, you need a method for gathering information and programming your firewall.

Here is a set of steps to use to do just that:

- *The Programme test*: What's the programme that wants to make a connection to the Internet? Although many programmes may need to make the same type of connection to the same Internet destination, you need to know the name of each. Avoid general rules that allow all programmes to make a connection. This often results in unwanted and unchecked behaviour.
- *The Location test*: What's the Internet location of the computer system to which your computer wants to connect? Locations consist of an address and a port number. Sometimes a programme is allowed to connect to any Internet location, such as a web browser connecting to any web server. Again, you want to limit programmes so that they only connect to specific locations where possible.
- *The Allowed test*: Is this connection allowed or denied? Your firewall rules will contain some of each.
- The Temporary test: Is this connection temporary or permanent? For example, if you're going to connect to this specific location more than five times each time you use the computer, you probably want to make the connection permanent. This means that you ought to add a rule to your firewall rules. If you

aren't going to make this connection often, you should define it as temporary.

With each connection, apply the PLAT tests to get the information you need to build a firewall rule. The answer to the PLAT tests tells you if you need to include a new firewall rule for this new connection. For most firewall programmes, you can temporarily allow a connection but avoid making it permanent by not including it in your rules. Where possible, allow only temporary connections.

As you run each programme on your home computer, you'll learn how it uses the Internet. Slowly you'll begin to build the set of rules that define what traffic is allowed into and out of your computer. By only letting in and out what you approve and denying all else, you will strike a practical balance between allowing everything and allowing nothing in or out. Along the way, you may come across exceptions to your rules. For example, you might decide that anybody who uses your home computer can visit any web site *except* a chosen few web sites. This is analogous to the security guard letting every employee pass except a few who need more attention first.

To do this with firewall rules, the exception rules must be listed before the general rules. For example, this means that the web sites whose connections are not allowed must be listed before the rules that allow all connections to any web site. Why? Most firewall programmes search their rules starting from the first through the last. When the firewall finds a rule that matches the packet being examined, the firewall honours it, does what the rule says, and looks no further. For example, if the firewall finds the general rule allowing any web site connections first, it honours this rule and doesn't look further for rules that might deny such a connection. So, the order of firewall rules is important.

Many firewalls can be programmed to require a password before changing the rules. This extra level of protection safeguards against unwanted changes no matter their source, that is, you, an intruder, or another user. Follow the guidance in assigning a password to your firewall.

Finally, make a backup of your firewall rules. You've probably taken a lot of time to build and tune them to match how your home computer is used. These rules are important to your computer's security, so back them up using the guidance in *Make Backups of Important Files and Folders*.

Firewalls come in two general types: hardware and software (programmes). The software versions also come in two types: free versions and commercial versions (ones that you purchase). At a minimum, you should use one of the free versions on your home computer. This is especially important if you have a laptop that you connect to your home network as well as a network at a hotel, a conference, or your office.

If you can afford a hardware firewall, you should install one of these too. We've recommended this as something to do later. (Firewall programmes are on our list of recommended actions, and hardware firewalls are The same issues apply to the hardware versions that apply to the software versions. Many can also be password protected against unwanted changes. Search the Internet with your browser to see what's available and what they cost. The price of hardware firewalls is coming down as the demand grows.

A firewall is your security guard that stands between your home computer and the Internet. It lets you control which traffic your computer accepts. It also controls which of your programmes can connect to the Internet. With a firewall, you define which connections between your computer and other computers on the Internet are allowed and which are denied. There are free firewall products that provide the capabilities you need to secure your home computer. Commercial versions have even more features that can further protect your computer.

Firewalls are an important part of your home computer's security defences:

- Use a worksheet to record your firewall decisions.
- Example: *Operating a Firewall Programme.*

BACKUPS

Whether you know it or not, you've divided everything

you own into two broad categories: those items you can replace and those you can't. For the items you can't replace, you've probably stored them in a safe place, either somewhere in your living space or elsewhere, in a lockbox at a bank, for example. In either case, you've probably also bought insurance that provides the funds you'd need to buy replacements. Your insurance policy covers almost everything you own.

On your home computer, have you similarly divided everything into the same categories? What have you done about the items – files in this case – that you can't replace? Examples are the files that make up your checking account records, that novel you've been writing for the past few years, and those pictures you took last summer with your digital camera. What happens if your computer malfunctions or is destroyed by a successful attacker? Are those files gone forever? Now think about your car for a moment. Do you have a spare tire? Is it inflated? When was the last time you used it? Can you imagine buying a car without a spare tire? Even if you bought a used car without a spare, how soon did you buy a spare so that you'd have one when you needed it?

Think back to your home computer. Do you have a "spare tire," meaning a way to continue computing when you have a "blowout" caused by a malfunction or an intruder? Said another way, can you back up your files onto some other media so that you can recover them if you need to? If you'd never buy a car without a spare tire, why did you buy a computer without a device to back up your files?

When deciding what to do about backing up files on your computer, ask these questions:

- *The Files question*: What files should you back up? The files you select are those that you can neither easily recreate nor reinstall from somewhere else, such as the CD-ROMs or the floppy disks that came with your computer.

Be realistic. That check register you printed does not constitute a backup from which you can easily recreate the files needed by your checking account programme. You're probably not going to re-enter all that data if the files are destroyed. Just as you protect your irreplaceable valuables, back up the files you cannot replace, easily or otherwise.

- *The Often question*: How often should you back them up? In the best of all cases, you should back up a file every time it changes. If you don't, you'll have to reintroduce all the changes that happened since your last backup. Just as you store your precious jewelry in a lockbox at the local bank lest the lucky robber find it in your jewelry box, you need to store your files safely (back them up) after every use (change in the file) lest an intruder destroys the file or there's a system catastrophe.
- *The Media question*: Where should you back them up to; that is, what media should you use to hold backed up files? The answer is: whatever you have. It's a question of how many of that media you have to use and how convenient it is. For example, most computers have a floppy disk drive. You could back up your irreplaceable files to floppies. That process just takes lots of time and may not be as convenient as using another media. Larger capacity removable disk drives and writable CD-ROMs also work well, take less time, and are more convenient.

If you don't have a backup device, there are alternatives. There are Internet services that let you back up your files to another Internet computer. Some of these services provide "transparent access" to the backups. That is, they look like another hard drive attached to your computer. You use the file copy scheme that your computer provides to back up files and recover them from backed up storage. To find these services, do some Internet searches using your browser.

Remember that the information you transfer across the Internet could be viewed and captured by others; that is, the information is in the clear. Be sensitive to that if you use an Internet-based backup computer. In addition, you need to be able to trust the information when you recover a file from that service.

- *The Store question*: Where should you store that media once it contains your backed up files? No matter how you back up your files, you need to be concerned about where those backed up copies live.

You already know that intruders try to break into your home computer to gain access to your files and your computer's resources. Another way to gain access to the same information is by stealing your backups. It is more difficult, though, since a robber must physically be where your backups are, whereas an intruder can access your home computer from literally anywhere in the world. The key is to know where the media is that contains your backed up files.

Just like important papers stored in a fireproof container at your house, you also need to be concerned about your backups being destroyed if your living space is destroyed or damaged. This means that you ought to keep a copy of your backed up files in a fireproof container or somewhere beyond your living space, your office for example. It is the eternal compromise between security and usability. If you need to recover a file and the backed up copies are at the office, that's inconvenient. However, while storing them at home is more convenient and more usable, they share the same risks that your computer faces should your living space be destroyed. Be aware of the issues and make a conscious decision, perhaps keeping copies in both places.

If you have that spare tire for your car or a lockbox for your valuables, you've already planned for the worst that can happen around your living space. Continue that good practice by backing up your critical files onto media that you can safely store elsewhere. Do those backups often enough that you can capture the changes you've made. With the FOMS questions, you have a structured approach to use to back up your critical files. You've now planned for the worst.

As you computerize the routine aspects of your daily life, making backup copies of important files and folders becomes critical. Even if you can't store the backup copies in a fireproof container or somewhere outside your home, make backups anyway. Any backup is better than none.

- Use a worksheet to record your important information about backups.

USE STRONG PASSWORDS

Your living space has doors and windows, and perhaps most of the time they're locked. For each lock that uses a key, chances are that each key is different. You know to lock up and not to share the keys with strangers, and probably not with most of your friends. You should not hide keys under the mat or in a flowerpot on your front porch.

Passwords for computers are much the same. For each computer and service you use (online purchasing, for example), you should have a password. Each password should be unique and unrelated to any of your other passwords. You shouldn't write them down nor should you share them with anyone, even your best friends.

Take a look at your front door key. It's pretty complicated. There are lots of notches and grooves. If there weren't so many possible variations, a thief could easily make a key for every possible combination and then try each on your front door. This trial-and-error method, (for computers, called *brute force*) is likely to be effective even if it takes a long time. Nonetheless, no matter how complicated, if the thief gets hold of your key, he or she can copy it and use that copy to open your door.

A password can also be complicated. Most schemes let you use any combination of letters, both upper and lower case, and numbers; and some also let you use punctuation marks. Lengths can vary. You can create a password to be as complicated as you want. The key (no pun intended) is to be able to remember this password whenever you need it without having to write it down to jog your memory.

Like the thief at your door, computer intruders also use trial-and-error, or brute-force techniques, to discover passwords. By bombarding a login scheme with all the words in a dictionary, they may "discover" the password that unlocks it. If they know something about you, such as your spouse's name, the kind of car you drive, or your interests, clever intruders can narrow the range of possible passwords and try those first. They are often successful. Even slight variations, such as adding a digit onto the end of a word or replacing the letter o (oh) with the digit 0 (zero), don't protect passwords. Intruders know we use tricks like this to make our passwords more difficult to guess.

Just like the front door key, even a complicated password can be copied and the copy reused. Remember the earlier discussion about information on the Internet being in the clear? Suppose that really strong password you took a long time to create – the one that's 14 characters long and contains 6 letters, 4 numbers, and 4 punctuation marks, all in random order – goes across the Internet in the clear. An intruder may be able to see it, save it, and use it. This is called *sniffing* and it is a common intruder practice.

The point is that you need to follow the practice of using a unique password with every account you have. Below is a set of steps that you can use to help you create passwords for your accounts:

- *The Strong test*: Is the password as strong (meaning length and content) as the rules allow?
- *The Unique test*: Is the password unique and unrelated to any of your other passwords?
- *The Practical test*: Can you remember it without having to write it down?
- *The Recent test*: Have you changed it recently?

In spite of the SUPR tests, you need to be aware that sniffing happens, and even the best of passwords can be captured and used by an intruder. You should use passwords not only on your home computer but also for services you use elsewhere on the Internet. All should have the strongest passwords you can use and remember, and each password should be unique and unrelated to all other passwords.

A strong password is a password that is longer than it is short, that uses combinations of uppercase and lowercase letters, numbers, and punctuation, and that is usually not a word found in a dictionary. Also remember that no matter how strong a password is, it can still be captured if an intruder can see it "in the clear" somewhere on the Internet. When you buy an appliance, you give little thought to it doing you or your house any harm. Why? Because there are organizations likeUnderwriters Laboratories that set standards and certify products. When you see a certifier's label, you have more confidence that a product will be safer than a competing product that does not carry the same label. You're willing to accept the risk because you believe the product has met some standards and has been certified by a respected authority.

Unfortunately, the Internet is not the same. There are neither standards nor many certification organizations. Anyone who writes a programme can distribute it through any means available, such as through the web or by sending you a copy. Speaking of that, have you ever received a CD-ROM in the mail? How do you know that it contains what the label says? The answer is: you don't know. More importantly, it's difficult to know.

No matter how you acquire a programme, it runs on your computer at the mercy of the program's author. Anything, any operation, any task that you can do, this programme can also do. If you're allowed to remove any file, the programme can too. If you can send e-mail, the programme can too. If you can install or remove a programme, the programme can too. Anything you can do, the intruder can do also, through the programme you've just installed and run.

Sometimes there's no explanation of what a programme is supposed to do or what it actually does. There may be no user's guide. There may be no way to contact the author. You're on your own, trying to weigh a program's benefits against the risk of the harm that it might cause. What's the problem you're trying to solve here? You are trying to determine if the programme you've just found satisfies your needs (say it provides a service that you want or you're just experimenting) without causing harm to your computer and ultimately the information you have on the computer. How do you decide if a programme is what it says it is? How do you gauge the risk to you and your computer by running this programme?

You address these same risk issues when you purchase an appliance; you may just not have realised that's what you were doing. When you make that purchase, you buy from either a local store you know or a national chain with an established reputation. If there's a problem with your purchase, you can take it back to the store and exchange it or get your money back. If it causes you harm, you can seek relief through the legal system. The reputation of the merchant, the refund/return policy, and the availability of the legal system reduce your risk to a point where you make the purchase.

Apply these same practices when you buy a programme. You should:

- Learn as much as you can about the product and what it does before you purchase it.
- Understand the refund/return policy before you make your purchase.
- Buy from a local store that you already know or a national chain with an established reputation.

Presently, it is not as clear what the legal system's role is for a programme that causes harm or does not work as advertised. In the meantime, the LUB practices are a good first step. Today's Internet has a feature that standard products don't have, or at least have but to a lesser extent. This feature is free programmes. There is a multitude of free programmes available for all types of systems, with more available each day. The challenge is to decide which programmes deserve your confidence and are, therefore, worth the risk of installing and running on your home computer.

So then, how do you decide if a programme is worth it? To decide if you should install and run a programme on your home computer, follow these steps:

- *The Do test*: What does the programme do? You should be able to read a clear description of what the programme does. This description could be on the web site where you can download it or on the CD-ROM you use to install it. You need to realise that that if the programme was written with malicious intent, the author/intruder isn't going to tell you that the programme will harm your system. They will probably try to mislead you. So, learn what you can, but consider the source and consider whether you can trust that information.

- *The Changes test*: What files are installed and what other changes are made on your system when you install and run the programme? Again, to do this test, you may have to ask the author/intruder how their programme changes your system. Consider the source.
- *The Author test*: Who is the author? (Can you use e-mail, telephone, letter, or some other means to contact them?) Once you get this information, use it to try to contact them to verify that the contact information works. Your interactions with them may give you more clues about the programme and its potential effects on your computer and you.
- *The Learn test*: Has anybody else used this programme, and what can you learn from him or her? Try some Internet searches using your web browser. Somebody has probably used this programme before you, so learn what you can before you install it.

If you can't determine these things – the DCAL tests for short – about the programme you'd like to install, then strongly consider whether it's worth the risk. Only you can decide what's best. Whatever you do, be prepared to rebuild your computer from scratch in case the programme goes awry and destroys it. Task 5 - *Make Backups of Important Files and Folders* tells you how to make a copy of your important information should you need it.

Your anti-virus programme prevents some of the problems caused by downloading and installing programmes. However, you need to remember that there's a lag between recognizing a virus and when your computer also knows about it. Even if that nifty programme you've just downloaded doesn't contain a virus, it may behave in an unexpected way. You should continue to exercise care and do your homework when downloading, installing, and running new programmes.

- Use a worksheet to record important information about programmes you install on your computer.

INSTALL AND USE A HARDWARE FIREWALL

Complement your firewall programme by installing a hardware firewall. Together, these two firewalls stand between your home computer and the Internet. This is another place where your money is well spent.

Please go to Task 4 - *Install and Use a Firewall Programme* to learn more about firewalls. That section concentrates primarily on firewall programmes, but much of the information applies to hardware firewalls as well. To find out what hardware firewall products are available, search the Internet with your web browser.

- Use a worksheet to record the ruleset for your hardware firewall.

FILE ENCRYPTION PROGRAMME

Let's return to your living space and our original analogy. Think about your checkbook, your insurance policies, perhaps your birth certificate or passport, and other important documents you have at home. Where are they? They're probably stored in a filing cabinet or a safe, either of which that can be or is routinely locked. Why do you store these important items in a locked container?

Without realizing it, you are satisfying one of the three components of information security – *confidentiality*. Confidentiality means keeping secrets secret. Only those who are supposed to see that information should have access to it. You are keeping information sensitive to you and others away from those who should not be able to get to it, for example a family member or an intruder.

You further protect information confidentiality when you enforce it by using an *access control device,* namely the lock on your filing cabinet or safe. This device stands between the information and those seeking access, and it grants access to all who have the combination, the key, or whatever tool unlocks the container. When several layers of access control devices are used (called "defence in depth") – you might also find that these containers are themselves in locked rooms.

Would-be intruders must pass through several levels of protection before finally gaining access to the information they seek. Now, think back to your home computer. The problem is to control access to files and folders. The access control device here is the *access control list* or *ACL*. ACLs define who can perform actions on a file or folder: reading and writing, for example. ACLs are equivalent to a locked filing cabinet for paper documents.

Different computer systems provide different types of ACLs. Some have fine-grained controls while others have virtually none. The key is to use all the controls that are available on your computer.

Frequently, vendors define ACLs that are overly permissive. This satisfies their need to ensure that access limitations don't get in the way of using their systems. Your challenge is to tighten those ACLs so that they properly restrict access to only those who need access. This means that you need to modify the ACLs from the settings set by the vendor. We'll talk more about how to do this shortly.

Returning to the home environment, do you remember a time when adults in your house wanted to say something to one another in front of their children but in such a way that the children couldn't understand what was being said? Perhaps they spelled their message or used Pig Latin (ig-pay Atin-lay) to conceal the meaning. This worked for a while, until the children learned to spell or could otherwise understand what was being said. What's really happening here?

Very simply, the adults could not control who could hear their conversation. It was inconvenient or perhaps impossible for them to go to another room where they couldn't be heard. They had to talk in a way that only those who knew the concealing scheme could understand what was being said.

On a computer, when access to information can't be limited, such for an e-commerce transaction over the Internet, that information is concealed through a mathematical process called encryption. Encryption transforms information from one form (readable text) to another (encrypted text).

Its intent is to hide information from those who have neither the transformation method nor the particulars (the decryption keys) to transform the encrypted text into readable text. The encrypted text appears to be gibberish and remains so for people who don't have the scheme and the keys. Back on the home front, the children eventually learned how to spell and perhaps also learned the trick to using Pig Latin. They can now understand the conversations the adults are having. While they could also understand the conversations held weeks, months, or even years before, the information in those conversations is no longer important. The encryption scheme – spelling or Pig Latin – is strong enough to guard the information during its useful lifetime.

Computer-based encryption schemes must also withstand the test of time. For example, if a credit card encryption scheme needs six months of computer time to break, the resulting clear text credit card number is probably still valid and, therefore, useful to an intruder. In this case, the encryption scheme isn't strong enough to guard the information for its entire useful lifetime.

So, to guard paper or computer files, you need to limit who has access to them by using the access control devices, whether filing cabinets and safes for paper or access control lists for information on a computer system. For assets whose access cannot be sufficiently limited, you need to encrypt them strongly enough so that the time it takes to decrypt them is longer than their useful life.

Now, what can you do? First, if more than one person uses your computer, you can adjust the ACLs that control access to sensitive files and folders. Your goal is to allow the correct type of access to the files and folders that each user needs, and nothing more. The steps below help you to decide how to adjust the ACLs for files and folders:

- *The Who test*: Who – which users – need access to files besides you?
- *The Access test*: What type of access do they need? Read? Write?
- *The Files/Folders test*: Which files and folders need special access? Just like your firewall rules, your general policy should be to limit access to only you first, and then grant access beyond that where needed.

By applying the WAF tests, you can limit access to sensitive files on your computer to only those who need it.

Setting proper ACLs is not a trivial task. Be prepared to repeat it a few times until you get it right for the way your computer is used. It's worth the time spent, but know that it may take longer than you expect.

For very sensitive files and for files that are on a laptop, don't rely solely on file and folder ACLs. You need to go further and use encryption. Some vendors provide encryption with their systems right from the start. This means that all you have to do is follow the vendor's instructions on how to use those features, but be certain to use them.

On systems where encryption is not included, you need to install additional encryption programmes. For encryption programmes that you download from the Internet, be sure to follow the instructions in . Also follow the instructions in for additional guidance on passwords required by encryption programmes. There are free and commercial encryption programmes, and in most cases, the free versions suffice. However, commercial programmes may provide more features and may keep up better with newer and, therefore, stronger encryption methods. If you rely on a laptop computer, you should consider purchasing a commercial file encryption programmes. Whether paper files around your living space or files and folders on your computer, limit access where you can. On your computer, use encryption programmes either when you can't restrict access to the extent that you'd like or when you want even more security protecting your computer files and folders. The line between a 'business' and 'home' computer market segments has blurred, since the computers typically use the same operating systems, processor architectures, applications and peripherals. Another change from the home computer era is that the once-common endeavour of writing one's own software programmes has almost vanished from home computer use

SECURITY AGREEMENT

DEFINITION

The agreement aims at establishing a general framework at European level concerning the employment conditions of teleworkers and at reconciling the needs for flexibility and security shared by employers and workers. It grants teleworkers the same overall level of protection as workers who carry out their activities at the employer's premises.

The agreement defines telework as a form of organising and/or performing work, using information technology, in the context of an employment contract/relationship, where work, which could also be performed at the employer's premises, is carried out away from those premises on a regular basis.

Since telework covers a wide and fast evolving spectrum of circumstances, the social partners have chosen a definition of telework that includes various forms of regular telework. The agreement focuses on several key areas in which the specific nature of telework must be taken into account, viz:

Voluntary Nature of Teleworking

Telework is voluntary for the worker and the employer concerned. Telework may be required as part of a worker's initial job description or it may be engaged in as a voluntary arrangement subsequently. In both cases, the employer provides the teleworker with relevant written information in accordance with Directive 91/533/EEC;

Employment Conditions

Teleworkers benefit from the same rights as comparable workers at the employer's premises. These rights are guaranteed by applicable legislation and collective agreements. In order to take into account the particularities of telework, specific agreements may be necessary;

Data Protection

The employer is responsible for taking the appropriate measures to ensure the protection of data used and processed by the teleworker for professional purposes. The employer informs the teleworker in particular of any restrictions on the use of equipment and of sanctions in the case of non-compliance;

Privacy

The employer respects the teleworker's privacy. If any kind of monitoring system is put in place, it needs to be proportionate to the objective and introduced in accordance with Directive 90/270 on visual display units;

Equipment

As a general rule, the employer is responsible for providing, installing and maintaining the equipment necessary for regular telework unless the teleworker uses his/her own equipment. The employer has the liability, in accordance with national legislation and collective agreements, regarding costs for loss and damage to the equipment and data used by the teleworker;

Health and Safety

The employer is responsible for the protection of the occupational health and safety of the teleworker in accordance with Directive 89/391 and relevant daughter directives, national legislation and collective agreements.

In order to verify that the applicable health and safety provisions are correctly employed, the employer, workers' representatives and/or relevant authorities have access to the telework place, within the limits of national legislation and collective agreements. If the teleworker is working at home, such access is subject to prior notification and his/her agreement. The teleworker is entitled to request inspection visits;

Organisation of Work

Within the framework of applicable legislation, collective agreements and company rules, the teleworker manages the organisation of his/her working time. The workload and performance standards of the teleworker are equivalent to those of comparable workers at the employer's premises;

Training of Teleworkers

Teleworkers have the same access to training and career development as comparable workers at the employer's premises and are subject to the same appraisal policies as these are their workers. Teleworkers receive appropriate training targeted at the technical equipment at their disposal and at the characteristics of this form of work organisation;

The Collective Rights of Teleworkers

Teleworkers have the same collective rights as workers at the employer's premises. No obstacles are put to communicating with workers' representatives.

IMPLEMENTATION AND FOLLOW-UP

This European framework agreement will be implemented within three years after the date of signature by the members of UNICE/UEAPME, CEEP and ETUC (and the Liaison Committee EUROCADRES/CEC).

Member organisations will report on the implementation of this agreement to an ad-hoc group set up by the signatory parties, under the responsibility of the Social Dialogue Committee. Within four years after the date of signature of this agreement, this ad-hoc group will prepare a joint report on the implementation measures taken. The signatory parties will review the agreement five years after the date of signature if requested by one of the signatory parties.

CONTEXT

This new agreement directly supports the strategy defined at the Lisbon European Council and the transition to a knowledge-based economy and society, in line with the

Lisbon objectives. In July 1997, the European Commission adopted a raft of policy recommendations on the labour market and the social dimension of the information society. The recommendations included commitments to promote teleworking in Europe and to study teleworking within the Commission.

In 1998 a pilot project was launched by the Directorate General for Employment, Social Affairs and Equal Opportunities and the Directorate-General for the Information Society. It includes three telework types of a part-time nature: working both from home and in the office, working whilst on the move during official missions, and occasional work in another Commission building.

The promotion of telework opportunities is one of the components of the Commission's proposals for an employment strategy in the information society. The Commission supports the work of the social partners with a view to establishing framework conditions and practical rules so as to allow telework to be introduced on a large scale.

WHAT IS TELEWORKING

Telework occurs when information and communications technologies (ICTs) are applied to enable work to be done at a distance from the place where the work results are needed or where the work would conventionally have been done. It includes:

- Home-based telework or "telecommuting", when an employee or contractor works at home instead of travelling to an employer's or a customer's premises.
- Mobile telework, when executives, professionals or service staffs using ICTs to enable them to spend more time with customers and to deliver "on the road" a range of services and capabilities that previously would have involved office based staff or visits to the company offices;
- Telecentres, providing local office facilities for people who prefer not to work at home but wish to avoid the cost, time and inconvenience of commuting;

- Telecottages, which provide local communities with access to skills development, high performance ICTs, and the networking and socialisation aspects of work that may be missed by a home based worker.
- Functional relocation, where business functions that previously were located close to the customer are concentrated and delivered at a distance; examples include both "front office" (selling activities previously done in the High Street, now delivered by phone or computer networks) and "back office" (service and maintenance work previously done "on site", which may now be done anywhere in the world using remote access to systems).

Telework also affects some kinds of "outsourcing", in that many kinds of work can now be done from thousands of miles away and "outsourced" across national borders. Telework has also been said to include "dispersed team working", in which (for example) an engineering company uses three or more teams in different time zones to work 24 hours a day on a time-sensitive customer tender, with each team "passing the baton" to the next at the end of its working day.

As well as affecting the individual and the enterprise telework has significant economic and trade implications, for example many jobs in computer programing that might previously have been done in California or in Sweden are now done in Bangalore. Understanding telework in all its ramifications is essential to the future of work and jobs.

ELECTRONIC MAIL

INTRODUCTION

For many people, electronic mail is still a novel experience. Many people sign up for an e-mail account, get some mail programme like Eudora or one of the Microsoft mail programmes, play around for a while, and then just about forget it, leaving mail to collect unanswered. Even big companies are offenders here. In those cases where such people do send or answer mail, the quality of the message is frequently poor. They often contain misspellings, irrelevant quotes, or poor layout ("formatting").

Don't underestimate the effect of such a mail message. Your mail message is all that many people see of you, and if it's poorly formatted, one line per paragraph, badly spelt, or full of errors, it will give people a poor impression of you. E-mail use is just now becoming mainstream, but many hackers have been using it for 20 years or more.

In the impersonal world of the Internet, your mail messages are the most tangible thing about you. Send out a well thought out, clear and legible message, and you will leave a good impression. Send out a badly formulated, badly formatted and badly spelt message, and you will leave a bad impression.

Problems in mail fall into a number of categories. Select the link for more details of each category:

- Format problems. In extreme cases, messages can be barely legible. Microsoft "Outlook" seems to have taken this problem to new heights.
- Character set problems. Traditionally, Mail was written in US-ASCII, a character set which only suffices to represent English correctly. Even most of the optional English letters, such as æ and French accents é, è and friends are missing.
- Message layout issues. These are entirely in your hands, and they reflect most on your personality. Use them well and you'll make a good impression. Use them badly and you'll make a bad impression. Who decides what good and bad are? The reader does, and you don't get a say in the matter.

One of the most prominent uses of networking since the first networks were devised, has been electronic mail. It started as a simple service that copied a file from one machine to another, and appended it to the recipient's *mailbox* file. Basically, this is still what e-mail is all about, although an ever growing net with its complex routing requirements and its ever increasing load of messages has made a more elaborate scheme necessary.

Various standards of mail exchange have been devised. Sites on the Internet adhere to one laid out in RFC-822, augmented by some RFCs that describe a machine-independent way of transferring special characters, and the like. Much thought has also been given recently to "multi-media mail", which deals with including pictures and sound in mail messages. Another standard, X.400, has been defined by CCITT.

Quite a number of mail transport programmes have been implemented for systems. One of the best-known is the University of Berkeley's sendmail, which is used on a number of platforms. The original author was Eric Allman, who is now actively working on the sendmail team again. There are two ports of sendmail-5.56c available, one of which will be described.

Compared to sendmail, smail is rather young. When handling mail for a small site without complicated routing requirements, their capabilities are pretty close. For large sites, however, sendmail always wins, because its configuration scheme is much more flexible. Both smail and sendmail support a set of configuration files that have to be customised. Apart from the information that is required to make the mail subsystem run (such as the local hostname), there are many more parameters that may be tuned.

Sendmail's main configuration file is very hard to understand at first. It looks as if your cat had taken a nap on your keyboard with the shift key pressed. smail configuration files are more structured and easier to understand than sendmail's, but don't give the user as much power in tuning the mailer's behaviour. However, for small UUCP or Internet sites the work required in setting up any of them is roughly the same.

USING MAILER

Your choice of MUA ("mailer") is personal—maybe. You can only choose from what's available. If you use UNIX or a compatible operating system, there are dozens of mailers available, some of them good. I personally prefer mutt.

If you use Microsoft, you'll also find several mailers, but most of them are bad, at least from the point of view of what the recipient sees. My personal hate list (in order of decreasing capability to annoy) is:

- Lotus Notes
- Microsoft "Outlook" Express
- Microsoft "Outlook"

Netscape Communicator is better, but not much. None of these mailers is capable of both producing correct formats and not mutilating quoted text. "Outlook" Express apparently insists on displaying in a proportionally spaced font, so you can't even decide where to insert a manual line break. Most of them discard headers, which may contain important information—it's rather like receiving conventional ("snail mail") letters without the envelope.

MAIL MESSAGE

A Mail message generally consists of a message body, which is the text the sender wrote, and special data specifying recipients, transport medium, etc., very much like what you see when you look at a letter's envelope.

This administrative data falls into two categories; in the first category is any data that is specific to the transport medium, like the address of sender and recipient. It is therefore called *the envelope*. It may be transformed by the transport software as the message is passed along.

The second variety is any data necessary for handling the mail message, which is not particular to any transport mechanism, such as the message's subject line, a list of all recipients, and the date the message was sent. In many networks, it has become standard to prepend this data to the mail message, forming the so-called *mail header*. It is offset from the *mail body* by an empty line. Most mail transport software in the world uses a header format outlined in a RFC-822. Its original purpose was to specify a standard for use on the ARPANET, but since it was designed to be independent from any environment, it has been easily adapted to other networks, including many UUCP-based networks. RFC-822 however is only the greatest common denominator. More recent standards have been conceived to cope with growing needs as, for example, data encryption, international character set support, and multi-media mail extensions (MIME).

In all these standards, the header consists of several lines, separated by newline characters. A line is made up of a field name, beginning in column one, and the field itself, offset by a colon and white space. The format and semantics of each field vary depending on the field name. A header field may be continued across a newline, if the next line begins with a TAB. Fields can appear in any order.

A typical mail header may look like this:

```
From brewhq.swb.de!ora.com!andyo Wed Apr 13
00:17:03 1994
   Return-Path:
   Received:from brewhq.swb.de by monad.swb.de
   with uucp
   (Smail3.1.28.1 #6) id m0pqqlT-00023aB; Wed,
13 Apr 94 00:17
   Received: from ora.com (ruby.ora.com) by
   brewhq.swb.de with
   smtp(Smail3.1.28.1 #28.6) id; Tue, 12 Apr
   94 2
   Received: by ruby.ora.com (8.6.8/8.6.4) id
   RAA26438; Tue, 12
Apr 94
   Date: Tue, 12 Apr 1994 15:56:49 -0400
   Message-Id: <199404121956.PAA07787@ruby>
   From: andyo@ora.com (Andy Oram)
   To: okir@monad.swb.de
   Subject: Re: Your RPC section
```

Usually, all necessary header fields are generated by the mailer interface you use, like elm, pine, mush, or mailx. Some however are optional, and may be added by the user. elm, for example, allows you to edit part of the message header. Others are added by the mail transport software. A list of common header fields and their meaning are given below:

- *From*: This contains the sender's e-mail address, and

possibly the "real name". A complete zoo of formats is used here.

- *To*: This is the recipient's e-mail address.
- *Subject*: Describes the content of the mail in a few words. At least that's what it should do.
- *Date*: The date the mail was sent.
- *Reply-To*: Specifies the address the sender wants the recipient's reply directed to. This may be useful if you have several accounts, but want to receive the bulk of mail only on the one you use most frequently. This field is optional.
- *Organization*: The organization that owns the machine from which the mail originates. If your machine is owned by you privately, either leave this out, or insert "private" or some complete non- sense. This field is optional.
- *Message-ID*: A string generated by mail transport on the originating system. It is unique to this message.
- *Received*: Every site that processes your mail (including the machines of sender and recipient) inserts such a field into the header, giving its site name, a message id, time and date it received the message, which site it is from, and which transport software was used. This is so that you can trace which route the message took, and can complain to the person responsible if something went wrong.
- *X-anything*: No mail-related programmes should complain about any header which starts with X-. It is used to implement additional features that have not yet made it into an RFC, or never will. This is used by the Linux Activists mailing list, for example, where the channel is selected by the X-Mn-Key: header field.

The one exception to this structure is the very first line. It starts with the keyword From which is followed by a blank instead of a colon. To distinguish it from the ordinary From: field, it is frequently referred to as From_. It contains the route the message has taken in UUCP bang-path style (explained below), time and date when it was received by the last machine having processed it, and an optional part specifying which host it was received from. Since this field is regenerated by every system that processes the message, it is sometimes subsumed under the envelope data.

The From_ field is there for backward compatibility with some older mailers, but is not used very much anymore, except by mail user interfaces that rely on it to mark the beginning of a message in the user's mailbox. To avoid potential trouble with lines in the message body that begin with "From ", too, it has become standard procedure to escape any such occurrence by preceding it with

MAIL DELIVERED

Generally, you will compose mail using a mailer interface like mail or mailx; or more sophisticated ones like elm, mush, or pine. These programmes are called *mail user agents*, or MUA's for short. If you send a mail message, the interface programme will in most cases hand it to another programme for delivery. This is called the *mail transport agent*, or MTA. On some systems, there are different mail transport agents for local and remote delivery; on others, there is only one. The command for remote delivery is usually called rmail, the other is called lmail (if it exists).

Local delivery of mail is, of course, more than just appending the incoming message to the recipient's mailbox. Usually, the local MTA will understand aliasing (setting up local recipient addresses pointing to other addresses), and forwarding (redirecting a user's mail to some other destination). Also, messages that cannot be delivered must usually be *bounced*, that is, returned to the sender along with some error message.

For remote delivery, the transport software used depends on the nature of the link. If the mail must be delivered over a network using TCP/IP, SMTP is commonly used. SMTP stands for Simple Mail Transfer Protocol, and is defined in RFC-788 and RFC-821. SMTP usually connects to the recipient's machine directly, negotiating the message transfer with the remote side's SMTP daemon. In UUCP networks, mail will usually not be delivered directly, but rather be forwarded to the destination host by a number of intermediate systems. To send a message over a UUCP link, the sending MTA will usually execute rmail on the forwarding system using uux, and feed it the message on standard input.

Since this is done for each message separately, it may produce a considerable work load on a major mail hub, as well as clutter the UUCP spool queues with hundreds of small files taking up an unproportional amount of disk space. Some MTAs therefore allow you to collect several messages for a remote system in a single batch file.

The batch file contains the SMTP commands that the local host would normally issue if a direct SMTP connection was used. This is called BSMTP, or *batched* SMTP. The batch is then fed to the rsmtp or bsmtp programme on the remote system, which will process the input as if a normal SMTP connection had occurred.

E-MAIL ADDRESSES

For electronic mail, an address is made up of at least the name of a machine handling the person's mail, and a user identification recognized by this system. This may be the recipient's login name, but may also be anything else. Other mail addressing schemes, like X.400, use a more general set of "attributes" which are used to look up the recipient's host in an X.500 directory server.

The way a machine name is interpreted, i.e. at which site your message will finally wind up, and how to combine this name with the recipient's user name greatly depends on the network you are on. Internet sites adhere to the RFC-822 standard, which requires a notation of user@host.domain, where host.domain is the host's fully qualified domain name. The middle thing is called an "at" sign. Because this notation does not involve a route to the destination host but gives the (unique) hostname instead, this is called an *absolute* address.

In the original UUCP environment, the prevalent form was path!host!user, where path described a sequence of hosts the message had to travel before reaching the destination host. This construct is called the *bang path* notation, because an exclamation mark is loosely called a "bang". Today, many UUCP-based networks have adopted RFC-822, and will understand this type of address.

Now, these two types of addressing don't mix too well. Assume an address of hostA!user@hostB. It is not clear whether the '@' sign takes precedence over the path, or vice versa: do we have to send the message to hostB, which mails it to hostA!user, or should it be sent to hostA, which forwards it to user@hostB?

Addresses that mix different types of address operators are called *hybrid addresses*. Most notorious is the above example. It is usually resolved by giving the '@' sign precedence over the path. In the above example, this means sending the message to hostB first.

However, there is a way to specify routes in RFC-822-conformant ways: <@hostA,@hostB:user@hostC> denotes the address of user on hostC, where hostC is to be reached through hostA and hostB (in that order). This type of address is frequently called a *route-addr address*.

Then, there is the '%' address operator: user% host B@hostA will first be sent to hostA, which expands the rightmost (in this case, only) per cent sign to an '@' sign. The address is now user@hostB, and the mailer will happily forward your message to hostB which delivers it to user. This type of address is sometimes referred to as "Ye Olde ARPANET Kludge", and its use is discouraged. Nevertheless, many mail transport agents generate this type of address.

Other networks have still different means of addressing. DECnet-based networks, for example, use two colons as an address separator, yielding an address of host:user.Lastly, the X.400 standard uses an entirely different scheme, by describing a recipient by a set of attribute-value pairs, like country and organization. On FidoNet, each user is identified by a code like 2:320/204.9, consisting of four numbers denoting zone (2 is for Europe), net (320 being Paris and Banlieue), node (the local hub), and point (the individual user's PC).

Fidonet addresses can be mapped to RFC-822; the above would be written as Thomas. Quinot@ p9. f204. n320. z2.fidonet. org. Now didn't I say domain names are easy to remember?

There are some implications to using these different types of addressing which will be described throughout the following sections. In a RFC-822 environment, however, you will rarely use anything else than absolute addresses like user@host.domain.

HOW DOES MAIL ROUTING WORK

The process of directing a message to the recipient's host is called *routing*. Apart from finding a path from the sending site to the destination, it involves error checking as well as speed and cost optimization.

There is a big difference between the way a UUCP site handles routing, and the way an Internet site does. On the Internet, the main job of directing data to the recipient host (once it is known by it's IP-address) is done by the IP networking layer, while in the UUCP zone, the route has to be supplied by the user, or generated by the mail transfer agent.

Mail Routing on the Internet

Mail Routing on the Internet On the Internet, it depends entirely on the destination host whether any specific mail routing is performed at all. The default is to deliver the message to the destination host directly by looking up its IP address, and leave the actual routing of the data to the IP transport layer.

Most sites will usually want to direct all in-bound mail to a highly available mail server that is capable of handling all this traffic, and have it distribute this mail locally. To announce this service, the site publishes a so-called MX record for their local domain in the DNS database. MX stands for *Mail Exchanger* and basically states that the server host is willing to act as a mail forwarder for all machines in this domain. MX records may also be used to handle traffic for hosts that are not connected to the Internet themselves, like UUCP networks, or company networks with hosts carrying confidential information.

MX records also have a *preference* associated with them. This is a positive integer. If several mail exchangers exist for one host, the mail transport agent will try to transfer the message to the exchanger with the lowest preference value, and only if this fails will it try a host with a higher value. If the local host is itself a mail exchanger for the destination address, it must not forward messages to any MX hosts with a higher preference than its own; this is a safe way of avoiding mail loops.

Suppose that an organization, say Foobar Inc., want all their mail handled by their machine called mailhub. They will then have an MX record like this in the DNS database:

```
foobar.com IN MX 5 mailhub.foobar.com
```

This announces mailhub.foobar.com as a mail exchanger for foobar.com with a preference value of 5. If there's no MX with a preference smaller than 5, the message will be delivered to mailhub, which then dispatches it to greenhouse.

Mail Routing in the UUCP World

Mail routing on UUCP networks is much more complicated than on the Internet, because the transport software does not perform any routing itself. In earlier times, all mail had to be addressed using bang paths. Bang paths specified a list of hosts through which to forward the message, separated by exclamation marks, and followed by the user's name. To address a letter to Janet User on a machine named moria, you would have used the path eek!swim!moria!janet. Whis would have sent the mail from your host to eek, from there on to swim and finally to moria.

The obvious drawback of this technique is that it requires you to remember much about the network topology, fast links, etc. Much worse than that, changes in the network topology—like links being deleted or hosts being removed— may cause messages to fail simply because you weren't aware of the change. And finally, in case you move to a different place, you will most likely have to update all these routes. One thing, however, that made the use of source routing necessary was the presence of ambiguous hostnames: For instance, assume there are two sites named moria, one in the U.S., and one in France. Which site now does moria!janet refer to? This can be made clear by specifying what path to reach moria through.

The first step in disambiguating hostnames was the founding of *The UUCP Mapping Project*. It is located at Rutgers University, and registers all official UUCP hostnames, along with information on their UUCP neighbours and their geographic location, making sure no hostname is used twice. The information gathered by the Mapping Project is published as the *Usenet Maps,* which are distributed regularly through Usenet. A typical system entry in a Map (after removing the comments) looks like this.

```
moria
bert(DAILY/2),
swim(WEEKLY)
```

This entry says that moria has a link to bert, which it calls twice a day, and swim, which it calls weekly. We will come back to the Map file format in more detail below.

Using the connectivity information provided in the maps, you can automatically generate the full paths from your host to any destination site. This information is usually stored in the paths file, also called *pathalias database* sometimes. Assume the Maps state that you can reach bert through ernie, then a pathalias entry for moria generated from the Map snippet above may look like this:

```
moria  ernie!bert!moria!%s
```

If you now give a destination address of janet @ moria. uucp, your MTA will pick the route shown above, and send the message to ernie with an envelope address of bert!moria!janet.

Building a paths file from the full Usenet maps is however not a very good idea. The information provided in them is usually rather distorted, and occasionally out of date. Therefore, only a number of major hosts use the complete

UUCP world maps to build their paths file. Most sites only maintain routing information for sites in their neighborhood, and send any mail to sites they don't find in their databases to a smarter host with more complete routing information. This scheme is called*smart-host routing*. Hosts that have only one UUCP mail link (so-called *leaf sites*) don't do any routing of their own; they rely entirely on their smart-host.

Mixing UUCP and RFC-822

The best cure against the problems of mail routing in UUCP networks so far is the adoption of the domain name system in UUCP networks. Of course, you can't query a name server over UUCP. Nevertheless, many UUCP sites have formed small domains that coordinate their routing internally. In the Maps, these domains announce one or two host as their mail gateways, so that there doesn't have to be a map entry for each host in the domain. The gateways handle all mail that flows into and out of the domain. The routing scheme inside the domain is completely invisible to the outside world.

This works very well with the smart-host routing scheme described above. Global routing information is maintained by the gateways only; minor hosts within a domain will get along with only a small hand-written paths file that lists the routes inside their domain, and the route to the mail hub. Even the mail gateways do not have to have routing information for every single UUCP host in the world anymore. Beside the complete routing information for the domain they serve, they only need to have routes to entire domains in their databases now. For instance, the pathalias entry shown below will route all mail for sites in the sub.org domain to smurf:

```
.sub.org  swim!smurf!%s
```

Any mail addressed to claire@jones.sub.org will be sent to swim with an envelope address of smurf!jones!claire.

The hierarchical organization of the domain name space allows mail servers to mix more specific routes with less specific ones. For instance, a system in France may have specific routes for subdomains of fr, but route any mail for hosts in the us domain towards some system in the U.S. In this way, domain-based routing (as this technique is called) greatly reduces the size of routing databases as well as the administrative overhead needed.

The main benefit of using domain names in a UUCP environment, however, is that compliance with RFC-822 permits easy gatewaying between UUCP networks and the Internet. Many UUCP domains nowadays have a link with an Internet gateway that acts as their smart-host. Sending messages across the Internet is faster, and routing information is much more reliable because Internet hosts can use DNS instead of the Usenet Maps.

In order to be reachable from the Internet, UUCP-based domains usually have their Internet gateway announce an MX record for them (MX records were described above). For instance, assume that moria belongs to the orcnet.org domain. gcc2.groucho.edu acts as their Internet gateway. moria would therefore use gcc2 as its smart-host, so that all mail for foreign domains is delivered across the Internet. On the other hand, gcc2 would announce an MX record for orcnet.org, and deliver all incoming mail for orcnet sites to moria.

The only remaining problem is that the UUCP transport programmes can't deal with fully qualified domain names. Most UUCP suites were designed to cope with site names of up to eight characters, some even less, and using non-alphanumeric characters such as dots is completely out of the question for most.

Therefore, some mapping between RFC-822 names and UUCP hostnames is needed. The way this mapping is done is completely implementation-dependent. One common way of mapping FQDNs to UUCP names is to use the pathalias file for this:

```
moria.orcnet.org  ernie!bert!moria!%s
```

This will produce a pure UUCP-style bang path from an address that specifies a fully qualified domain name. Some mailers provide a special files for this; sendmail, for instance, uses the uucpxtable for this. The reverse transformation (colloquially called domainizing) is sometimes required when sending mail from a UUCP network to the Internet. As long as the mail sender uses the fully qualified domain name in the destination address, this problem can be avoided by not removing the domain name from the envelope address when forwarding the message to the smart-host. However, there are still some UUCP sites that are not part of any domain. They are usually domainized by appending the pseudo-domain uucp.

PATHALIAS AND MAP FILE FORMAT

The pathalias database provides the main routing information in UUCP-based networks. A typical entry looks like this (site name and path are separated by TABs):

```
moria.orcnet.org  ernie!bert!moria!%s
moria  ernie!bert!moria!%s
```

This makes any message to moria be delivered via ernie and bert. Both moria's fully qualified name and its UUCP name have to be given if the mailer does not have a separate way to map between these name spaces.

If you want to direct ali messages to hosts inside some domain to its mail relay, you may also specify a path in the pathalias database, giving the domain name as target, preceded by a dot. For example, if all hosts in the sub.org may be reached through swim!smurf, the pathalias entry might look like this:

```
\&.sub.org  swim!smurf!%s
```

Writing a pathalias file is acceptable only when you are running a site that does not have to do much routing. If you have to do routing for a large number of hosts, a better way is to use the pathalias command to create the file from map files. Maps can be maintained much easier, because you may simply add or remove a system by editing the system's map entry, and re-create the map file. Although the maps published by the Usenet Mapping Project aren't used for routing very much anymore, smaller UUCP networks may provide routing information in their own set of maps.

A map file mainly consists of a list of sites, listing the sites each system polls or is polled by. The system name begins in column one, and is followed by a comma-separated list of links. The list may be continued across newlines if the next line begins with a tab. Each link consists of the name of the site, followed by a cost given in brackets. The cost is an arithmetic expression, made up of numbers and symbolic costs. Lines beginning with a hash sign are ignored.

As an example, consider moria, which polls swim.twobirds.com twice a day, and bert.sesame.com once per week. Moreover, the link to bert only uses a slow 2400bps modem. moria's would publish the following maps entry:

```
moria.orcnet.org
  bert.sesame.com(DAILY/2),
  swim.twobirds.com(WEEKLY+LOW)
moria.orcnet.org = moria
```

The last line would make it known under its UUCP name, too. Note that it must be DAILY/2, because calling twice a day actually halves the cost for this link. Using the information from such map files, pathalias is able to calculate optimal routes to any destination site listed in the paths file, and produce a pathalias database from this which can then be used for routing to these sites.

Pathalias provides a couple of other features like site-hiding (i.e. making sites accessible only through a gateway) etc. See the manual page for pathalias for details, as well as a complete list of link costs. Comments in the map file generally contain additional information on the sites described in it. There is a rigid format in which to specify this, so that it can be retrieved from the maps. For instance, a programme called uuwho uses a database created from the map files to display this information in a nicely formatted way.

When you register your site with an organization that distributes map files to its members, you generally have to fill out such a map entry.

Below is a sample map entry (in fact, it's the one for my site):

```
#N monad, monad.swb.de, monad.swb.sub.org
#S AT 486DX50; Linux 0.99
#O private
#C Olaf Kirch
#E okir@monad.swb.de
```

```
#P Kattreinstr. 38, D-64295 Darmstadt, FRG
#L 49 52 03 N/ 08 38 40 E
#U brewhq
#W okir@monad.swb.de (Olaf Kirch); Sun Jul
25 16:59:32 MET DST
#
monad brewhq(DAILY/2)
# Domains
monad = monad.swb.de
monad = monad.swb.sub.org
```

The white space after the first two characters is a TAB. The meaning of most of the fields is pretty obvious; you will receive a detailed description from whichever domain you register with. The L field is the most fun to find out: it gives your geographical position in latitude/longitude and is used to draw the postscript maps that show all sites for each country, as well as world-wide.

CONFIGURING ELM

ELM stands for "electronic mail" and is one of the more reasonably named tools. It provides a full-screen interface with a good help feature. We won't discuss here how to use elm, but only dwell on its configuration options. Theoretically, you can run elm unconfigured, and everything works well—if you are lucky. But there are a few options that must be set, although only required on occasions. When it starts, elm reads a set of configuration variables from the elm.rc file in/usr/lib/elm. Then, it will attempt to read the file.elm/elmrc in your home directory. You don't usually write this file yourself. It is created when you choose "save options" from elm's options menu. The set of options for the private elmrc file is also available in the global elm.rc file. Most settings in your private elmrc file override those of the global file.

Global Elm Options

In the global elm.rc file, you must set the options that pertain to your host's name. For example, at the Virtual Brewery, the file for vlager would contain the following:

```
#
# The local hostname
hostname = vlager
#
# Domain name
hostdomain =.vbrew.com
#
# Fully qualified domain name
hostfullname = vlager.vbrew.com
```

These options set elm's idea of the local hostname. Although this information is rarely used, you should set these options nevertheless. Note that these options only take effect when giving them in the global configuration file; when found in your private elmrc, they will be ignored.

National Character Sets

Recently, there have been proposals to amend the RFC-822 standard to support various types of messages, such as plain text, binary data, Postscript files, etc. The set of standards and RFCs covering these aspects are commonly referred to as MIME, or Multipurpose Internet Mail Extensions. Among other things, this also lets the recipient know if a character set other than standard ASCII has been used when writing the message, for example using French accents, or German umlauts. This is supported by elm to some extent.

The character set used by internally to represent characters is usually referred to as ISO-8859-1, which is the name of the standard it conforms to. It is also known as Latin-1. Any message using characters from this character set should have the following line in its header:

```
Content-Type: text/plain; charset=iso-8859-1
```

The receiving system should recognize this field and take appropriate measures when displaying the message. The default for text/plain messages is a charset value of us-ascii. To be able to display messages with character sets other than ASCII, elm must know how to print these characters. By default, when elm receives a message with a charset field other than us-ascii (or a content type other than text/plain, for that matter), it tries to display the message using a command called metamail. Messages that require metamail to be displayed are shown with an 'M' in the very first column in the overview screen.

Since ' native character set is ISO-8859-1, calling metamail is not necessary to display messages using this character set. If elm is told that the display understands ISO-8859-1, it will not use metamail but will display the message directly instead. This can be done by setting the following option in the global elm.rc:

```
displaycharset = iso-8859-1
```

Note that you should set this options even when you are never going to send or receive any messages that actually contain characters other than ASCII. This is because people who do send such messages usually configure their mailer to put the proper Content-Type: field into the mail header by default, whether or not they are sending ASCII-only messages.

However, setting this option in elm.rc is not enough. The problem is that when displaying the message with its built-in pager, elm calls a library function for each character to determine whether it is printable or not. By default, this function will only recognize ASCII characters as printable, and display all other characters as "?". You may overcome this by setting the environment variable LC_CTYPE to ISO-8859-1, which tells the library to accept Latin-1 characters as printable. Support for this and other features is available since libc-4.5.8. When sending messages that contain special characters from ISO-8859-1, you should make sure to set two more variables in the elm.rc file:

```
charset = iso-8859-1
textencoding = 8bit
```

This makes elm report the character set as ISO-8859-1 in the mail header, and send it as an 8 bit value (the default is to strip all characters to 7 bit).

SYNOPSIS

Electronic Mail", better known as e-mail, is one of the most widely used forms of communication today. This chapter provides a basic introduction to running a mail server on FreeBSD, as well as an introduction to sending and receiving e-mail using FreeBSD; however, it is not a complete reference and in fact many important considerations are omitted.

E-COMMERCE

DEFINITION

E-commerce (electronic commerce or EC) is the buying and selling of goods and services on the Internet. In practice, this term and e-business are often used interchangeably. For online retail selling, the term e-tailing is sometimes used.

Aspects of e-commerce include:

- E-tailing or "virtual storefronts" on websites with online catalogs.
- The gathering and use of demographic data through Web contacts.
- Electronic Data Interchange (EDI), the business-to-business exchange of data.
- E-mail, <term>instant messaging</term> and <term>social networking</term> as media for reaching prospects and established customers.
- Business-to-business buying and selling.
- The security of business transactions.

E-TAILING OR THE VIRTUAL STOREFRONT AND THE VIRTUAL MALL

As a place for direct retail shopping, with its 24-hour availability, a global reach, the ability to interact and provide custom information and ordering, and multimedia prospects, the Web is a multi-billion dollar source of revenue for the world's businesses.

As early as the middle of 1997, Dell Computers reported orders of a million dollars a day. By early 1999, projected e-commerce revenues for business were in the billions of dollars and the stocks of companies deemed most adept at e-commerce were skyrocketing.

MARKET RESEARCH

In early 1999, it was widely recognized that because of the interactive nature of the Internet, companies could gather data about prospects and customers in unprecedented amounts -through site registration, questionnaires, and as part of taking orders. The issue of whether data was being collected with the knowledge and permission of market subjects had been raised.

ELECTRONIC DATA INTERCHANGE (EDI)

EDI is the exchange of business data using an understood data format. It predates today's Internet. EDI involves data exchange among parties that know each other well and make arrangements for one-to-one (or point-to-point) connection, usually dial-up. EDI may be replaced by one or more standardXML formats, such as ebXML.

E-MAIL, SOCIAL NETWORKING AND INSTANT MESSAGING

E-commerce is also conducted through e-mail, instant messaging and social networking sites such as <term>Facebook</term>. To avoid the perception of spam, Opt-In E-mail is an option in which Web users voluntarily sign up to receive e-mail, usually sponsored or containing ads, about product categories or other subjects they are interested in.

BUSINESS-TO-BUSINESS BUYING AND SELLING

Thousands of companies that sell products to other companies have discovered that the Web provides not only a 24-hour-a-day showcase for their products but a quick way to reach the right people in a company for more information.

THE SECURITY OF BUSINESS TRANSACTIONS

Security includes authenticating business transactors, controlling access to resources such as Web pages for registered or selected users,encrypting communications, and, in general, ensuring the privacy and effectiveness of transactions. Among the most widely-used security technologies is the Secure Sockets Layer (SSL), which is built into Web browsers.

PURCHASING ONLINE

ONLINE

You must be logged into informaworld and click on the HTML or PDF link to view your purchase. If you are denied access, you may have been timed out of your informaworld session, and should sign-out and then sign-in from the homepage before clicking the link again. Please note that 3 days begins at the time of purchase (and not when you first access the content). For full details of the payment process please see the checkout help page.

How do I purchase a subscription online? You can purchase journal subscriptions online. eBook and Encyclopedia subscriptions must be purchased offline. For more information on purchasing options for all publications please search for the publication you require, and select the *subscribe* tab.

For journals, the subscription options will be shown to you, with currency and tax applied as appropriate. Select *Buy Now* to go directly to checkout. Select *Add to Cart* to continue to make selections before paying. For more information on purchasing journal subscriptions offline, please read the journal subscriptions help page.

I only see prices in GBP, USD or EUR. Can I purchase in another currency? You can only make online purchases in GBP (Pounds Sterling), USD (US Dollars) or EUR (Euros). You can purchase some subscriptions offline in other currencies. For more information on how to purchase in other currencies please read the journal subscriptions help page. I am VAT registered. Do I have to pay VAT on articles? You can pay the VAT at the point of purchase and claim it back. Please contact us for a VAT receipt. To avoid paying VAT in future please contact us with your VAT number and informaworld account details. Please ensure that you always use this account for purchasing otherwise we may charge you VAT.

HELP: ONLINE ACCESS

I cannot access an article I have previously purchased. The system is only recognizing me as a 'Guest User' This message is displayed when a user has not logged in, or is not affiliated to any licenses. Please sign in with the username and password you used to purchase the article. For more help on usernames and passwords see Sign In help.

Note that once purchased, you can only view an article for 3 days. I cannot access any of my organization's subscriptions.

Here are some possible reasons and solutions:

- You have not signed in: Click the sign-in button and sign in using the username and password provided by your institution. For more help on usernames and passwords see Sign In help
- Your IP address is not registered with us. Check with your librarian that the computer you are using should allow you access to the subscriptions.
- The license that your institution holds does not cover the requested content. Check with your librarian

What do the access indicators mean? Online Access Help for Institutional Account Administrators:

How to I get online access to my journal subscription? If you are an existing online customer your subscription will be added to your account. The only exception to this will be when we receive a new order with an address that does not match our system. In this case you will receive an e-mail. You will be asked to select a link within the e-mail in order to add the subscription to your online account.

If you are a new customer, or have not previously taken up your online access, please ensure you have provided an e-mail address with your order. We will send you an e-mail inviting you to access your online subscriptions. You will be asked to select a link within the e-mail in order to confirm your online account and provide IP details. How do I check the IP ranges that I have registered? Sign in with your administrator username and password. Go to My Account, and select *edit logins*.

Your registered IP ranges will be displayed:

- If these appear to be incorrect, please update using the form. Any changes will not be active until they have been authorised by our online support team. This should take place within 24 hours.
- If the IP ranges appear to be correct but you are still experiencing problems, please use the web form to submit the following details:
  - IP address of terminal being used to access informaworld.
  - Browser version you are using.
  - Journal or Book title, Volume/Issue number and page number you are trying to access
  - Date and Time you attempted the access.
  - If you receive an error message, the exact details of this. If possible please provide a screen print.

How do I set my institution up to use Athens on informaworld^{TM}? To register your Athens details visit your My Account pages and edit your registration details. More information can be found in Registration help.

The Risks

Purchasing online presents risks that aren't encountered at a local fish shop. Not being able to select the fish ahead of time or observe the condition of the shop itself are enough to keep many people from purchasing online. An even bigger concern is stress the fish experience when shipped. Will the fish arrive alive and healthy? What happens if they are lost, or arrive dead or dying? All of these concerns are quite valid.

Reasons for Online Purchases

Before considering an online purchase think about your reasons for buying online versus a local fish shop. Price should not be the issue, as lower online prices will be offset by the addition of shipping fees. Ordering online because you are can't find a specific species of fish locally, isn't always necessary. Most good pet shops will order fish upon request, and if the fish dies during shipping, the cost is generally not passed on to you.

Lastly, if you order online because you live far away from a fish shop, odds are you probably just as far from a major airport. The fish may be subjected to a lengthy transit time, which is very stressful. It may be in your best interest to drive to a fish shop even if it is a few hours away, rather than ordering online and risk losing the fish during shipping. At least you can control the temperature in your car, and assure that the fish arrive at your home as quickly as possible.

Precautions to Take

If you still want to order live fish online, you can be increase your chances for success by taking a few precautionary steps. Keep the following things in mind before placing your order:

- *Find an expert*: Companies that specialize in shipping live fish directly to customers do a better job of packing the fish, and expediting the shipment.
- *Ask about guarantees*: A number of online suppliers offer 'arrive alive' provisions. If they make no guarantees at all, you are taking a big risk.
- *Get a firm price with shipping*: Don't settle for undefined shipping costs when placing your order. Often the shipping can be far more than the cost of the fish itself.
- *Go to the airport*: If you live near a major airport, consider opting to pick up the package there. The cost will often be less, and there will be no risk of the fish sitting in a delivery truck for a long period of time.
- *Consider the weather*: If there are temperature extremes consider placing your order at another time. Keep in mind that although your weather may be good, the plane may travel through areas of not so pleasant temperatures. Fish are usually shipped in a cargo bay that is neither heated or cooled.

- *Order with others*: See if anyone else in your area is interested in ordering fish online. By combining your order you can save on shipping costs.
- *Order Securely*: Treat the order like any online purchase-very carefully. Personally I'd call my credit card or bank information in to the company if I had a choice. That way there is less chance of your information falling into the wrong hands. If you do fill out an online form, make sure it is a secure one.

4

Information Security

INTRODUCTION

PROCESS

Information security is the process of protecting information. It protects its availability, privacy and integrity. Access to stored information on computerdatabases has increased greatly. More companies store business and individual information on computer than ever before. Much of the information stored is highly confidential and not for public viewing.

Many businesses are solely based on information stored in computers. Personal staff details, client lists, salaries, bank account details, marketing and sales information may all be stored on a database. Without this information, it would often be very hard for a business to operate. Information security systems need to be implemented to protect this information.

Effective information security systems incorporate a range of policies, security products, technologies and procedures. Software applications which provide firewall information security and virus scanners are not enough on their own to protect information. A set of procedures and systems needs to be applied to effectively deter access to information.

There are people who make a living from hacking or breaking through information security systems. They use their technological skills to break into computer systems and access private information. Firewalls, which are designed to prevent access to a computer's network, can be bypassed by a hacker with the right hardware. This could result in the loss of vital information, or a virus could be planted and erase all information. A computer hacker can gain access to a network if a firewall is shut down for only a minute.

One of the biggest potential threats to information security is the people who operate the computers. A workplace may have excellent information security systems in place, but security can be easily compromised. If a help desk worker gives out or resets passwords without verifying who the information is for, then anyone can easily gain access to the system. Computer operators should be made fully aware of the importance of security.

Simple security measures can be used by everyone to keep data secure. Changing passwords on your computer, and using combinations of letters and numbers, makes it harder for hackers to gain access. Also, do not keep a note of your password where it can be easily accessed. This is the same idea as not keeping you bank card and PIN number together. You would not want anyone to have access to the information or funds in your bank account, and it is the same with your computer.

There has never been such a thing as a totally secure system. Hackers will always find more sophisticated ways to gain access. However, with technology implementing higher levels of information security, such as iris recognition systems, security systems should keep them out for a little longer.

SECURITY AWARENESS

An organization's people, information, operations, and systems are critical assets. Protecting the safety, confidentiality, integrity, and availability of these assets is essential to maintaining profitability, compliance, public image, and a competitive edge. Companies face threats to their employees, systems, operations, and information every day. These threats include computer viruses, network attacks, fraud, industrial espionage, and even natural disasters. Companies implement tools and procedures to protect against these threats and to comply with laws and regulations. Unfortunately, even the best tools and procedures can be defeated by a user who is unaware how to use them, or how important security is.

THE SMART WAY TO SECURITY

In order for the organization's security programme to operate effectively, all employees must help the organization to secure its assets. Security Awareness provides the greatest return on investment, and has the greatest positive impact on a company's security. The cost of a Security Awareness Programme is quickly realised when tools and procedures are followed, and employees understand how to be more secure.

Consider the quotes from the following security experts:

- "There is probably no more effective countermeasure, dollar for dollar, than a good security awareness programme."
- "Although it is important for an awareness programme to ensure that the right things are covered, the critical success factor for an awareness programme is the delivery methods. The advice must be simple. It must be made personal...Advice that is realistic, understandable, actionable, and repeated is useful."
- "There is only one way to keep your product plans safe and that is by having a trained, aware, and a conscientious workforce. This involves training on the policies and procedures, but also-and probably even more important-an ongoing awareness programme."

INFOSECURITYLAB IS THE INDUSTRY LEADER

Our Security Awareness solutions arc developed with one purpose in mind: "Provide Security Awareness solutions that are meaningful to every employee." Our team draws on over one hundred man-years of information and physical security experience. Our products and solutions are developed using our extensive knowledge of security standards including ISO/ IEC 27001:2005, PCI-DSS, Sarbanes-Oxley, BS 25999, NIST,

CIS, and numerous other government, industry, and organizational standards. Our work spans Home Security Awareness, Information Security Awareness, Business Continuity and Disaster Management Awareness, Awareness of Compliance and Regulations, and Privacy Awareness.

Our products span a wide range of solutions that include e-Learning training modules, posters, images, screensavers, newsletters and films. We also provide expert consultants who can help you build your Security Awareness programme for you using our state of the art tools, and expertise.

IMPORTANCE OF INFORMATION SECURITY

Information is the crown jewels of business. Your business partners want to know if you have done enough to protect your information assets. The BS 7799 Information Security Management System outlines the best practices that one should follow and is a benchmark for security certification in business. by Avinash Kadam Name a key ingredient that drives your business. All those who said 'information' got it right. That's because most businesses cannot function if this ingredient is not available or is unreliable. Availability, integrity and confidentiality of information are paramount concerns today. How do you know that your organization is taking good care of all the information it has so diligently acquired, over the years?

The manufacturing records, sales records, financial records, customer records are all kept on computers. In today's networked world, these may be accessible from anywhere, via the Internet. You can't be too sure that all your digitized information is secure. Your personal and confidential records will be with banks, finance and insurance companies; your medical records are with hospitals and laboratories; your credit card details have to be tendered whenever you buy something on the Internet. Is there any guarantee that all this information is really kept confidential? Shouldn't there be a way to tell if an organization can be entrusted with confidential information and if it maintains Information Security? In fact there is. Heard of the BS 7799 Information Security Management System?

BS 7799 standard

Anyone who wants to ascertain the quality of a business process will look for an ISO 9001:2000 certificate. This gives an assurance that the organization has achieved the minimum requirements for establishing a Quality Management System (QMS). Similarly, the British Standards Institute (BSI) has established a standard for Information Security Management System (ISMS). The BS 7799 was first issued in 1995 and was revised in 1999. Latest revision i.e. BS 7799 -2 2002 is due on 5th Sept. 2002.

The BS 7799 standard comprises two parts:

1. *Part 1*: Code of Practice for Information security management.
2. *Part 2*: Specifications of Information Security Management Systems.

Part 1 outlines the recommended best practices that one should follow and Part 2 gives the specifications against which an organization will be evaluated to determine whether it deserves to be certified.

Assessing your Security Requirements

BS7799 depends heavily on risk assessment. You are expected to carry out a thorough risk evaluation exercise. To prepare for this exercise, you have to take a complete inventory of all your information assets. These include not only the usual suspects like hardware assets—servers and networking devices, but also software assets like programmes and databases. Also consider paper assets and infrastructure assets like power, light and air-conditioning. A risk like 'Denial of Service' is usually attributed to an external attack from the Internet, but it can also be an internal attack—someone can remove the power fuse in the server room.

The next step is to classify all the information assets according to their sensitivity and criticality, with respect to business needs. A risk evaluation exercise helps to identify the risk scenarios. The probability and consequences of a particular risk scenario in terms of business losses needs to be documented. If the losses could be quantified, that's good.

Otherwise, these could be categorized into high, medium and low categories.

Security Domains and Control Objectives

After risk categorization and prioritization, the next obvious step is risk mitigation. This is where we revisit BS 7799 controls. These are given in BS 7799 Part 2: Specification for Information Security Management System.

These are divided into 10 domains:

1. Security policy.
2. Security organization.
3. Asset classification and control.
4. Personnel Security.
5. Physical and environmental security.
6. Communication and operations management.
7. Access control.
8. System development and maintenance.
9. Business continuity management.
10. Compliance

These are further categorized into 36 control objectives, which are to be achieved by fulfilling 127 specified controls. As an example of this hierarchy, let us look at the domain of 'Communication and operations management.' This domain has seven control objectives to be fulfilled. One of these seven control objectives is 'Exchange of information and software.' The objective is 'To prevent loss, modification or misuse of information exchanged between organizations.'

The steps to achieve this objective are:

- *Step 1*: Does the risk analysis point out that there is a business risk in exchange of information? Is this control objective applicable for protection of your business?
- *Step 2*: If the answer is no, prepare a statement justifying the exclusion.
- *Step 3*: If the answer is yes, look at each of the seven control statements under this particular control objective.

Each of these control statements has the word 'shall',

which means compliance with the requirements is mandatory, unless you have a valid justification.

For example, one control is: "Electronic commerce security: Electronic commerce security shall be protected against fraudulent activity, contract dispute and disclosure or modification of information." So if you have E-Commerce activity, you will have to prove that you are protected against each of the stipulated risk factors.

- Step 4: Select the appropriate policy, procedure, process or product that will fulfill the requirement of each applicable control. You should be able to prove that the control is effective in reducing the risk, which you have identified.

You will realise that there's not much to help you decide what is required to be done. The control statements are extremely general in nature. They do not provide any further recommendations, technical or otherwise. On one hand, this makes the standard independent of technology but on other hand, it introduces subjectivity of interpretation.

Advantages of BS 7799 Certification

Despite these shortcomings, BS 7799 presents the following advantages:

1. You will have a structured, risk based approach to information security.
2. Your employees will have to take security seriously as you will have framed adequate policies and penalties for any breach of security.
3. Your clients will be assured about your security seriousness.
4. Foreign companies that are paranoid about information security, may feel comfortable dealing with you, if they have not already made it mandatory for you to get certified or audited by a security consultant.
5. Since availability is one of the critical components of information security, you would have set up adequate business continuity management plans.

6. You may do all of the above things without aiming for a certification, but you may even get a marketing advantage if you are certified.
7. And finally, you will definitely sleep better.

How to Proceed

You can aspire for BS 7799 certification with the following steps:

- *Step 1*: Establish importance of information security in the organization. In the current scenario, this should not be difficult. However, it will help if you identify the critical business processes, which are dependent on information, and what is the business risk if any—check if the three pillars of information security are compromised (i.e. confidentiality, integrity and availability).
- *Step 2*: Set up a Security Organization. You will need organizational involvement to define and implement security measures. A steering committee for BS 7799 project, a security forum with representation of key business and technology departments, appointment of an Information Security Officer and defining security responsibilities for protection of various assets will have to be done.
- *Step 3*: Define the Security Policy for the company. This should be endorsed by top management and should convey their concern and commitment.
- *Step 4*: Define the scope of Information Security Management System (ISMS). This could be business specific, location specific or function specific.
- *Step 5*: Undertake risk assessment. Start with business risk assessment. This will help you in identifying the risk areas for detailed risk evaluation. Identify and prioritize all the risks.
- *Step 6*: Identify the controls objectives and the control options.
- *Step 7*: Select appropriate controls to fulfill the control objectives. These controls will be in the form of

security policies, procedures and products. Prepare guidelines on how to implement these controls.

- *Step 8*: Implement and monitor the controls. You should be able to prove adequacy of the controls in reducing the risks.
- *Step 9*: Make a table of all the 127 controls and map the controls implemented by you against relevant control objectives. One control may address more than one control objective. If there are some gaps, find out, whether these are omissions or there are no requirements of controls. Fill up all the gaps.
- *Step 10*: Make statement of applicability, which justifies the controls in place as well as those, which really are not required. For all exclusions, you should have a justification backed by risk assessment.
- Step 11: Invite a certification body for pre-assessment. Some of the accredited certification agencies are DNV, BSI, STQC.
- Step 12: Take appropriate measures to comply with all observations.
- Step 13: Get the final assessment done.
- Step 14: Acquire the coveted certificate, which is valid for three years. An external audit will be done once a year.

How to Implement the Standard

If you perform all the 14 steps mentioned above, you will have implemented the standard. Alternatively, if you are short of manpower or expertise, employ an external agency to implement it for you. This will be especially useful while performing a detailed and objective risk analysis. A consultant will use a risk analysis questionnaire, which has been enhanced by his experience. The period taken for entire implementation depends on the size of the organization. It could be between 3 to 9 months.

Difference between BS 7799 and ISO 17799

ISO has adapted the BS 7799 Part 1 and numbered it as

ISO 17799. As we discussed earlier, Part 1 covers the Code of Practice and as such only provides guidelines. ISO has not yet adapted the BS 7799 Part 2. So, there are no specifications, which an implementer or an auditor can refer to. An organization cannot be evaluated or certified today as an ISO 17799 compliant organization, but it can be certified as a BS 7799 compliant organization.

Why BS 7799 Certification?

BS 7799 may not be a perfect security certification but it provides excellent guidelines for information security management. It presents a yardstick for measuring a company's security practices. The risk-oriented approach ensures that the organization does not become complacent after getting the certificate.

If the risk has not been controlled, the ISMS may not be effective. So, apart from a periodic audit by an external auditor, the management could get regular feedback about the state of information security in the organization through the security management infrastructure created in the process of implementation of BS 7799.

Where to get the Standard?

You can order the Standard from www.c-cure.org for £94.00. In India, you may enquire with bsb@giasdl01.vsnl.net.in.

You may get more information about BS 7799 at www.bsi-global.com. Another site giving FAQs on BS 7799 is www.dnv.com. You can also down load the 'DNV Interpretation guide to BS 7799' from this site.

PRIVACY AND PASSWORDS

DEFINITION

To keep strangers from finding out when you're online, set ICQ to require your authorization before others can add you to their contact list. To do so, click the box in the lower-left of the window that reads ICQ. Select *Security and*

Privacy. Head to the Security tab and select "My authorization is required." Click Save. You can also head to the Ignore List tab and check "Accept messages only from users on my contact list" to block unsolicited messages from strangers.

You can also password-protect your ICQ programme so others can't sit down at your PC and pose as you on the Net. Click *ICQ, Security and Privacy*. Click the Security tab. Type in a new password and uncheck Save Password. Under Security Level select High. Now, every time ICQ loads, it will prompt you for your password before letting the world know that you're online.

Nowadays, you need a password for just about everything. Your bank and credit card accounts all require a Personal Identification Number (PIN); most subscriber internet sites require passwords to log in; your e-mail requires a password; your computer or your network may require a password; popular computer programmes and sites require passwords (eBay, PayPal, etc); and just about any place that offers you an 'account' of any sort requires a password to log on. As the internet becomes more of the standard for doing business, technology increases, and so do the hackers and nefarious sorts who try to break into accounts that have financial information.

One of the easiest ways to do this is to 'crack' a password and log on to your account in your name, without your knowledge. For example, Associated Content provides payment for articles through PayPal. If someone where able to break into AC's member's accounts, it would be easy to redirect payments to another PayPal Account. While that would probably be easy enough to trace, consider someone breaking into the actual PayPal account itself. Or perhaps eBay. Or maybe even your online banking account.

As many of you read this, you will be thinking, "That would never happen to me!" You may be right, but how much is it worth to you to find out that you may be wrong?

Most of us are aware of a technique known as 'phishing'. Yet, though many of us are aware of it and will say that you understand what this means, every time a phishing e-mail for PayPal or eBay or a large bank is emailed out, several hundreds and sometimes even thousands of consumers still click on those links in the e-mail and provide the spammers/ hackers with their log in information. A few seconds is all it takes to drain an account of funds.

The Nigerian Scam, and others like it, are all about receiving your personal banking information directly, instead of stealing passwords. This scam actually requires you to send someone your bank routing and account number in order to fall for this. One would think that in today's day and age we would all know better than to send someone we do not know our personal banking information, but still, every year, thousands of people fall for this.

Now, all hope isn't lost and the internet is not as unsafe as all this makes it sound. All you have to do is be informed and think before you take action and the internet is really a safe place to do business, as much as shopping in any retail store would be, and sometimes even safer. The first thing to remember is this: never give your personal information to anyone! eBay and PayPal and many other sites out there all have password recovery tools in case you forget your password.

They will not under any circumstances ever ask you for your password. So if someone claiming to be from one of theses sites does ask you, don't take the bait. They can be very convincing, and often will tell you that your account has been compromised and you've already lost thousands of dollars, or some other scary story to get you to act first and think later. Don't ever believe them! Always go directly to the site – never through a link in an e-mail.

What many people don't seem to realise is that eBay and PayPal both keep copies of all emails they send to you in your account when you log in. Never use a link to these sites from your e-mail – always type the URL in your browser to go to the main page and log in manually before you do anything. If there is no indication that PayPal or eBay sent you an e-mail in your account once you are logged in, you have been phished. eBay and PayPal both have spoof and abuse accounts to send copies of these emails so they can help protect other less informed consumers. If you are ever in doubt, or truly, even if you are not in doubt, never, ever click directly on a link in an e-mail to take you to a banking site, eBay, PayPal, or any other site that might contain personal or financial information.

The next thing you can do to protect your information is safeguard it behind a good password. Technology has created password crackers that take very little time to get your password if you use normal or dictionary based words and only add digits. Many sites allow you to use case sensitive passwords, so if a site allows this, always use at least one upper or lower case letter. If a site allows symbols, use them.

As a general rule, a password should be at least 6 characters in length, and many experts will recommend at least 8 characters. Use a combination of letters and numbers, or symbols if they are allowed, and upper and lower case if the password is case sensitive. A password that closely resembles your log in name will be one of the first things a hacker will try. Never do this!

Target21 is easy to guess or crack, but Ta2rGe1t4 is much harder to guess and crack, and Cg1f45rQz is even harder to crack. Now granted, it's also harder to remember too. There are password encryption programmes out there where you can encrypt and store your passwords on your computer in case you don't remember them and many browsers do automatically save passwords for you, but your best bet might simply be to write the passwords down somewhere and keep them with your other important documents, but not in easy view or reach of the computer itself.

If you share your computer with someone else or if you access personal information from a public computer, such as your place of employment or a public library, never – ever – check the box to save your password information on that computer. In fact, my recommendation would be to never access personal financial information from any public computer if you can help it. One last word of warning: many people use the same exact password for every account, or a similar one with only one number of letter changed. Don't do this. Hackers know that people do this and once they have one password for you that works, they are going to continue to target your other accounts at other places to see if you have done this. It takes very little time for them to do this, but it will take you a long time to recover from it if they do.

Use a different password for every site that contains any personal or confidential or financial information. While it may be a bit more inconvenient for you now, keeping hard to guess and multiple passwords will be a lot less inconvenient than having to file police reports and try to recover your lost money once your accounts become compromised.

BACKING UP DATA

This is one of the most important, yet also one of the most neglected areas of computing. Backing up your data should be at the top of your computer maintenance list, right next to Virus Protection. Without data backup or virus protection, you are running the risk of losing your data. And it will happen, don't think that you don't have to worry about it.

WHY SHOULD YOU BACK UP

Data loss can happen in many ways. One of the most common causes is physical failure of the media the data is stored on. You probably have everything saved on your PCs hard drive. That hard drive will not live forever. To quote a friend of mine, "there are only two types of hard drives-the ones that have failed and the ones that will fail." Yes, normally hard drives will live for years without incident.

But eventually they will die. It might happen gradually, by more and more bad clusters accumulating until most of the drive is unusable. Or it might happen suddenly, the hard drive just dies without warning. Another bad storage media are floppy disks. They are good for temporary storage and maybe transporting information, but not for permanent data storage. I've lost count of how many floppies I've tossed because they were bad.

And I have talked to countless people who saved

valuable data to a floppy only to find out when they needed to access it that the floppy was bad and the data inaccessible.

Another possible cause for data loss is power failure or spikes. It can result in loss of the document you are currently working on because you did not save it before the power failed and your PC shut down, or in loss of your entire hard drive because a power surge fried your motherboard and destroyed the file allocation table of your hard drive. Also worth mentioning is data loss through virus attacks. There are plenty of nasty computer viruses out there that will delete files on an infected machine. That's why Virus Protection is just as important.

WHAT DATA SHOULD YOU BACK UP

You might think that you probably don't really have anything worth backing up, nothing important, no big deal. Let's go through just a few items to jog your memory. Let's start with your favourite places on the Internet and that long list of bookmarks. Do you want to lose all those? How about the e-mail addresses from all your friends? That would take a long time to accumulate those again. What about that to-do list you wrote? Or about that nice picture somebody e-mailed you and that you saved?

How about that family history you collected over the years and put into a database? Maybe you have a document for work, like a presentation or a spreadsheet that you created at home and don't have a copy on your work PC? Think about that saved game of your favourite game where it took you weeks or months to get to that level. These are just the most common examples, and I know that after thinking about it for a while you will realise that there is a lot of information you don't want to lose. That's why you should back up your data.

HOW TO BACK UP

Backing up means to keep a copy of your important files in a separate location for retrieval in case of an emergency. Keeping a copy of it in another folder on the same hard drive though is not a good idea. It means to put it on a separate media. Preferably, you have two backups on two separate types of media in two places. The oldest and worst way to back up is to save your data to floppy. As I said before, floppies fail rather quickly and are not a reliable storage media. Bad idea. use them only for temporary storage or data transportation if there is no other way.

Another older and very popular way was to use a tape drive. They could store several Gigabytes of data. The disadvantage of tape drives are that they are slow and that the tapes are somewhat sensitive to heat, magnetism etc. which does not make them the most reliable media either.

Then a few years ago, the Zip drive from iomega came out. It became very popular overnight for several reasons. It is easy to use, just like a floppy drive. Insert a disk, copy the data, eject the disk, done. It is also very mobile if you have an external Zip drive. Just take it with you, plug it in, install the software if needed and you're set.

The Zip disks are relatively reliable (yes, there was the click of death but it supposedly affected less than 1% of all Zip drives according to iomega) and can store 100 Megabytes, that's about 70 floppies worth. Recently iomega released a new version that can store 250 MB. However, the disks are still somewhat pricey, and a lot of times several disks are required for a complete backup.

Recently, recordable and re-writable CD burners have flooded the consumer market and offered another way of data storage. A good burner can be had for $200-$300, the disks cost $1 for recordable and $2-$3 for re-writable ones. The disks hold approximately 650MB of data. The advantage is that the media is pretty cheap and very reliable, but the burners cost more than a tape or Zip drive. I've been using a CD burner for a while now for backups and found it to be very reliable and convenient.

Another way of backing up data is to another hard drive. If you have multiple PCs at home and they are networked, you can copy data files to the hard drive of another PC on the network for backup. That way, if one PC goes down, you still have the data on the other PC. The advantage is that it is pretty quick and easy to do, but it takes away some hard drive space and it does not allow off-site storage of the backups which is a problem if your house burns down and all PCs on your home network go up in flames. I always back up my data to my laptop as well by connecting my laptop to my home network or by using Direct Cable Connection.

Recently I have seen some ads for online backup storage, where you can rent disk space online and upload your data for backup. I am still a little skeptical about this concept, because you depend on your ISP and the disk space provider to be up and running for data retrieval, if you have lots of data and only a 56k modem, upload will take quite some time, and lastly, you put all your info on a strangers machine.

BE ORGANIZED

To make backing up your data easier, it helps if your data is organized. If you save all your data in the programme folder of the programme the data is used in, e.g. Word documents in C:\Office\Word, Excel documents in C:\Office\Excel, you will have a lot of fun hunting down all your files and making sure you didn't forget anything when backing up.

Believe me, it gets old real fast. Instead, you should make a point of saving all your documents, no matter what it is, in one central location. That's what the My Documents folder is for. You can make subfolders called Private andBusiness, and subcategorize those more. This way 95% of your backup will be done by simply copying the

TIPS FOR DATA BACKUP

- There are many ways to backup data on your computer-the least effective of which (for obvious reasons) is having the only backup location on your actual hard drive. Instead, use external hardware such as a disk, CD, zip drive, or memory stick.
- Online backup is another option. This requires the use of an Internet-based data backup storage service.
- If space on your computer is limited, be selective

with the data you choose to backup. For example, you may choose to only backup personal data. As a general rule, there's no need to backup entire programmes, as in the event that they are deleted, you can simply reinstall them with original software. For this reason, it's important to keep a copy of your operating system on hand.

All in all, computer data backup doesn't have to be a complex and painful process. In fact, although it may seem more time consuming now, just imagine the time it will take to get all your important data back-or worse, have to start from scratch-in the event that all of it is deleted.

BACKUP STRATEGIES

With as much data as is stored on a modern computer system, how do you decide what to backup? Should you just put the entire system on a CD or tape and be done with it? There are several problems with putting your entire system in a backup, not the least of which is cost of tapes and CDs. Also, the time to perform a backup is increased when the entire system is stored.

As long as you have the original CDs for your software, there is no need to include the programmes themselves in backups. For example, your operating system and word processor shouldn't be backed up. The data files, however, cannot be recreated so you should include them in backups.

You do want to backup:

- All your web pages, databases, and anything that you made or would have trouble replacing
- All the information from your financial software
- All the information from inventory control, customer databases, or other specialist business software
- Important correspondence
- Internal documents (important memos and the like)
- Anything you would suffer for lack of if it lost

You might want to backup:

- Your e-mail, especially if it has customer queries, contact data, or other business-critical information

- Preferences or bookmarks from web browsers
- Your personal settings for how *your* computer works
- Anything that would be a nuisance if it was lost

You probably don't need to backup:

- Your operating system, so long as you have the original disks
- Your software, so long as you have the original disks
- Strictly temporary files (like a webcache, or anything in the trash can)
- Anything that you are certain you won't need if the entire computer becomes rubbish.

How many days worth of information could you afford to lose if your computer crashed? What about if your office or home burned down? What about if most of your city was wiped out by a tornado or a flood? The answers to these questions will tell you how often you should do a backup, and roughly where you should store them.

The computer crash one is for your most frequent backup-usually a daily backup, stored in your office or home. The office-burned-down is for your next most frequent backup, usually a weekly backup stored in a secure place in another building-possibly a friend's place, or a friendly business whose backups you store. (Exchange backups each week.) The final is often a monthly or six-monthly backup, and is stored somewhere distant-and in some cases, isn't done at all. It's a matter of choice, and what risks you want to take.

IMPLICATIONS

INTRODUCTION

There are several ways in which patient confidentiality may be breached such as theft, break-ins and poor disposal of confidential waste. All breaches should be investigated and reported accordingly. This guidance suggests mechanisms for handling security incidents where patient confidentiality has been or may have been breached. The majority of IM&T security breaches are innocent and unintentional such as the user not 'logging out' at the end of the day. However 'near misses', where no actual harm results from the incident, should still be reported and analysed to look for possible ways of preventing an actual incident occurring in the future.

DEFINITIONS

An IM&T security incident is defined as any event that has resulted or could result in: the disclosure of confidential information to any unauthorised individual the integrity of the system or data being put at risk the availability of the system or information being put at risk

An adverse impact can be defined for example as:

- Threat to personal safety or privacy
- Legal obligation or penalty
- Financial loss
- Disruption of HA business
- An embarrassment to the HA

TYPES OF SECURITY INCIDENTS

The types of security incidents likely to affect patient confidentiality are variable. Data security incidents may take many forms including the following:

- Theft of equipment holding confidential information – PCs, dicta-phones, case-notes, etc.
- Unauthorized access to a building or areas containing unsecured confidential information.
- Access to patient records by an authorised user who has no work requirement to access the records.
- Authorized access which is misused (staff).
- Electronic access (hacking) and viruses.
- Misuse of equipment such as faxes, text messages on mobiles and e-mails.
- Inadequate disposal of confidential material (paper, PC hard drive, disks/tapes, etc).
- Car theft / break-ins to on-call staff carrying patient records.
- Unauthorized access to records away from premises (e.g. laptops and notes when travelling between clinics to home-visits etc).

5

Security Insructions

INTRODUCTION

You certainly agree that the most important thing a microprocessor has to do is to actually execute the instructions of the software it's running. Thus it's about time that we are getting to this stage. You cannot really see it in the block diagrams, but Pentium III has 11 (+1) parallel execution units, Athlon has even more. Those units are executing the OPs, and since it's so many in parallel, you can imagine why we are talking of 'out-of-order' execution here. Executing one OP after another would obviously not make any use of parallel execution units. To make sure that the out-of-order execution is actually working, Intel is using the 'Renamer and Allocator' as well as the 'Reorder-Unit'. The 'Integer/FP Renamer/ Allocator' is found before the Reservation Station, and as the name already says it, this unit is responsible for integer as well as FP and multimedia OPs. Athlon does this work a bit more sophisticated. The units that take care of the out-of-order execution are the Integer Scheduler and the FP Scheduler, both able to hold a quite impressive number of OPs (18/36).

The control unit is the part of a computer that controls the computer's operation. Basically, each part of the computer requires control signals to arrive at particular times for each instruction of the computer's software. The control unit provides those control signals.

At one time control units were ad-hoc logic, and they were difficult to design. Now they are designed as a microprogram that is stored in a control store. Words of the microprogram are selected by a sequencer and the bits from those words directly control the different parts of the computer, including the registers, arithmetic and logic unit, instruction register, bus, input/output and computer storage. In modern computers, each of these subsystems may have its own subsidiary controller, but the control unit is the top dog that controls the computer overall.

A control unit for a CISC ISA can... have to deal with instructions that involve tens and even hundreds of minor states. There would thus be thousands of logic expressions to generate the control signals. CAD tools can simplify and minimize these and even lay them out on the silicon automatically, but it is still a large block of irregular logic on the chip.

The control unit is a finite state machine that takes as its inputs the IR, the status register (which is partly filled by the status output from the ALU), and the current major state of the cycle. Its rules are encoded either in random logic, a Programmable Logic Array (PLA), or Read-Only Memory (ROM), and its outputs are sent across the processor to each point requiring coordination or direction for the control unit.

For example the outputs needed for the portion of the instruction/data path shown in Discussion 13 are Jump/Branch/NextPC, IR Latch, Read Control, Load Control, ALU Function Select, Load/Reg-Reg, Reg R/W.

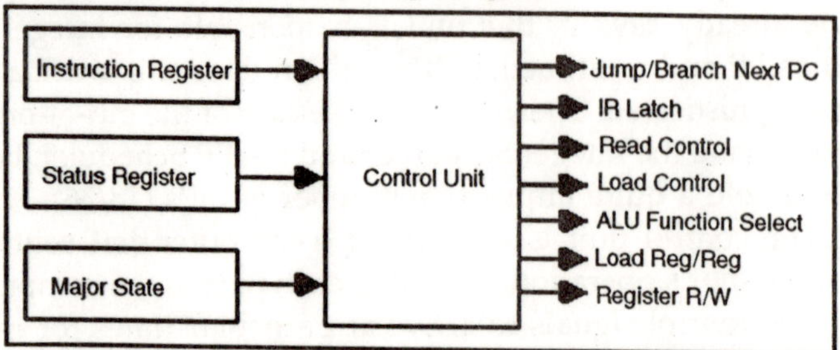

The ALU function select takes the instruction op code and translates it into a given function of the ALU (either one line per ALU function or a compact binary code for the function). The Jump/Branch/PC depends on the instruction type and in a RISC architecture these may be directly coded in the op code. Read control occurs at the start of an instruction cycle. IR latch and occurs at the end of the fetch state. Load control happens at the end of the data fetch state of a load instruction. Load Reg/Reg again depends on the op-code. Register R/W is in the start of the data fetch stage and at the write back stage of an operation. It thus depends on the major state and the instruction.

A CISC architecture typically uses a more complex control unit. As we've noted before, the IR is often multiple words, and the control unit has to look at different parts of the IR at different stages of execution. In fact, the entire IR may not be available at once, requiring interlocks with fetch logic to ensure the contents of the IR are valid.

There are many more control signals coming out of a CISC control unit, partly to control the more complex addressing logic, but also to directly connect to the many special purpose registers. In a RISC architecture, the registers are accessed uniformly in a block so a simple decoder in the register file can select the particular register. In a CISC architecture, there are restrictions on the particular registers that can be used by a given instruction and these are enforced by the control unit.

To begin the design of a control unit, we start by listing every control signal in the instruction/data path of the processor. This becomes a list of the control unit's outputs. As input, it has the instruction register, any status information (such as branch flags, interrupts, etc.) from the processor, and a "major state" which simply keeps track of where we are in the execution of an instruction. We always begin an instruction with state 0, which corresponds to Fetch. During that state, the control unit outputs the necessary signals to route the contents of the PC to the memory address port, to select and clock the memory until it responds with data from that location, and then cause this data to be latched into the IR> In a CISC architecture, the Fetch may only retrieve the first part of an instruction, and (depending on bits in the IR that are then decoded by the control unit) more words may need to be fetched. In a RISC architecture, a single Fetch retrieves a complete instruction, so we may proceed to the next major state, which is usually to begin fetching data from the registers, while we decode the instruction.

In a RISC architecture, "decoding an instruction" mainly means that the instruction type field determines what the control unit will do for the remainder of the instructions. If you think of the CU as a finite state machine, the bits in the type field select the next state following the decode.

In terms of a program's logic, this is like selecting a branch in a Switch statement – each branch of the Switch contains the series of steps to be performed for one type of instruction. For example, after decoding a Jump instruction, the control unit outputs the signals required to combine the address portion of the instruction with the upper bits of the PC and load the result back into the PC. The CU then returns to the Fetch step. Thus, a Jump has three major states (Fetch, Decode, Complete). For a memory Load instruction, the CU first sends one of the selected register values (the address) to the address port of the memory (via a multiplexer) and signals the memory to fetch this location. When the memory returns the value, then the CU sends signals to the necessary multiplexer(s) and the register file so that the memory data goes over the Dest bus and is stored in the designated register. Thus, a Load has four major states (Fetch, Decode, Memory, Write Back).

So, for each type of instruction, and for each major state in each type of instruction, we look at the list of control signals and decide what value each signal must have. In some cases, the value doesn't matter (*e.g.*, if memory isn't selected, it doesn't matter whether it is set to read or write, because it simply won't do anything in either case). You can think of this as a large 2-dimensional table indexed by instruction type and major state. Within each cell of the table is a list of the control signal and their values.

One last bit of control output that we've neglected is the control of the major state itself. This is usually a register, as shown above, that is input to the CU. But it also receives its next value on each clock from the CU. In the above example, the Jump proceeds from State 0 (Fetch) to State 1 (Decode) to State 3 (Complete) and then goes back to State 0. While a Load adds a State 4. In some designs, the state register also encodes the instruction type. Thus, it is really referring to the different states of the finite state machine (FSM) rather than the major steps of the instructions. So, for example, the FSM states for a Load might be the sequence 0, 1, 12, 13. The latter two distinguish Memory and Write Back from the Complete stage of the Jump. In other designs, we might see Jump going through states 0, 1, 2, and Load going through 0, 1, 2, 3, with the type field used to distinguish the different behaviour of the latter states. This is all just a matter of using somewhat different ways of naming the same things. The important point is just that the CU has the inputs it needs to know what it is supposed to be doing on the present clock and what it will do next. In the CU design process, this translate to ensuring that one of the control signals on the list is the "next state" signal, and that we always specify this in every cell of our table.

Unlike the way this is drawn in the text, it is quite obvious here that each level of the controller's finite state machine corresponds to a clock cycle (or major state). This view clearly shows the commonality of the first two major states, prior to the decoding of the instruction. The third stage is a typical fanning out of the finite state machine to deal with the different cases of the instruction types. Thus, we can see that the machine is arranged in a table where the rows are major states, and the columns are major instruction types. Because the new PC values have been computed, the Jump and Branch types can be finished early. The memory read takes the longest (5 major states).

Each of these states produces a set of control signals that cause the multiplexers to select the appropriate inputs, and the various registers to latch at the proper time. This is determined by looking at each device requiring control and determining for each state whether it is necessary to issue a signal on that particular control line. Note that in the text, the circuitry controlled by the status from the ALU is shown external to the control for simplicity. But in a more general controller that must handle multiple conditions, this logic would not be separated. Because there are ten distinct states, and the book chooses to encode the instruction type in the major state (really the FSM state number) the state register for this machine must have four bits.

One common approach to implementing a controller is to have the major state be implemented by a counter register and within each of these states the different columns are represented by the state register (which in a RISC architecture could just be the instruction type code). The major state counter simply increments on each clock cycle, and when a column of states finishes early, its last state generates a reset signal to the major state counter.

Another issue that is not addressed here is what happens when there is a memory delay. We are still assuming that memory returns in a single cycle. The simplest case is to stall the finite state machine until the fetch is complete. This is done by having a memory wait signal that is input to the finite state machine. Each memory fetch state has a next state arc that loops back to itself whenever memory wait is asserted.

Microcode

In many CISC architectures the control unit can feed back to the major (and minor) states and has internal registers and a ROM. It can thus cause portions of an instruction to be extended or repeated as necessary. The minor states, registers. additional control logic, and ROM form a finite state machine called a microcode engine. In the microcode engine, the op-code from the IR becomes a jump address into the ROM. A micro-PC can be used to step through a series of fetches from the ROM starting at that point, with each fetch resulting in control signals being sent out and providing feedback to the major and minor state values.

An alternative to using a micro-PC is to have each instruction explicitly specify the address of its successor. Thus, one of the fields in the micro-op may be the address of the next instruction. This allows jumps to be used anywhere in the microcode with no time penalty — consider that if a separate instruction had to be employed for a jump, it would add a cycle to the execution of the ISA instruction.

The microcode instruction set can contain a subroutine jump so that common sequences of control outputs can be reused. This is typically present in systems that employ a microPC rather than a next instruction field. There is typically just one subroutine return register, so nesting of subroutines is not allowed. Thus, the subroutine jump may be implemented as a normal jump with a signal issued that stores the current micro-PC value into the return register. And the subroutine ends with a Return operation rather than a jump to another location. The Return operation issues a signal that loads the return register back into the micro-PC. In a system with an explicit next instruction field, the current address plus one is stored into the return register and it is implicit that the next location holds the next instruction following the subroutine call. (An alternative is to have both a subroutine jump address and a next instruction address, and simply return to the same instruction, but this requires the instruction format to be larger than necessary for most operations.

Microinstruction Format Design

From the preceding discussion of how sequential execution, jumps, and calls are executed we can gather that the microinstruction needs to include control information for the microengine itself. But what else does it store?

In the simplest microinstruction formats, each bit represents a control signal that is sent out to the datapath. Thus, when a microinstruction is fetched, the bits in the instruction are connected to control wires and cause actions to occur in the datapath.

For example, in our PDP-8 example, there are 14 control signals that are driven by a single bit, and three others that each require multiple bits, for a total of 23 bits. Each of the first 20 bits of this microinstruction corresponds to a control signal in the PDP-8. For example, bit 0 might be the Halt, bit 1 the No defer, bit 2 the Max St., bit 3 Acc. Load, bit 4 Acc.

clear, etc. This simple representation is effective but inefficient. For example, it uses 4 bits to select the ALU function but only one of those bits should be asserted at any time. Thus, we can save some memory by storing the number of the active bit and using an external "decoder" circuit to translate the two bits into the four lines that control the ALU.

In a simple design such as the PDP-8, it may seem that this (two bit) savings is trivial, but in a CISC ISA, the number of control signals can be quite large and it is important to minimize the number of bits in the microinstruction format. Every location in the microcode memory has to store the same set of bits, so any waste of bits is multiplied by the number of words.

Microinstruction format designs are often classified by the width of the word employed. One approach is to have a very wide word that contains all of the control signals necessary to drive the system. Such a design is referred to as a "horizontal" microinstruction format. Another approach is to use a narrower word, with a sequence of microinstructions being required to drive all of the control signals. This is called a "vertical" microinstruction format.

At first glance, it appears that a vertical microinstruction is inherently slower — it takes a sequence of operations to accomplish what the horizontal microinstruction can do in a single cycle. But consider that in many cases, individual control lines are asserted only in certain minor states. If all of these are grouped together by minor state, then they can reuse some of the bits of the microword by having their outputs first fed to a "demultiplexer" that steers them to the proper signal lines according to the current minor state (which may itself be part of the instruction). In effect the microinstruction format is using multiple instruction formats to reduce redundancy.

Horizontal microcode has been employed in massively parallel array processors where every processor in the system shares a single controller. Often the controller is itself a full-fledged computer, and so the microinstruction both contains traditional machine code for the controller itself as well as the control signals that are distributed to the processors that make up the array. A typical horizontal microinstruction for this type of machine is 128 bits wide (16 bytes). Thus, every effort is made to reduce the number of words required. It is important to note, however, that this is an unusual application of microcode.

One other problem with horizontal microcode is that it is difficult to drive such a large number of signals simultaneously. The switching of so many drivers at once can cause the power supply voltage to sag momentarily (the same as when your lights dim as you turn on a big appliance). This in turn causes noise to appear on signal lines that can cause erroneous behaviour in other parts of the computer. Avoiding this requires careful circuit design and sometimes clever tricks, such as ensuring that the signals are asserted in a series of slightly offset time steps.

Microcode

Of course, the whole reason for using microcode is to manage the complexity of a CISC ISA's control unit. Most RISC designs, even those that have fairly complex implementations, are still sufficiently regular that their control units can be directly constructed from a FSM built with combinational logic. (The advantage of using çombinational logic is that it is easier to build a fast decoder with it than with a microcode ROM.)

However, for a CISC ISA, the speed decrease resulting from the use of microcode is often outweighted by the need to manage the complexity of controlling the architecture (a slow processor is, after all, more useful than a faster one that doesn't work). In a CISC architecture there may be a large number of instruction types, each with different fields referring to a wide range of registers that have asymmetrical functions, or referring to one or more memory operands with as many as 20 different addressing modes. (The DEC VAX, Intel 80X86/Pentium, and Intel iAPX 432 are prime examples).

A control unit for a CISC ISA can thus have to deal with instructions that involve tens and even hundreds of minor states. There would thus be thousands of logic expressions to generate the control signals. CAD tools can simplify and minimize these and even lay them out on the silicon automatically, but it is still a large block of irregular logic on the chip.

More importantly, if a mistake is discovered later (*i.e.*, one of the logic expressions is wrong), then it may be necessary to resimplify the entire design and lay it out again, which could mean a redesign of the rest of the chip to accommodate a change in the size of the control unit. This is obviously a very costly error. Unfortunately, it is also common. Even with the best design and simulation tools, several commercial chips have gone into production with errors that were discovered later. An early 68000 design had a bug that would cause the processor to hang in certain cases, Intel shipped half a million Pentium processors with an error in the floating-point division instruction before it was caught, and has had bugs in earlier processors.

Since errors do occur, manufacturers of CISC processors use microcode to reduce the cost of correcting the errors (and to help simplify the initial design, which in itself helps to reduce errors). A bug-fix in a microcoded controller is just a matter of changing the ROM, which does not affect the size of the controller at all. It is a very low-cost correction. In addition, a microcoded design is easier to enhance because unused op-codes can be turned into new machine instructions by simply extending the microcode. This simplicity of extension may be another factor that has lead to the increasingly complex ISAs produced by CISC manufacturers.

At one point, it was even thought that allowing the user to add to the microcode was a good idea. If a user has a particular operation that they want to accelerate, they can code it up as a new instruction in the microcode. Such machines were said to have "writeable control stores." The VAX 11/780, the first model in the VAX line, was one of the most widely sold of these machines. However, the feature was rarely used for two reasons: first, the compilers could not take advantage of the custom instructions so the user had to programme in assembly language; second, the microcode is tied to the machine implementation (it refers to the particular control signals in the design) so it is not even portable to another model of the same architecture.

Nanocode

In some cases, such as the Motorola 68000, there is also a nanocode engine. The 68000 uses 544 17-bit words in its microengine and 336 68-bit words in its nanocode engine. It thus has 32,096 bits of ROM. If everything had been done with 68-bit words, it would have required 36,992 bits.

The M68000 microcode is very unusual in that the microcode implicitly calls the nanocode. Each microcode instruction causes a corresponding nanocode engine instruction to be fetched automatically. The nanocode bits are actually the control signals that get distributed across the machine. The microcode instructions thus have only to determine what the next instruction will be. They have two formats, one for an unconditional jump (perhaps just to the next location) or a conditional jump (two bits of the jump address are reserved for the result of the conditional test). This would seem to imply that there are as many nanocode instructions as microcode instructions. Yet we can see that there are 208 fewer. This is accomplished by carefully assigning the addresses so that common nanocode operations can have multiple microcode locations corresponding to them. The address space allows for 1024 instructions, and they are arranged so that if a bit (or several) is ignored, the same nanocode address is produced. Essentially the engineers mapped the microcode operations into locations so that certain of the address bits are "don't cares" and all of those locations are then mapped to the same nanocode address. The don't cares are achieved by removing selected transistors in the address decoders of the nanocode ROM.

Comparison of Some Microcode Engines

- *Motorola* 68000: 544 17-bit microwords, plus 336 68-bit nanowords

- *DEC LSI*-11: 2048 22-bit microwords
- *IBM* 3033 *mainframe*: 2048 108-bit microwords plus 2048 126-bit microwords
- *Texas instruments* 8800: 32K 128-bit microwords in user-programmable RAM
- *UMass/Hughes IUA*-2: 64K 128-bit microwords in RAM

The startech SD6 tuning kit consists of a computer-controlled auxiliary control unit. Thanks to an included model-specific wire harness and detailed installation instructions the plug-and-play module can be installed in less than 30 minutes by any authorized Chrysler/Jeep dealer.

At one time control units were ad-hoc logic, and they were difficult to design. Now they are designed as a microprogram that is stored in a control store. Words of the microprogram are selected by a sequencer and the bits from those words directly control the different parts of the computer, including the registers, arithmetic and logic unit, instruction register, bus, input/output and computer storage.

FORMATS

ACTIONS

- *A disk controller for a disk having spirally formed tracks, comprising*:
  - Buffer memory for temporarily storing write data to be recorded on said disk or read data derived from said disk,
  - First register for temporarily storing current sector information representative of a sector currently accessible, said current sector information being changed each time a currently accessible sector varies in accordance with rotation of said disk,
  - Second register for temporarily storing target sector information representative of a sector from which a data read/write operation starts, comparator means for comparing said current

sector information with said target sector information and for producing a coincident signal when said current sector information coincides with said target sector information, monitor means coupled to said buffer memory for producing a ready signal when said write data is stored in said buffer memory or when said buffer memory has a vacancy for accepting said read data, and control means coupled to said comparator means and said monitor means for generating a jump back signal when said coincident signal is produced while said ready signal is not being produced, said control means further generating said jump back signal when said monitor means stops producing said ready signal after said data read/write operation on said disk starts.

- *The disk controller as claimed in claim 1, further comprising*:
  - Third register loaded with the current sector information stored in said first register each time said jump back signal is generated, the current sector information stored in said first register being thereafter changed, and means for generating an additional coincident signal when the contents of said first and third registers become equal to each other, said control means generating said jump back signal again when said additional coincident signal is generated while said ready signal is not being produced.
- The disk controller as claimed in claim 2, further comprising selector means responsive to said control means for selecting the contents of said second or third register for comparing with the contents of said first register, the contents of said first register being selected prior to said jump back signal being generated and the contents of said third register being selected after such time as said jump back signal is generated.

- The disk controller as claimed in claim 2, wherein said disk controller performs a write-verify operation in which data written on the disk in response to a write command is thereafter read from the disk and the data read out is checked for errors, said control means comprising counter means for causing said jump back signal to be generated a number of times to return the read/write head to a track at which data recorded in response to said write command began to be recorded.
- The disk controller as claimed in claim 4, wherein said counter means comprises: Sector register means for temporarily storing a number corresponding to a number of sectors to be subjected to data recording in response to said write command; first down counter means initially loaded with the number temporarily stored in said sector register means for counting down to zero in response to data being recorded in a sector; track register means for temporarily storing a number corresponding to a number of tracks to be backed up upon completion of data recording for a write command; and second down counter means initially loaded with the number temporarily stored in said track register means for counting down to zero in response to said jump back signal being repeatedly generated.
- In a disk controller for a disk having spirally formed tracks and driven by a servo controller which moves a read/write head to one of said tracks in response to control information supplied by a drive controller, said drive controller being responsive to seek information generated by a system controller from data read and write commands, said disk controller comprising: Buffer memory means for temporarily storing write data to be recorded on said disk or read data derived from said disk,
  - First register means for temporarily storing current sector information representative of a

sector currently accessible, said current sector information being changed each time a currently accessible sector varies in accordance with rotation of said disk,

- Second register means for temporarily storing target sector information representative of a sector from which a data read/write operation starts,
- Comparator means for comparing said current sector information with said target sector information and for producing a coincident output signal taking an active level when said current sector information coincides with said target sector information,
- Monitor means coupled to said buffer memory for producing a ready signal when said write data is stored in said buffer memory means or when said buffer memory means has a vacancy for accepting said read data, and

Control means coupled to said comparator means and said monitor means for generating a jump back signal when said coincident signal is produced while said ready signal is not being produced, said control means further generating said jump back signal when said monitor means stops producing said ready signal after said data read/write operation on said disk starts, said jump back signal being supplied directly to said servo controller without intervention of the system controller and the drive controller, said servo controller responding directly to the jump back signal to perform a jump back operation.

- A disk controller for a disk apparatus which includes a disk having spirally formed tracks each containing a plurality of sectors, head circuit means for tracing each track to perform a data recording operation for recording write data supplied thereto to each sector or a data reading-out operation for reproducing read data from each sector, said head circuit means further producing current sector information indicative of a sector currently accessible and updating said current sector information each time the sector currently accessible varies, and a servo control unit for controlling, in response to a jump back signal supplied thereto, said head circuit means such that said head circuit means jumps back from a track currently being traced to a track precedent thereto, said disk controller comprising:

- Buffer memory means for temporarily storing said write data to be supplied to said head circuit means or said read data reproduced from each sector,
- Memory control unit coupled to said buffer memory for producing a ready signal when said write data is actually stored in said buffer memory or when said buffer memory has a vacancy for accepting said read data,
- Register for temporarily storing target sector information indicative of a target sector from which said data recording operation or said data reading-out operation starts, and
- Control circuit coupled to said head circuit means, said memory control unit and said register for allowing said head circuit means to start said data recording operation or said data reading-out operation when the current sector information from said head circuit means becomes equal to said target sector information while said ready signal is being produced and for generating and supplying said jump back signal to said servo control unit to thereby inhibit said head circuit means from starting said data recording operation or said data reading-out operation when the current sector information from said head circuit means becomes equal to said target sector information while said ready signal is not being produced.

• The disk controller as claimed in claim 7, wherein

said control circuit includes an additional register loaded with and temporarily storing the current sector information each time said head circuit means updates the current sector information and a comparator for comparing the current sector information stored in said additional register with said target sector information to detect that the current sector information becomes equal to said target sector information.

- A disk controller for a disk apparatus which includes a disk having spirally formed tracks each containing a plurality of sectors, head circuit means for tracing each track to perform a data recording operation for recording write data supplied thereto on each sector or a data reading-out operation for reproducing read data from each sector, said head circuit means producing current sector information indicative of a sector currently accessible and updating said current sector information each time the sector currently accessible varies, and a servo control unit for controlling, in response to a jump back signal supplied thereto, said head circuit means such that said head circuit means jumps back from a track currently being traced to a track precedent thereto, said disk controller comprising:
  - Buffer memory for temporarily storing said write data to be supplied to said head circuit means or said read data reproduced from said disk,
  - Memory control unit coupled to said buffer memory for producing a ready signal when said buffer memory actually stores said write data or when said buffer memory has a vacancy for accepting said read data,
  - Register for temporarily storing suspended sector information indicative of a suspended sector at which said data recording operation or said data reading-out operation is suspended, and
  - Control circuit coupled to said head circuit

means, said memory control unit and said register for allowing said head circuit means to resume the suspended data recording operation or the suspended reading-out operation when the current sector information from said head circuit means becomes equal to said suspended sector information while said ready signal is being produced and for generating and supplying said jump back signal to said servo control means to thereby inhibit said head circuit means from resuming the suspended data recording operation or the suspended data reading-out operation when the current sector information from said head circuit mean becomes equal to said suspended sector information while said ready signal is not being produced.

- The disk controller as claimed in claim 9, wherein said control circuit includes an additional register loaded with and temporarily storing the current sector information each time said head circuit means updates the current sector information and a comparator comparing the current sector information stored in said additional register with said suspended sector information to detect that the current sector information becomes equal to said suspended sector information.

DISK CONTROLLER FORMAT

The present invention relates to a disk controller and, more particularly, to an optical disk controller for an optical disk having a spirally formed track. An optical disk is employed as one of the data storage units in an information processing system. An optical disk controller performs a data transfer operation between the disk and a host processor.

The optical disk controller includes in general a buffer memory for temporarily storing write data from the host processor and read data from the disk, a format control unit for converting the write data from the buffer memory into data to be recorded on the disk and the data reproduced from the disk into the read data, and a system controller for responding to commands from the host processor to control the data transfer flow. Further included in the disk controller are a servo controller for controlling the focus and tracking of an optical beam on the disk and a drive controller for ordering, under the control of the system controller, the servo controller to perform a seek operation in which the optical beam moves to a target track and a jump operation in which the optical beam jumps to the adjacent track.

When the system controller receives a data transfer command from the host processor, it requests the seek operation of the drive controller, so that the optical beam moves rapidly to the target track. At a time when a target sector on that track is searched, the format controller starts to operate in a data write mode to record the write data from the buffer memory on the disk and in a data read mode to supply the buffer memory with the read data responsive to the data recorded on the disk. In the data write mode, the write data is transferred from the host processor to the buffer memory, and in the data read mode, the read data is transferred from the buffer memory to the host processor. Thus, the data transfer is executed between the disk and the host processor.

However, sometimes in the data write mode no write data has been transferred to the buffer memory at a time the target sector is searched and that the write data transfer to the buffer memory is suspended. Also in the data read mode, the buffer memory is often filled with the read data which are not transferred to the host processor yet. In such cases, the data read/write operation is of course suspended until the write data arrives in the buffer memory or until the buffer memory has a vacancy for accepting the read data. On the other hand, the disk continues to rotate. Since the track on the disk is formed spirally, therefore, the accessible sector advances in sequence, so that the target sector is not searched again even when the write data is transferred to the buffer memory or the vacancy for the read data is formed in the buffer memory. Therefore, the format controller informs the system controller of a fact that the data read/write operation is suspended due to the above reason. In response thereto, the system controller requests the jump operation of the drive controller to back the optical beam up by one track. To back the optical beam up is called hereinafter "jump back".

However, this jump back operation is performed after the response time of the system controller and the drive controller has elapsed, resulting in lowering in an access speed. Moreover, the system controller must be designed to handle the request from the format controller, and hence the load thereof is made large.

PRESENTATION

Therefore, an object of the present invention is to provide an improved disk controller. Another object of the present invention is to provide a disk controller which can prevent lowering the access speed even when a data read/write operation is suspended. Still another object of the present invention is to provide a disk controller which can achieve a jump back processing operation without increasing the loading of the system controller. A disk controller according to the present invention is characterized in that a format control unit generates directly a jump back signal and a servo controller responds directly to that signal to perform a jump back operation.

More specifically, the format control unit comprises a first register for temporarily storing current sector information which indicates a currently accessible sector on a disk and is changed in accordance with the location of the disk, a second register for temporarily storing target sector information indicative of a target sector from which a data read/write operation starts, comparator means for comparing the information stored in the first register with the information stored in the second register to produce a comparison output signal taking an active level when the former information coincides with the latter information, and a sequence controller receiving the comparison output signal and a ready signal which takes an active level when write data is already stored in a buffer memory or when the buffer memory has a vacancy for accepting read data and generating the jump back signal when the ready signal is in an inactive level when the comparison output signal takes the active level, the sequence controller further generating, after the comparison output signal takes the active level, the jump back signal when the ready signal is in the inactive level when the information stored in the first register is changed.

Thus, the format control unit initiates the jump back operation to prevent lowering the access speed due to the delay of system and drive controllers.

When the sequence controller generates the jump back signal, the sector information at that time is temporarily retained, and the comparator means thereafter compares the current sector information with the retained sector information. The generation of the jump back signal is then controlled in response to the comparison output signal and the ready signal.

DESCRIPTION

The commands such as a data write command and a data read command from the host processor 14 are supplied to a system controller 11 via a controller bus 13. The system controller 11 responds to the commands thus supplied and calculates ID (Identification) information indicative of a physical address of a sector from which a data read/write operation starts and the number of sectors to be subjected to the data read/write and further generates seek information for moving rapidly an optical beam 31 to a target track on an optical disk 1. The seek information is supplied via a bus 110 to a drive controller 6, whereas read/write command information is supplied via a bus 13 to a format control unit 7 and a memory control unit 10. The data to be written into the disk 1, *i.e.* write data from the host processor 14, are temporarily stored into a buffer memory 9 through the interface circuit 8 and an internal bus 12. The buffer memory 9 is of a FIFO (first-in first-out) type. The data to be transferred to the host processor 14, i.e. read data derived from the disk 1, are also temporarily stored into the buffer memory 9 and then transferred to the host processor 14 through the interface circuit 8 and the system bus 15. The memory control unit 10 manages the buffer memory 9 through a control line 10 and thus detects the presence/absence of the write data into the memory 9 and the presence/absence of a vacancy for the read data in the memory 9. The detection output is outputted as ready information 102.

On the other hand, the disk 1 is rotated by a spindle motor 2 and the data read/write is carried out by an optical beam 31 from an optical head circuit 3. This circuit 3 produces focus and tracking information 32 for the beam 31, which information is in turn supplied to a servo controller 5. In response thereto, the controller 5 performs the rotation speed control of the motor 2 and the focus and tracking control of the beam 31 through control data 51 and 52. The servo controller 5 is further supplied with a seek control information and track jump information 61 from a drive controller 6. In response thereto, the servo controller 5 opens the servo control loop to move the beam 31 as the seek operation and the track jump operation.

The optical head circuit 3 communicates via a data line 71 with a format control unit 71 with respect to data to be recorded on the disk 1 and data reproduced from the disk 1. The format control unit 7 receives the write data from the buffer memory 9 in the data write mode and then supplies them to the head circuit 3 as data to be recorded. In the data read mode, on the other hand, it receives the data from the head circuit 3 and then supplies them to the buffer memory 9 as the read data. In accordance with the present invention, the format control unit 7 generates a jump back signal 72 by itself, and the jump back signal 72 is in turn supplied directly to the servo controller 5 without intervention of the system controller 11 and the drive controller 6.

The serial data are further supplied to a synchronizing pattern detector 704. This detector 704 detects predetermined patterns such as a sector mark indicative of the beginning of a sector, an address mark indicative of the beginning of ID information and a data mark indicative of the beginning of data and supplies this detection information to a sequence controller 710 via a bus 7041 to synchronize the controller 710. When ID information indicative of a current sector is obtained in the conversion circuit 702, it is transferred to a current ID register 705. The read-out data obtained in the circuit 703 in the data read mode is transferred to the buffer memory 9 via the bus 12. In the data write mode, on the other hand, the write data from the buffer memory 9 is transferred to the conversion circuit 703 and then converted into serial data which are in turn encoded or modulated by an encoder 701. Serial data 7011 to be recorded on the disk 1 are thus obtained and supplied to the head circuit 3.

ID information stored in the current ID register 703 is changed each time an accessible sector is changed. The ID information is compared by a comparator 706 with an output of a selector 707. This selector 707 selects and outputs the content of a target ID register 708 when a selection signal 7071 is at the low level. On the other hand, the high level of the signal 7071 causes the selector 707 to select and output the content of a suspended ID register 709. The target ID register 708 is loaded by the system controller 11 with ID information indicative of a sector from which data read/write operation starts. The suspended ID register 709 captures the content of the current ID register 705 in response to an ID fetch signal 7091.

The output 7061 of the comparator 706 is supplied to the sequence controller 710 which also receives a read ready signal 1021 and a write ready signal 1022 as data ready information 102 from the memory control unit 10. The sequence controller 710 responds to the synchronizing information 7041, the comparison output signal 7061, data ready information 102 and command information from the controller 11 and generates a set of sequence control signals 7101 for performing a sequence of operations. The sequence control signals 7101 contain the selection signal 7071 and ID fetch signal 7091. The controller 710 further generates the jump back signal 72 which is in turn supplied directly to the servo controller 5. There is shown a tracking servo loop circuit and a jump back control circuit in the servo controller 5 and a part of the optical head circuit 3. A laser beam 31 from a laser diode 305 as an optical source is applied to the disk 1 through a beam splitter 303 and a lens 301. The laser beam reflected from the disk 1 is supplied to a read-out control circuit 304 by the beam spritter 303. The circuit 304 produces the serial data 7021 to be supplied to the format control unit 7. The circuit 304 further produces tracking information of the beam 31 and supplies it to a tracking error producing circuit 305 in which tracking error information is produced and then supplied through a phase compensation circuit 306, a selector 307 and a driver 308 to a tracking actuator 302 to carry out a tracking control. The circuit 306 compensates the phase delay of the actuator 302. The serial data 7011 to be recorded is supplied to a recording control circuit 316 to drive the laser diode 305.

The selector 307 receives the tracking error compensation signal from the circuit 306, a jump back drive signal 721 from a jump back circuit 720 and a seek drive signal 611 from the drive controller 6 and selects and outputs one of them in response to the levels of a jump back instruction signal 722 and a seek instruction signal 612. Specifically, when only the signal 722 takes the active level, the jump back drive signal 721 is selected and outputted. The seek drive signal 611 is selected when the signal 612 is at the active level. When both the signals 612 and 722 are at the inactive level, the tracking error compensation signal is selected.

The jump back circuit 720 includes two S-R type flip-flops 310 and 311, a NAND gate 312, an AND gate 313, a P-channel transistor 314, an N-channel transistor 315, a delay circuit 309 and a tracking cross detector 318 which are connected as shown. Accordingly, the jump back signal 72 from the sequence controller 710 of the format control unit 7 sets both flip-flops 310 and 311 to change the signal 722 to the active level and turn the transistor 314 ON. The tracking servo loop is thereby made open. The actuator 302 is driven by the

V_{DD} level, so that the laser beam 31 starts to move back to a track that is just before the current track. When the laser beam 31 crosses an intermediate point between two tracks, the detector 318 produces the detection output to reset the flip-flop 311. The transistor 314 is thereby turned OFF, whereas the transistor 315 is turned ON to stop the lens 301. The output of the detector 318 is delayed by a predetermined time by the delay circuit 309, and the delayed output resets the flip-flop 310. As a result, the tracking servo loop is formed again. The one-track jump back operation is thus completed.

An operation will be described below with reference to illustrating the track configuration on the disk 1. When the host processor 14 issues data read/write command, the system controller 11 responds to command and produces and stores into the target ID register 708 ID information indicative of the physical address of a sector from which the data read/write operation starts, denoted by a read/write commencement sector 101 in. The system controller 11 further requests the sequence controller 710 to initiate a sequence flow for data read or write and supplies the drive controller 6 with seek information for moving the laser beam 31 to the neighborhood of the read/write commencement sector 101 by the seek operation.

In response thereto, the drive controller 6 produces the seek drive signal 611 with making the signal 612 active, so that the laser beam 31 moves to the neighborhood of the sector 101. The signal 612 is thereafter changed to the inactive level to activate the tracking servo loop. The serial data 7021 from the read-out control circuit 304 are thereby supplied to the decoder 702 and the synchronizing pattern detector 704. As described above, ID information to be stored in the current ID register 705 is changed each time the accessible sector varies. Since the selection signal 7071 is at the low level in an initial state, the content of the target ID register 708, i.e. the ID information of the data read/write commencement sector 101, is compared by the comparator 706 with the content of the current ID register 705. When the comparator 706 produces the active level signal 7061 to inform that the read/

write commencement sector 101 is accessible, the sequence controller 710 checks the level of data ready information 1021 before requesting the memory control unit 10 to transfer data between the buffer memory 9 and the conversion circuit 703. The write ready signal 1022 of the data ready information 102 is in the active level when write data is stored in the buffer memory 9 in the data write mode, and the read ready signal 1021 thereof is in the active level when the buffer memory 9 has a vacancy for accepting the read-out data in the data read mode. The sequence controller 710 monitors the ready signal 1021 or 1022 in accordance with the operation mode to be executed. When the monitored ready signal 1021 or 1022 is in the inactive level at a time the comparison output signal 7061 becomes active, the data read/write cannot be performed. Therefore, the sequence controller 710 generates the jump back signal 72. Consequently, as already described with reference the laser beam 31 jumps back to a track 105 that is just before a track 104 on which the read/write commencement sector 101 exists.

The sequence controller 710 further generates the ID fetch signal 7091, so that ID information of the read/write commencement sector 101 is stored in the suspended ID register 709 as a read/write-suspended sector information. The selection signal 7071 is thereafter changed to the high level to cause the selector 707 to select the register 709.

When the laser beam 31 shifts from the track 105 to the track 104 by the rotation of the disk 1 and the ID information of the sector 101 is then stored in the current ID register 705, the comparator 706 generates again the active level output signal 7061. Assuming that the write data is stored in the buffer memory 9 from the host processor 14 or the buffer memory 9 has a vacancy for accepting the read data before the active level signal 7061 is generated again, the monitored ready signal 1021 or 1022 is at the active level at a time the signal 7061 becomes active.

Accordingly, the sequence controller 710 requests the data transfer of the memory control unit 10. In the data write mode, the write data is thereby transferred from the buffer memory 9 to the conversion circuit 703. In the data read mode, on the other hand, the read data is transferred from the conversion circuit 703 to the buffer memory 9. If the monitored ready signal 1021 or 1022 is still at the inactive level when the signal 7061 comes active again, the jump back operation is repeated.

After the data read/write operation starts from the sector 101, the sequence controller 710 checks the monitored ready signal 1021 or 1022 irrespective of the level of the comparison signal 7061 each time the content of the current ID register 705 changes.

As denoted by a suspended sector 102 in assume that the mentioned ready signal 1021 or 1022 is at the inactive level when the ID information indicative of the sector 102 is stored in the current ID register 705. The sequence controller 710 therefore generates the jump back signal 72 to back the track to be accessed by one. The ID information of the sector 102 is stored into the suspended ID register 709. After the jump back operation is completed, the content of the current ID register 705 changes in sequence. When the current ID register 705 stores the ID information indicative of the suspended sector 102, the comparison output signal 7061 becomes active. In response thereto, the sequence controller 710 requests again the jump back operation or requests the data transfer for the sector 102 in accordance with the monitored ready signal 1021 or 1022.

After the data read/write operation for the sector 102 is completed, the sequence controller 710 checks the ready signal 1021 or 1022 irrespective of the comparison output signal 7061 each time the content of the current ID register changes, as described hereinbefore.

Thus, the format control unit 7 detects whether or not the data read/write for the currently accessible sector is performed and then generates by itself, the jump back signal 72 when the data read/write is disabled. The jump back signal 72 controls directly the jump back circuit 720 to perform one-track jump back operation. Therefore, the access time is free from delay due to the response time of the system controller

11 and the drive controller 6. Moreover, the processing load of the system controller 6 is reduced. The disk controller is required to execute a write-verify operation in which data from the host processor are recorded on the disk and thereafter the recorded data is read out and checked for errors. This operation is executed in general as follows.

That is, the format control unit informs the system controller of the completion of data recording. In response thereto, the system controller requests the seek operation of the drive controller to back the optical beam by a predetermined number of tracks. Thereafter, the format control unit receives a verifying command from the system control.

In such an operation, as if the data write commencement sector 101 is close to a data write end sector 103, while it is sufficient to back the beam 31 by two tracks, due to the delay of response time of the controllers 11 and 6, the beam 31 has already passed the write commencement sector 101 at the time the beam 31 is backed by two tracks. For this reason, the beam 31 requires to be backed by three tracks, resulting in that the initiation of the verifying operation is delayed.

A circuit construction for solving as another embodiment of the present invention, in which the same components as those are denoted by the same reference numerals to omit further description thereof. The format control unit according to the present embodiment further includes an S-R type flip-flop 750, an AND gate 751, a down counter 752 and a sector register 753, and a track register 754 is provided in the sequence controller 710. The sector register 753 is loaded with the number of sectors to be subjected to data recording from the system controller 11. The track register 754 is loaded with the number of tracks to be backed up from the system controller 11.

The jump back operation which may be performed in the data write mode responsive to the write-verify operation is omitted because it is the same as the former embodiment. By the generation of the comparison output signal 7061 due to the write commencement sector 101 becoming accessible, the flip-flop 750 is set to open the AND gate 751 and the content of the sector register 753 is loaded to the down counter 752. The sequence controller generates a count signal 7511 every time the write data is recorded on the sector, so that the content of the down counter 752 is decremented one by one. When the count value reaches zero, i.e. when the data write operation to the write end sector 103 is completed, the sequence controller 710 outputs the content, of the track register 754 onto the data line 7541 and thereafter generates the jump back signal 72.

Turning to, the jump back circuit 720 according to the present embodiment further includes a down counter 760, a zero detector 761, an AND gate 762 and an OR gate 763. The data on the line 7541 is loaded to the down counter 760. By the jump back signal 72 being thereafter generated, one-track jump back operation is executed and the content of the down counter 760 is decremented by one.

The signal from the delay circuit 309 representative of the completion of one-track jump back operation passes through the AND gate 762 and then sets the flip-flops 310 and 311 as the jump back signal. The one-track jump back operation is thereby performed again. Since the content of the down counter 760 reaches zero, the detector 761 closes the AND gate 762. The output from the delay circuit 309 is thereby masked. Thus, the jump back operation for backing the beam 31 by two tracks is performed immediately. The comparator 706 thereafter generates the active level output signal 7061 for initiating the verifying operation.

It is apparent that the present invention is not limited to the above embodiments but may be modified and changed without departing from the scope and spirit of the invention. For example, in place of the selector 707, two comparators can be provided, one of which compares the current ID register with the target ID register and the other of which compares the current ID register with the suspended ID register, one of outputs of these comparator being selected. Moreover, a part of the buffer memory can be provided in the format control unit.

INSTRUCTION CYCLES

INTRODUCTION

In order to programme at an elementary level, it is not necessary to understand in detail the internal structure of the processor that one is using. However, in order to do efficient programming, such an understanding is required. The purpose is to present the basic hardware concepts necessary for understanding the operation of the Z80 system. The complete microcomputer system includes not only the microprocessor unit (here the Z80), but also other components.

ARCHITECTURE

The architecture of the microcomputer system appears in Figure. The microprocessor unit (MPU), which will be a Z80 here, appears on the left of the illustration. It implements the functions of a *central-processing unit* (CPU) within one chip: it includes an *arithmetic-logical unit* (ALU), plus its internal registers, and a*control unit* (CU), in charge of sequencing the system. The MPU creates three *buses*: an 8-bit bidirectional *data bus*, which appears at the top of the illustration, a 16-bit unidirectional *address bus*, and a *control bus*, which appears at the bottom of the illustration. Let us describe the function of each of the buses.

The *data bus* carries the data being exchanged by the various elements of the system. Typically, it will carry data from the memory to the MPU or from the MPU to the memory or from the MPU to an input/output chip. (An input/output chip is a component in charge of communicating with an external device.) The *address bus* carries an address generated by the MPU, which will select one internal register within one of the chips attached to the system. This address specifies the source, or the destination, of the data which will transit along the data bus.

The *control bus* carries the various synchronization signals required by the system. Having described the purpose of the buses, let us now connect the additional components required for a complete system.

Every MPU requires a precise timing reference, whichis supplied by a *clock* and a *crystal*. In most "older" microprocessors, the clock-oscilator is external to the MPU and requires an extra chip. In most recent microprocessors, the clock-oscilator is usually incorporated within the MPU. The quartz crystal, however, because of its bulk, is always external to the system.

The ROM is the *read-only memory* and contains the *programme* for the system. The advantage of the ROM memory is that its contents are permanent and do not disappear whenever the system is turned off. The ROM, therefore, always contains a *bootstrap* or a *monitor* programme (their function will be explained later) to permit initial system operation. In a process-control environment, nearly all the programmes will reside in ROM, as they will probably never be changed. In such a case, the industrial user has to protect the system against power failure; programmes must not be volatile. They must be in ROM.

However, in a hobbyist environment, or in a programme-development environment (when the programmer tests his programme), most of the programmes will reside in RAM, so that they can be easily changed. Later, they may remain in RAM, or be transferred into ROM, if desired. RAM, however, is volatile. Its contents are lost when power is turned off.

The RAM (*random-access memory*) is the read/write memory for the system. In the case of a control system, the amount of RAM will typically be small (for data only). On the other hand, in a programme development environment, the amount of RAM will be large, as if will contain programmes plus development software. All RAM contents must be loaded prior to use from an external device. Finally the system will contain one or more interface chips so that it may communicate with the external world. The most frequently used interface chip is the PIO or*parallel input/ output* chip. It is the one shown on the illustration. This PIO, like all other chips in the system, connects to all three buses and provides at least two 8-bit ports for communication with the outside world. For more details on how and acutal PIO works, refer to book C201 or, for specifics of the Z80 system. All the chips are connected to all three buses, including the control bus. The functional modules which have been described need not necessarily reside on a single LSI chip. In fact, we could use *combination chips*, which may include both PIO and a limited amount of ROM or RAM. Still more components will be required to build a real system. In particular, the buses need to be *buffered*. Also *decoding logic* may be used for the memory RAM chips, and, finally, some signals may need to be amplified by *drivers*. These auxiliary circuits will not be described here as they are not relevant to programming.

SECURITY IN MICROPROCESSOR

The large majority of all microprocessor chips on the market today implement the same architecture. This "standard" architecture will be described here. It is shown in Figure below. The modules of this standard microprocessor will now be detailed, from right to left.

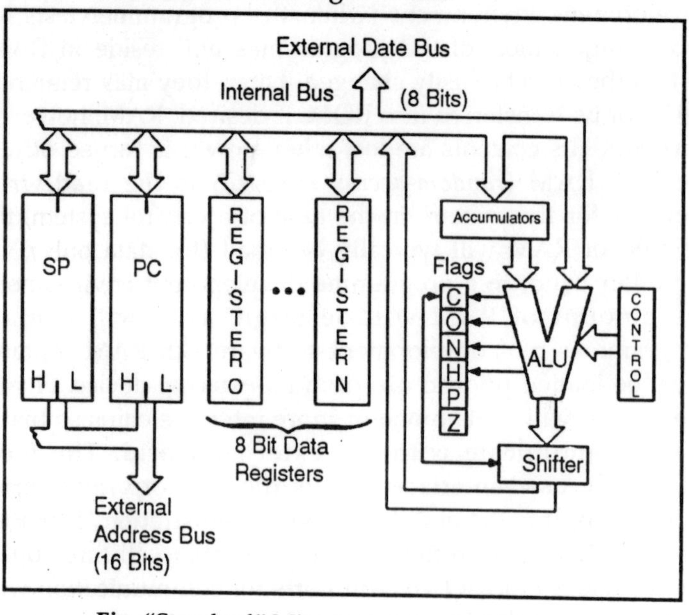

Fig. "Standard" Microprocessor Architecture.

The *ALU* performs arithmetic and logic operations. A special register equips one of the inputs of the ALU, the left input here. It is called the accumulator. (Several accumulators may be provided.) The accumulator may be referenced as input and output within the same instruction.

Setting Flags

Most of the instructions executed by the processor will modify some or all of the flags. It is important to always refer to the chart provided by the manufacturer listing which bits will be modified by the instructions. This is essential in understanding the way a programme is being executed. Such a chart for the Z80 is shown in Figure.

The Registers

Let us look now at above Figure. On the left of the illustration, the registers of the microprocessor appear. Conceptually, one can distinguish the *general-purpose registers* and the *address registers.*

The General-Purpose Registers

General-purpose registers must be provided in order for the ALU to manipulate data at high speed. Because of restrictions on the number of bits which is reasonable to provide within an instruction, the number of (directly addressable) registers is usually limited to fewer than eight. Each of these registers is a set of eight flip-flops, connected to the bidirectional internal data bus. These eight bits can be transferred simultaneously to or from the data bus. The implementation of these registers in MOS flip-flops provide the fastest level of memory available, and their contents can be accessed within tens of nanoseconds.

Internal registers are usually labeled from 0 to n. The role of these registers is not defined in advance: they are said to be "general-purpose." They may contain any data used by the programme. These general-purpose registers will normally be used to store eight-bit data. On some microprocessors, facilities exist to manipulate two of these registers at a time.

They are then called "register pairs." This arrangement facilitates the storage of 16-bit quantities, whether data or addresses.

The Address Registers

Address registers are 16-bit registers intended for the storage of addresses. They are also often called *data counters* or *pointers*. They are double registers, *i.e.*, two eight-bit registers. Their essential characteristic is to be connected to the address bus. The address registers create the address bus. The address bus appears on the left and the bottom part of the illustration in Figure below.

The only way to load the contents of these 16-bit registers is via the data bus. Two transfers will be necessary along the data bus in order to transfer 16 bits. In order to differentiate between the lower half and the higher half of each register, they are usually labelled as L (low) or H (high), denoting bits 0 through 7, and 8 through 15, respectively.

PROGRAMME COUNTER (PC)

The *programme counter* must be present in any processor. It contains the address of the next instruction to be executed. The presence of the programme counter is indispensable and fundamental to programme execution. The mechanism of programme execution and the automatic sequencing implemented with the programme counter will be described in the next section. Briefly, execution of a programme is normally sequential. In order to access the next instruction, it is necessary to bring it from the memory into the microprocessor. The contents of the PC will be deposited on the address bus, and transmitted towards the memory. The memory will then read the contents specified by this address and send back the corresponding word to the MPU. This is the instruction. In a few exceptional microprocessors, such as the two-chip F8, there is no PC on the microprocessor. This does not mean that the system does not have a programme counter. The PC happens to be implemented directly on the memory chip, for reasons of efficiency.

Stack Pointer (SP)

The *stack* has not been introduced yet and will be described in the next section. In most powerful, general-purpose microprocessors, the stack is implemented in "software", *i.e.,* within the memory. In order to keep track of the top of this stack within the memory, a 16-bit register is dedicated to the *stack pointer* or *SP*. The SP contains the address of the top of the stack within the memory. It will be shown that the stack is indispensable for interrupts and for subroutines.

Index Register

Indexing is a memory-addressing facility which is not always provided in microprocessors. The various memory-addressing techniques will be described. Indexing is a facility for accessing blocks of data in the memory with a single instruction. An *index register* will typically contain a displacement which will be automatically added to a base (or it might contain a base which would be added to a displacement). In short, indexing is used to access any word within a block of data.

The Stack

A *stack* is formally called an LIFO structure (last-in, first-out). A stack is a set of registers, or memory locations, allocated to this data structure. The essential characteristic of this structure is that it is a *chronological* structure. This first element introduced into the stack is always at the bottom of the stack. The element most recently deposited in the stack is on top of the stack. The analogy can be drawn with a stack of plates on a restaurant counter. There is a hole in the counter with a spring in the bottom. Plates are piled up in the hole. With this organization, it is guaranteed that the plate which has been put first in the stack (the oldest) is always at the bottom. The one that has been placed most recently on the stack is the one which is on top of it. This example also illustrates another characteristic of the stack. In normal use, a stack is only accessible via two instructions: "push" and "pop" (or "pull"). The *push* operation results in depositing one element on top of the stack (two in case of the Z80). The *pull* operation consists of removing one element from the stack. In the case of a microprocessor, it is the *accumulator* that will be deposited on top of the stack. The *pop* will result in a transfer of the top element of the stack into the accumulator. Other specialized instructions may exist to transfer the top of the stack between other specialized registers, such as the status register. The Z80 is more versatile than most in this respect. We will simply assume at this point that the stack is a required facility in every computer system.

A stack may be implemented in two ways:

- A fixed number of registers may be provided within the microprocessor itself. This is a "hardware stack." It has the advantage of high speed. However, it has the disadvantage of a limited number of registers.
- Most general-purpose microprocessors choose another approach, the software stack, in order not to restrict the stack to a very small number of registers. This is the approach chosen in the Z80. In the software approach, a dedicated register within the micropr-ocessor, here register SP, stores the stack pointer, *i.e.*, the address of the top element of the stack (or, sometimes, the address of the top element of the stack plus one). The stack is then implemented as an area of memory. The stack pointer will therefore require 16 bits to point anywhere in the memory.

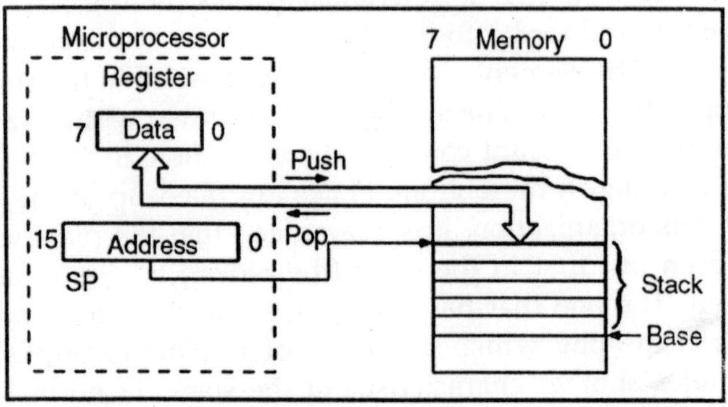

Fig. The Two Stack-Manipulation Instructions.

INSTRUCTION EXECUTION CYCLE

The microprocessor unit appears on the left, and the memory appears on the right. The memory chip may be a ROM or a RAM, or any other chip which happens to contain memory. The memory is used to store instructions and data. Here, we will fetch one instruction from the memory to illustrate the role of the programme counter. We assume that the programme counter has valid contents. It now holds a 16-bit address which is the address of the next instruction to fetch in the memory. Every processor proceeds in three cycles:

Fetch

Let us now follow the sequence. In the first cycle, the contents of the programme counter are deposited on the address bus and gated to the memory (on the address bus). Simultaneously, a read signal may be issued on the control bus of the system, if required. The memory will receive the address. This address is used to specify one location within the memory. Upon receiving the read signal, the memory will decode the address it has received, through internal decoders, and will select the location specified by the address. A few hundred nanoseconds later, the memory will deposit the eight-bit data corresponding to the specified address on its data bus. This eight-bit word is the instruction that we want to fetch. In our illustration, this instruction will be deposited on the data bus on top of the MPU box.

Let us briefly summarize the sequencing: the contents of the programme counter are output on the address bus. A read signal is generated. *The memory cycles,* and perhaps 300 nanoseconds later, the instruction at the specified address is deposited on the data bus (assuming a single byte instruction). The microprocessor then reads the data bus and deposits its contents into a specialized internal register, the IR register. The IR is the *instruction register*: it is eight-bits wide and is used to contain the instruction just fetched from the memory. The fetch cycle is now completed. The 8 bits of the instruction are now physically in the special internal register of the MPU, the IR register.

DECODING AND EXECUTION

Once the instruction is contained in IR, the control unit of the microprocessor will decode the contents and will be able to generate the correct sequence of internal and external signals for the execution of the specified instruction. There is, therefore, a short decoding delay followed by an execution phase, the length of which depends on the nature of the instruction specified. Some instructions will execute entirely within the MPU. Other instructions will fetch or deposit data from or into the memory. This is why the various instructions of the MPU require various length of time to execute. This duration is expressed as a number of (clock) cycles. Since various clock rates may be used, speed of execution is normally expressed in number of cycles rather than in number of nanoseconds.

FETCHING THE NEXT INSTRUCTION

We have described now, using the programme counter, an instruction can be fetched from the memory. During the execution of a programme, instructions are fetched *in sequence* from the memory. An automatic mechanism must therefore be provided by a simple incrementer attached to the programme counter. This is illustrated inFigure 2.7. Every time that the contents of the programme counter (at the bottom of the illustration) are placed on the address bus, its contents will be incremented and written back into the programme counter. As an example, if the programme counter contained the value "0", the value "0" would be output on the address bus. Then the contents of the programme counter would be incremented and the value "1" would be written back into the programme counter. In this way, the next time that the programme counter is used, it is the instruction at address 1 that will be fetched.

It must be stressed that the above descriptions are simplified. In reality, some instructions may be two- or even three-bytes long, so that successive bytes will be fetched in this manner from memory. However, the mechanism is identical. The programme counter is used to fetch successive bytes of an instruction as well as to fetch successive instructions themselves. The programme counter, together with its incrementer, provides an automatic mechanism for pointing to successive memory locations.

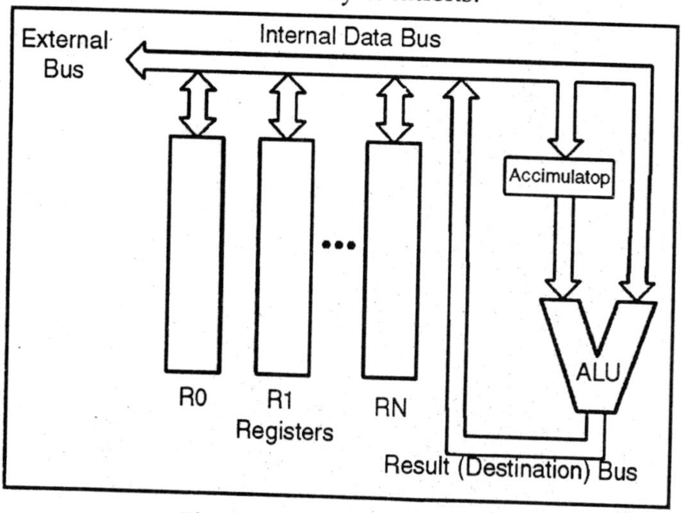

Fig. Single-Bus Architecture.

We will now execute an instruction within the MPU (see Figure above). A typical instruction will be, for example: R0 = R0 + R1. This means: "ADD the contents of R0 and R1, and store the results in R0." To perform this operation, the contents of R0 will be read from register R0, carried via the single bus to the left input of the ALU, and stored in the buffer register there. R1 then will be selected and its contents will be read onto the bus, then transferred to the right input of the ALU. This sequence is illustrated in Figures 2.9 and 2.10. At this point, the right input of the ALU is conditioned by R1, and the left input of the ALU is conditioned by the buffer register, containing the previous value of R0. The operation can be performed. The addition is performed by the ALU, and the result appears on the ALU output, in the lower right-hand corner of Figure. The result will be deposited on the single bus, and will be propagated back to R0. This means, in practice, that the input latch of R0 will be enabled, so that data can be written into it. Execution of the instruction is now complete. The results of the addition are in R0. It should be noted that the contents of R1 have not been modified by this operation. This is general principle: the contents of a register, or any read/write memory, are not modified by a read operation.

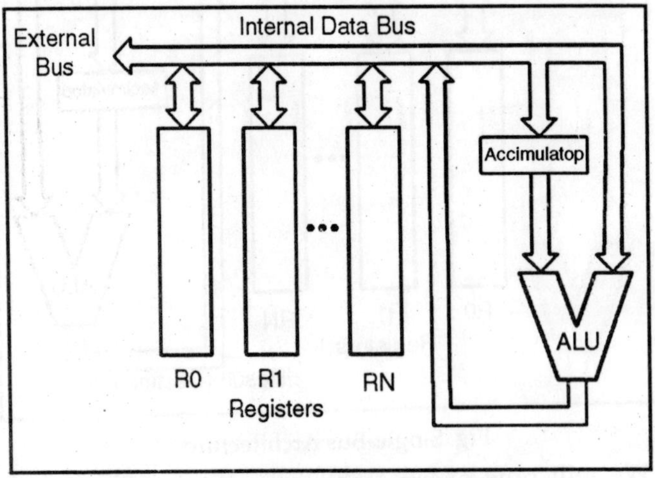

Fig. Execution of an Addition-R0 into ACC

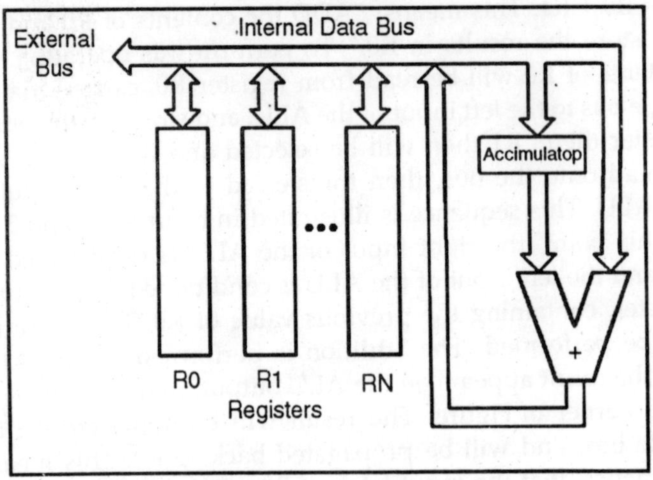

Fig. Addition-Second Register R1 into ALU

The buffer register on the left input of the ALU was

necessary in order to *memorize* the contents of R0, so that the single bus could be used again for another transfer. However, a problem remains.

INTERNAL ORGANIZATION

The terms necessary in order to understand the internal elements of the microprocessor have been defined. We will now examine in more detail the Z80 itself, and describe its capabilities. The internal organization of the Z80 is shown in figure below. This diagram presents a logical description of the device. Additional interconnections may exist but are not shown.

On the right part of the illustration, the *arithmetic-logical unit* (the ALU) may be recognized by its characteristic "V" shape. The accumulator register, which has been described in the previous section, is identified as A on the right input path of the ALU. It has been shown in the previous section that the accumulator should be equipped with a *buffer register*. This is the register labeled ACT (temporary accumulator). Here, the left input of the ALU is also equipped with a *temporary register*, called TMP. The operation of the ALU will become clear in the next section, where we will describe the execution of actual instructions.

The *flags register* is called "F" in the Z80, and is shown on the right of the accumulator register. The contents of the flags register are essentially conditioned by the ALU, but it will be shown that some of its bits may also be conditioned by other modules or events.

The accumulator and the flags registers are shown as double registers labeled respectively A, A′ and F, F′. This is because the Z80 is equipped internally with two sets of registers A + F, and A′ + F′. However, only *one* set of these registers may be used at any one time. A special instruction is provided to exchange the contents of A and F with A′ and F′. In order to simplify the explanations, only A and F will be shown on most of the diagrams which follow. The reader should remember that he has the option of switching to the alternate register set A′ and F′ if desired.

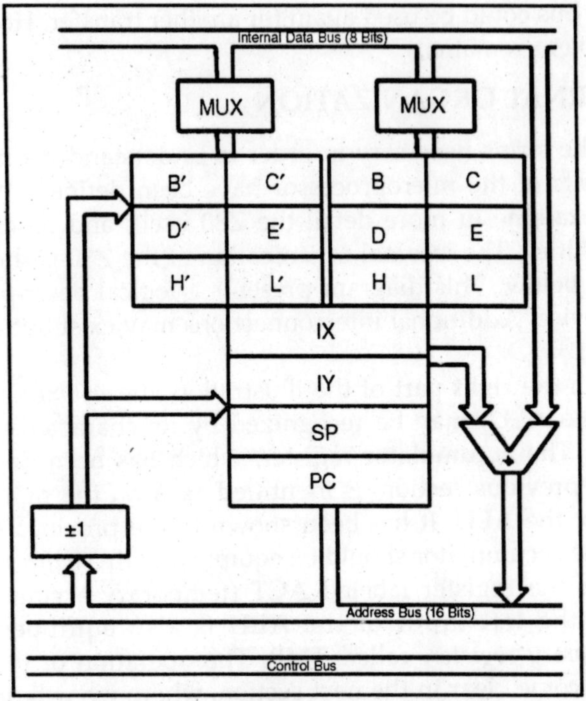

Fig. Center: Internal Z80 Organization (Register Block)

A large block of registers is shown at the center of the illustration. On top of the block of registers, two identical groups can be recognized. Each one includes six registers labeled B, C, D, E, H, L. These are the *general-purpose eight-bit registers* of the Z80. There are two peculiarities of the Z80 with respect to standard microprocessors which has been described. First, the Z80 is equipped with *two* banks of register, *i.e.,* two identical groups of 6 registers. Only six may be used at any one time. However, special instructions are provided to switch between the two banks of registers. One bank, therefore, behaves as an internal memory, while the other one behaves as a working set of internal registers. Conceptually, it will be assumed, for the time being, that there are only six working registers, B, C, D, E, H, and L, and the second register bank will temporarily be ignored, in order to avoid confusion. The MUX symbol which appears above the memory bank is an abbreviation for *multiplexer*. The data coming from the internal data bus will be gated through the multiplexer to the selected register. However, only one of these registers can be connected to the internal data bus at any one time.

A second characteristic of these six registers, in addition to being general-purpose eight-bit registers, is that they are equipped with a connection to the *address bus*. This is why they have been grouped in *pairs*. For example, the contents of B and C can be gated simultaneously onto the 16-bits address bus which appears at the bottom of the illustration. As a result, this group of 6 registers may be used to store either eight-bit data or else 16-bit *pointers* for memory addressing. The third group of registers, which appears below the two previous ones in the middle of figure above, contains four "pure" address registers. As in any microprocessor, we find the programme counter (PC) and the stack pointer (SP). Recall that the programme counter contains the address of the next instruction to be executed. The stack pointer points to the top of the stack in the memory. In the case of the Z80, the stack pointer points to the *last actual entry* in the stack. (In other microprocessors, the stack pointer points just above the last entry.) Also, the stack grows *"downwards"* i.e. towards the lower addresses.

This means that the stack pointer must be *decremented* any time a new word is *pushed* on the stack. Conversely, whenever a word is *removed* (popped) from the stack, the stack pointer must be *incremented* by one. In the case of the Z80, the "push" and "pop" always involve two words at the same time, so that the contents of the stack pointer will be decremented or incremented by two. Looking at the remaining two registers of this group of four registers, we find a new type of register which has not been described yet: two *index registers*, labeled IX (Index Register X) and IY (Index Register Y). These two registers are equipped with a special adder shown as a miniature V-shaped ALU on the right of these registers in Figure 2.14. A byte brought along the internal data bus may be added to the contents of IX or IY. This byte is called the *displacement,* when using an indexed instruction. Special instructions are provided which will automatically add this displacement to the contents of IX or IY and generate an address. Finally, a special box labeled "+/- 1" appears below and to the left of the block of registers. This is an increment/ decrement. The contents of any of the register pairs SP, PC, BC, DE, HL (the "pure address" registers) may be automatically incremented or decremented every time they deposit an address on the internal address bus. This is an essential facility for implementing automated *programme loops* which will be described in the next section. Using this feature it will be possible to access successive memory locations conveniently.

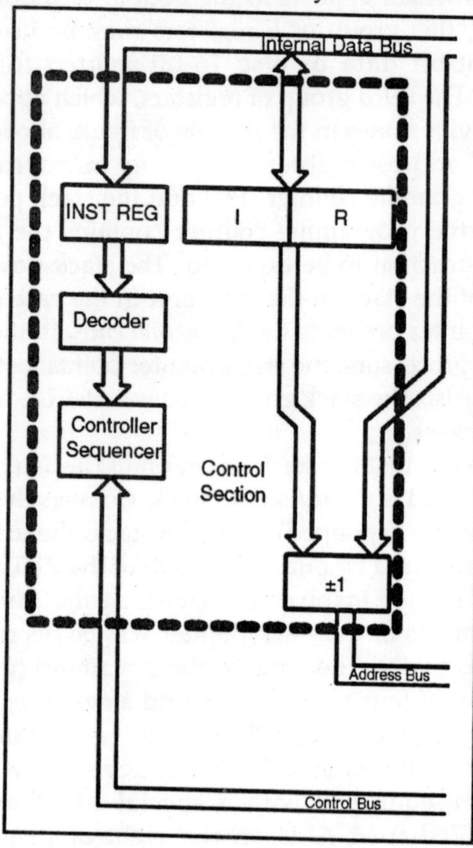

Fig. Left Side: Internal Z80 Organization (Control Section)

Let us move to the left side of the illustration. One register pair is shown, isolated on the left: I and R. The I register is called the *interrupt page address register*. It is used only in a special mode where an indirect call to a memory location is generated in response to an interrupt. The I register is used to store the high-order part of the indirect address. The lower part of the address is supplied by the device which generated the interrupt.

The R register is the *memory-refresh register*. It is provided to refresh dynamic memories automatically. Such a register has traditionally been located outside the microprocessor, since it is associated with the dynamic memory. It is a convenient feature which minimizes the amount of external hardware for some types of dynamic memories. It will not be used here for programming purposes, as it is essentially a hardware featurechniques" for a detailed description of memory refresh techniques). However, it is possible to use it as a software clock, for example.

Let us move now to the far left of the illustration. There the control section of the microprocessor is located. From top to bottom, we find first the *instruction register* IR, which will contain the instruction to be executed. The IR register is totally distinct from the "I, R" register pair described above. The instruction is received from the memory via the data bus, is transmitted along the internal data bus and is finally deposited into the instruction register. Below the instruction register appears the *decoder* which will send signals to the controller-sequencer and cause the execution of the instruction within the microprocessor and outside it. The *control ection* generates and manages the control bus which appears at the bottom part of the illustration.

The three buses managed or generated by the system, *i.e.*, the data bus, the address bus, and the control bus, propagate outside the microprocessor through its pins. The external connections are shown on the right-most part of the illustration. The buses are isolated from the outside through buffers shown in Figure above. All the logical elements in the Z80 have now been described. It is not essential to understand the detailed operation of the Z80 in order to start writing programmes. However, for the programmer who wishes to write efficient codes, the speed of a programme and its size will depend upon the correct choice of registers as well as the correct choice of techniques. To make a correct choice, it is necessary to understand how instructions are executed within the microprocessor. We will therefore examine here the execution of typical instructions inside the Z80 to demonstrate the role and use of the internal registers and buses.

INSTRUCTION FORMATS

The Z80 instructions may be formated in one, two, three or four bytes. An instruction specifies the operation to be performed by the microprocessor. From a simplified standpoint, every instruction may be represented as an opcode followed by an optional literal or address field, comprising one or two words. The opcode field specifies the operation to be carried out. In strict computer terminology, the opcode represents only those bits which specify the operation to be performed, exclusive of the register pointers which it might incorporate. In the microprocessor world, it is convenient to call opcode the operation code itself, as well as any register pointers which it might incorporate. This "generalized opcode" must reside in an eight-bit word for efficiency (this is the limiting factor on the number of instructions available in a microprocessor).

The 8080 uses instructions which may be one, two, or three bytes long. However, the Z80 is equipped with additional indexed instructions, which require one more byte. In the case of the Z80, opcodes are, in general, one byte long, except for special instructions which require a two-byte opcode. Some instructions require that one byte of data follow the opcode. In such a case, the instruction will be a two-byte instruction, the second byte of which is data (except for indexing, which adds an extra byte).

In other cases, the instruction might require the specification of an address. An address requires 16 bits and, therefore, two bytes. In that case, the instruction will be a three-byte or a four-byte instruction. For each byte of the instruction, the control unit will have to perform a memory fetch, which will require four clock cycles. The shorter the instruction, the faster the execution.

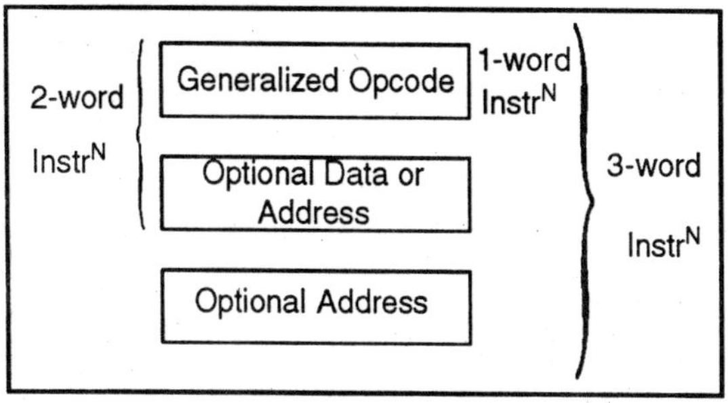

Fig. Typical Instruction Formats.

One-Word Instruction

One-word instructions are, in principle, fastest and are favored by the programmer. A typical such instruction for the Z80 is:

LD r,r′

This instruction means: "Transfer the contents of register r′ into r." This is a typical "register-to-register" operation. Every microprocessor must be equipped with such instructions, which allow the programmer to transfer information from any of the machine's registers into another one. Instructions referencing special registers of the machine, such as the accumulator or other special-purpose registers, may have a special opcode.

After execution of the above instruction, the contents of r will be equal to the contents of r′. The contents of r′ will *not* have been modified by the read operation.

Every instruction must be represented internally in a binary format. The above representation "LD r,r′ " is symbolic or *mnemonic*. It is called the *assembly-language*representation of an instruction. It is simply meant as a convenient symbolic representation of the actual binary encoding for that instruction. The binary code which will represent this instruction inside the memory is: 0 1 D D D S S S (bits 0 to 7).

This representation is still partially symbolic. Each of the letters S and D stands for a binary bit. The three D's, "D D D", represent the three bits pointing to the*destination* register. Three bits allow selection of one out of eight possible registers. The codes for these registers appear in Figure 2.16. For example, the code for register B is "0 0 0", the code for register C is "0 0 1", and so on.

Similarly, "S S S" represents the three bits pointing to the *source* register. The convention here is that register r′ is the source, and that register r is the destination. The placement of bits in the binary representation of an instruction is not meant for the convenience of the programmer, but for the convenience of the control section of the microprocessor, which must decode and execute the instruction. The *assembly-language* representation, however, is meant for the convenience of the programmer. It could be argued that LD r,r′ should really mean: "Transfer contents of r into r′." However, the convention has been chosen in order to maintain compatibility with the binary representation in this case. It is naturally arbitrary.

Two-Word Instruction

ADD A, n

This simple two-word instruction will add the contents of the second byte of the instruction to the accumulator. The contents of the second word of the instruction are said to be a "literal." They are data and are treated as eight bits without any particular significance. They could happen to be a character or numerical data. This is irrelevant to the operation.

The code for this instruction is:

- 1 1 0 0 0 1 1 0 followed by the 8-bit byte "n"

This is an *immediate* operation. "Immediate," in most programming languages, means that the next word, or words, within the instruction contains a piece of data which should not be *interpreted* (the way an opcode is). It means that the next one or two words are to be treated as a *literal*. The control unit is programmed to "know" how many words each instruction has. It will, therefore, always fetch and execute the right number of words for each instruction. However, the longer the possible number of words for the instruction, the more complex it is for the control unit to decode.

EXECUTION OF INSTRUCTIONS IN Z80

We have seen that all instructions are executed in three phases: fetch, decode, execute. We now need to introduce some definitions. Each of these phases will require several clock cycles. The Z80 executes each phase in one or more logical cycles, called a "machine cycle." The shortest machine cycle lasts three clock cycles. Accessing the memory requires three cycles for any operands, four clock cycles for the initial fetch. Since each instruction must be fetched first from memory, the fastest instruction will require four clock cycles. Each machine cycle is labeled M1, M2, etc., and will require three or more clock cycles, or "states," labeled T1, T2, etc.

FETCH Phase

The FETCH phase of an instruction is implemented during the first three states of machine cycle M1; they are called T1, T2, and T3. These three states are common to all instructions of the microprocessor, as all instructions must be fetched prior to execution. The FETCH mechanism is the following:

T1: PC OUT

The first step is to present the address of the next instruction to the memory. This address is contained in the programme counter (PC). As the first step of any instruction fetch, the contents of PC are placed on the address bus (see Figure below). At this point, an address is presented to the memory, and the memory address decoders will decode this address in order to select the appropriate location within the memory. Several hundred ns (a nanosecond is 10^{-9} second) will elapse before the contents of the selected memory location become available on the output pins of the memory, which are connected to the data bus.

6

Software Security

DESIGNING

The design of a piece of software is usually captured in some kind of document—all but the most trivial software projects benefit from good design documentation, particularly when there is more than one participant involved in the creation of the software.

The initial practice of designing software often focuses on creating work products that capture the desired requirements and specifications of the proposed software. There are many different approaches to software design, but most software will never reach a point where all of the desired requirements are met because the requirements will change and grow as soon as the software goes into use. So, software design is principally concerned with designing software that is expected to continuously evolve to meet an ever-changing list of requirements.

It is far easier to make sense of software design and development processes when this crucially important but subtle notion is grasped: good design is about creating software that can evolve and adapt over a long period of time and an indefinite number of versions, it is *not* chiefly concerned with creating a pristine finished product that is intended to remain untouched upon completion.

The first software was designed with a procedural paradigm in mind. The procedural paradigm envisions software simply as a list of instructions, usually contained across many files, to be executed. As computers became more powerful, programmes grew to a size that made this approach unmanageable without adopting designs specifying complex organizational procedures for keeping track of all of the files containing these instructions.

Since then, many programming paradigms have been envisioned, the most popular of which is the object oriented paradigm. Supporting the object oriented paradigm is the process of object oriented design, or OOD. OOD aims to design software such that it is broken up into manageable chunks called classes.

A class is a unit of code that contains information and defines behaviours that manage that information. In this way, the information managed by the class can only be changed by the outside world in the ways defined by the class.

The world outside that class need not understand the details of how such information must be manipulated; ensuring that the information is complete and consistent is managed within the class itself, greatly simplifying the task of working with that information for the outside world.

DESCRIPTION

The fundamental unit of an object oriented system is the class. A *class* is a set of data and the behaviours that operate upon that data. Each behaviour is captured in a method, which is a function associated with a class. A class defines a type of object that can exist within the system.

It is instructive to consider an example. An object is related to its class much in the same way a specific dog (let's call him Rover) is related to the class of all dogs. In the object oriented approach we say that Rover is an instance of a dog.

Similarly, we would refer to an object as an instance of a particular class. Just as Rover and Fido are two distinct instances of dogs, at any given time there may be many instances of a particular class existing in an object oriented system.

If we are designing an object oriented system designed to represent dogs, then, we would use this analogy to create a class called Dog. On this class we can define variables like hairColor, hairLength, eyeColor, weight, height, etc. We can also define behaviours that all dogs share such aseat(), sleep(), bark(), and run(). The behaviours we define may use the state stored in the variables to determine how to correctly carry out the behaviour (for instance, a large dog will eat more and bark louder than a small dog). When we instantiate, or create, a new dog we would initialize it with all the properties of the specific dog we wish to represent.

So, even though we'd have two instances of the Dog class in our system, fido and rover, they would exhibit the same behaviours in different ways based on their individual state. There are three principles fundamental to the definition of all object oriented software: encapsulation, inheritance, and polymorphism. We will discuss each in turn, but it's important to realise that all three principles work in combination to define a particular class.

The principle of *encapsulation* refers to the scope and visibility of state within a class. It is important for each class to define behaviours usable by the outside world in such a way that the internal state is not known outside the object, nor would it be necessary for that state to be known for objects of the class to serve a purpose within the system. Encapsulation goes hand-in-hand with the principle of information hiding, which says that any information that need not be known by outside agents should be hidden from view. In this way, the outside world sees only what it needs to see in order to use the object, simplifying its usage.

To use the example above, the eat() method of our Dog class might use a very complex algorithm based on the weight, height, and any other characteristics of that particular dog to calculate how much food it should eat when invoked. The outside world ought to regard the particular process used by the class with disinterest—it simply calls the eat() method and, from that outside perspective, the dog eats. *Inheritance* refers to a particular relationship that two or more classes can share. After we define our Dog class, we may wish to design some classes that represent particular breeds: German Shepherd, Pointer, and Retriever, for example. All of these are different kinds of dogs. As such, any behaviour or characteristic our more generic Dog class contains ought to also be contained by each of these classes. It would be a terrible waste of effort, however, to duplicate all of the work we've done defining those characteristics and behaviours on the Dog class. Furthermore, whenever we update such code shared by all dogs (such as when fixing a bug), we would have to apply the same update to all classes with copies of that same code.

Fortunately, because object oriented systems allow inheritance, we need not define the same functionality multiple times. We can simply say that the different breeds of dog extend or inherit from the Dog class, and instances of those classes automatically get all of the characteristics and behaviours defined on Dog. *Polymorphism* refers to a particular feature of classes that define an inheritance relationship. Above, we said that a Pointer is a specific kind of Dog, and therefore the Pointer class can extend the Dog class. Once this inheritance-type relationship is defined between these two classes, the outside world can treat any pointer specifically as a pointer, or it may also treat it more generally as simply a dog. When dealing with a particular instance, in fact, the outside world need not even know its dealing with a pointer. For example, if the Pointer class defines an additional behaviour unique to pointers, such as point(), when dealing with an instance of the Pointer class—let's call this particular dogpointy—we may invoke the point() method and observe Pointy point.

However, if we are only interested in requesting that Pointy do things that all dogs can do, such as eat() and sleep(), we may forget altogether that Pointy is in fact a Pointer and simply treat him just as though he were directly an instance of the Dog class. Polymorphism is the ability of objects to behave as though they are instances of a superclass.

OBJECT ORIENTED DESIGN

METHOD

The object-oriented approach to software development

extends and improves on traditional methods of system development. Object-oriented models effectively capture and communicate system requirements in a way that closely resembles the real world and which is extensible in response to change.

As part of learning such design techniques, students use elements of UML to describe how collections of collaborating objects, each with a well-defined and carefully-chosen set of responsibilities, can together realise the required behaviour of a software system under development. Students also learn how to express their software class discoveries using UML's class diagram and related notation.

Objectives:

- Analyse use cases and identify the important messages between external users and the internal software system;
- Design a collaboration of objects which implement these messages;
- Discover relevant software classes, including their attributes and methods which are part of an object of some class;
- Evaluate existing software class designs, identifying potential problems and possible solutions;
- Employ design heuristics, which give useful guidance in inventing good designs, as well as improving existing designs.

Includes:

- Review of domain class modeling and UML class diagrams.
- Introduction to Course Exercise (CE).
- Transforming use cases and domain models into working software: an overview.
- Discovering the important messages within a use case.
- Describing messages using a UML Sequence Diagram.
- Bridging the gap between analysis and design: responsibility-centered design of software classes.

- Some design guidance: the GRASP heuristics (General Responsibility Assignment Software Patterns) of C. Larman
- Core GRASP heuristics.
- Designing and diagramming a collaboration of objects.
- Designing with CRC Cards.
- Diagramming collaboration using UML Communication (Collaboration) Diagrams.
- Turning object collaborations into OO code.
- Other GRASP heuristics.
- Evaluating software designs.
- OO design heuristics
- Iterative development, software design, and design heuristics.
- Refactoring software designs
- Course review, summaries, and conclusions

DOWN AND BOTTOM DESIGN

OVERVIEW

Top-down and bottom-up are strategies of information processing and knowledge ordering, mostly involving software, but also other humanistic and scientific theories (see systemics). In practice, they can be seen as a style of thinking and teaching. In many cases *top-down*is used as a synonym of *analysis* or *decomposition,* and *bottom-up* of *synthesis*.

A top-down approach is essentially breaking down a system to gain insight into its compositional sub-systems. In a top-down approach an overview of the system is first formulated, specifying but not detailing any first-level subsystems. Each subsystem is then refined in yet greater detail, sometimes in many additional subsystem levels, until the entire specification is reduced to base elements.

A top-down model is often specified with the assistance of "black boxes", these make it easier to manipulate. However, black boxes may fail to elucidate elementary mechanisms or be detailed enough to realistically validate the model. A bottom-up approach is piecing together systems to give rise to grander systems, thus making the original systems subsystems of the emergent system.

In a bottom-up approach the individual base elements of the system are first specified in great detail. These elements are then linked together to form larger subsystems, which then in turn are linked, sometimes in many levels, until a complete top-level system is formed. This strategy often resembles a "seed" model, whereby the beginnings are small but eventually grow in complexity and completeness. However, "organic strategies" may result in a tangle of elements and subsystems, developed in isolation and subject to local optimization as opposed to meeting a global purpose.

Good engineering has a balance between top-down and bottom-up design, but there should generally be a bias towards top-down because your ultimate goal is to meet the system requirements which flow in at the top level. Bottom-up engineering is important to answer questions of technical feasibility or organisational capability, and ensure that the high level design decisions don't impose burdensome constraints on lower level components.

But too much bottom-up engineering can lead to missed requirements and the classic "integration problems" that occur when engineers realise too late in the process that the subcomponents aren't going to work together efficiently at the system level. While requirements flow down the system hierarchy, the balancing force is feasibility which flows back up to ensure that higher level design decisions don't result in downstream requirements which are excessively difficult or impossible to meet.

Including an experienced engineer on the design review team is often a more cost-effective way of answering questions of feasibility than bottom-up activities such as building a prototype or building an experimental ASIC. Engineers generally enjoy building things along the way during a large project, but bear in mind that the ultimate project goal is the final deliverables; all the throw-away prototypes and design revisions constructed along the way are simply steps towards that goal.

What counts is what the end customer gets. Multiple ASIC tape-outs, PCB revisions and software releases can simply point to an inefficient development process. Each of these has a cost associated with it, and only the final ASIC, PCB or software release actually gets delivered to the customer. Including design reviews in the process helps reduce the number of design iterations, prototypes and rework required to meet the end goal. In the Top-Down Model an overview of the system is formulated, without going into detail for any part of it. Each part of the system is then refined by designing it in more detail. Each new part may then be refined again, defining it in yet more detail until the entire specification is detailed enough to begin development.

By contrast in bottom-up design individual parts of the system are specified in detail, and may even be coded. The parts are then linked together to form larger components, which are in turn linked until a complete system is arrived at. Top down approaches emphasise planning, and a complete understanding of the system.

It is inherent that no coding can begin until a sufficient level of detail has been reached on at least some part of the system. Bottom up emphasises coding, which can begin as soon as the first module has been specified. However bottom-up coding runs the risk that modules may be coded without having a clear idea of how they link to other parts of the system, and that such linking may not be as easy as first thought.

Top-down design was promoted in the 1970s by IBM researcher Harlan Mills and by Nicklaus Wirth. Mills developed structured programming concepts for practical use and tested them in a 1969 project to automate the *New York Times* morgue index. The engineering and management success of this project led to the spread of the top-down approach through IBM and the rest of the computer industry.

Nicklaus Wirth, among other achievements the developer of Pascal programming language, wrote the influential paper

'Programme Development by Stepwise Refinement'. Top-down methods were favored in software engineeringuntil the rise of object-oriented programming in the late 1980s. Modern software design approaches usually combine both of these approaches. Although an understanding of the complete system is usually considered necessary for good design, leading theoretically to a top-down approach, most software projects attempt to make use of existing code to some degree. Pre-existing modules give designs a 'bottom-up' flavour. Some design approaches also use an approach where a partially-functional system is designed and coded to completion, and this system is then expanded to fulfill all the requirements for the project.

TECHNIQUES IN SOFTWARE DEVELOPMENT

Top-down approaches emphasize planning and a complete understanding of the system. It is inherent that no coding can begin until a sufficient level of detail has been reached in the design of at least some part of the system. The Top-Down Approach is done by attaching the stubs in place of the module.

This, however, delays testing of the ultimate functional units of a system until significant design is complete. Bottom-up emphasizes coding and early testing, which can begin as soon as the first module has been specified. This approach, however, runs the risk that modules may be coded without having a clear idea of how they link to other parts of the system, and that such linking may not be as easy as first thought.

The engineering and management success of this project led to the spread of the top-down approach through IBM and the rest of the computer industry. Among other achievements, Niklaus Wirth, the developer of Pascal programming language, wrote the influential paper *Programme Development by Stepwise Refinement*.

ince Niklaus Wirth went on to develop languages such as Modula and Oberon (where one could define a module before knowing about the entire programme specification), one can infer that top down programming was not strictly what he promoted. Top-down methods were favored in software engineering until the late 1980s, and object-oriented programming assisted in demonstrating the idea that both aspects of top-down and bottom-up programming could be utilized. Modern software design approaches usually combine both top-down and bottom-up approaches. Although an understanding of the complete system is usually considered necessary for good design, leading theoretically to a top-down approach, most software projects attempt to make use of existing code to some degree.

Pre-existing modules give designs a bottom-up flavour. Some design approaches also use an approach where a partially-functional system is designed and coded to completion, and this system is then expanded to fulfill all the requirements for the project

Programming

Top-down is a programming style, the mainstay of traditional procedural languages, in which design begins by specifying complex pieces and then dividing them into successively smaller pieces. Eventually, the components are specific enough to be coded and the programme is written. This is the exact opposite of the bottom-up programming approach which is common in object-oriented languages such as C++ or Java.

The technique for writing a programme using top-down methods is to write a main procedure that names all the major functions it will need. Later, the programming team looks at the requirements of each of those functions and the process is repeated. These compartmentalized sub-routines eventually will perform actions so simple they can be easily and concisely coded. When all the various sub-routines have been coded the programme is done.

By defining how the application comes together at a high level, lower level work can be self-contained. By defining how the lower level abstractions are expected to integrate into higher level ones, interfaces become clearly defined.

Top-down Approach

Practicing top-down programming has several advantages:

- Separating the low level work from the higher level abstractions leads to a modular design.
- Modular design means development can be self contained.
- Having "skeleton" code illustrates clearly how low level modules integrate.
- Fewer operations errors (to reduce errors, because each module has to be processed separately, so programmers get large amount of time for processing).
- Much less time consuming (each programmer is only involved in a part of the big project).
- Very optimized way of processing (each programmer has to apply their own knowledge and experience to their parts (modules), so the project will become an optimized one).
- Easy to maintain (if an error occurs in the output, it is easy to identify the errors generated from which module of the entire programme).

BOTTOM UP DESIGN

In accordance with this principle, a large programme must be divided into pieces, and the larger the programme, the more it must be divided. How do you divide a programme? The traditional approach is called *top-down design:* you say "the purpose of the programme is to do these seven things, so I divide it into seven major subroutines.

The first subroutine has to do these four things, so it in turn will have four of its own subroutines," and so on. This process continues until the whole programme has the right level of granularity— each part large enough to do something substantial, but small enough to be understood as a single unit. Experienced Lisp programmers divide up their programmes differently. As well as top-down design, they follow a principle which could be called *bottom-up design*— changing the language to suit the problem. In Lisp, you don't just write your programme down towards the language, you also build the language up towards your programme. As you're writing a programme you may think "I wish Lisp had such-and-such an operator." So you go and write it. Afterward you realise that using the new operator would simplify the design of another part of the programme, and so on.

Language and programme evolve together. Like the border between two warring states, the boundary between language and programme is drawn and redrawn, until eventually it comes to rest along the mountains and rivers, the natural frontiers of your problem. In the end your programme will look as if the language had been designed for it. And when language and programme fit one another well, you end up with code which is clear, small, and efficient.

It's worth emphasizing that bottom-up design doesn't mean just writing the same programme in a different order. When you work bottom-up, you usually end up with a different programme. Instead of a single, monolithic programme, you will get a larger language with more abstract operators, and a smaller programme written in it. Instead of a lintel, you'll get an arch.

In typical code, once you abstract out the parts which are merely bookkeeping, what's left is much shorter; the higher you build up the language, the less distance you will have to travel from the top down to it. This brings several advantages:

- By making the language do more of the work, bottom-up design yields programmes which are smaller and more agile. A shorter programme doesn't have to be divided into so many components, and fewer components means programmes which are easier to read or modify. Fewer components also means fewer connections between components, and thus less chance for errors there. As industrial designers strive to reduce the number of moving parts in a machine, experienced Lisp programmers use bottom-up design to reduce the size and complexity of their programmes.

- Bottom-up design promotes code re-use. When you write two or more programmes, many of the utilities you wrote for the first programme will also be useful in the succeeding ones. Once you've acquired a large substrate of utilities, writing a new programme can take only a fraction of the effort it would require if you had to start with raw Lisp.
- Bottom-up design makes programmes easier to read. An instance of this type of abstraction asks the reader to understand a general-purpose operator; an instance of functional abstraction asks the reader to understand a special-purpose subroutine.
- Because it causes you always to be on the lookout for patterns in your code, working bottom-up helps to clarify your ideas about the design of your programme. If two distant components of a programme are similar in form, you'll be led to notice the similarity and perhaps to redesign the programme in a simpler way.

Bottom-up design is possible to a certain degree in languages other than Lisp. Whenever you see library functions, bottom-up design is happening. However, Lisp gives you much broader powers in this department, and augmenting the language plays a proportionately larger role in Lisp style— so much so that Lisp is not just a different language, but a whole different way of programming. It's true that this style of development is better suited to programmes which can be written by small groups. However, at the same time, it extends the limits of what can be done by a small group. In *The Mythical Man-Month,* Frederick Brooks proposed that the productivity of a group of programmers does not grow linearly with its size. As the size of the group increases, the productivity of individual programmers goes down.

QUALITIES

In bottom-up organized organizations, *e.g.* ministries and their subordinate entities, decisions are prepared by experts in their fields, which define, out of their expertise, the policy they deem necessary. If they cannot agree, even on a compromise, they *escalate* the problem to the next higher hierarchy level, where a decision would be sought.

Finally, the highest common principal might have to take the decision. Information is in the debt of the inferior to the superior, which means that the inferior owes information to the superior. In the effect, as soon as inferiors agree, the head of the organization only provides his or her "face3 for the decision which their inferiors have agreed upon.Among several countries, the German political system provi des one of the purest forms of a bottom-up approach. The German Federal Act on the Public Service provides that any inferior has to consult and support any superiors, that he or she – only – has to follow "general guidelines" of the superiors, and that he or she would have to be fully responsible for any own act in office, and would have to follow a specific, formal complaint procedure if in doubt of the legality of an order.

The historical foundation of this approach lies with the fact that, in the 19th century, many politicians used to be noblemen without appropriate education, who more and more became forced to rely on consultation of educated experts, which (in particular after the Prussian reforms of Stein and Hardenberg) enjoyed the status of financially and personally independent, indismissable, and neutral experts as *Beamte* (public servants under public law).

A similar approach can be found in British police laws, where entitlements of police constables are vested in the constable in person and not in the police as an administrative agency, this leading to the single constable being fully responsible for his or her own acts in office, in particular their legality. The experience of two dictatorships in the country and, after the end of such regimes, emerging calls for the legal responsibility of the "aidees of the aidees" (*Helfershelfer*) of such regimes also furnished calls for the principle of personal responsibility of any expert for any decision made, this leading to a strengthening of the bottom-up approach, which requires maximum responsibility of the superiors. In the opposite, the French administration is based on a top-down approach, where regular public servants enjoy no other task than simply to execute decisions made by their superiors. As those superiors also require consultation, this consultation is provided by members of a *cabinet*, which is distinctive from the regular ministry staff in terms of staff and organization.

Those members who are not members of the *cabinet* are not entitled to make any suggestions or to take any decisions of political dimension. The advantage of the bottom-up approach is the great level of expertise provided, combined with the motivating experience of any member of the administration to be responsible and finally the independent "engine" of progress in that field of personal responsibility. A disadvantage is the lack of democratic control and transparency, this leading, from a democratic viewpoint, to the deferment of actual power of policy-making to faceless, if even unknown, public servants.

Even the fact that certain politicians might "provide their face" to the actual decisions of their inferiors might not mitigate this effect, but rather strong parliamentary rights of control and influence in legislative procedures (as they do exist in the example of Germany). The advantage of the top-bottom principle is that political and administrative responsibilities are clearly distinguished from each other, and that responsibility for political failures can be clearly identified with the relevant office holder.

Disadvantages are that the system triggers demotivation of inferiors, who know that their ideas to innovative approaches might not be welcome just because of their position, and that the decision-makers cannot make use of the full range of expertise which their inferiors will have collected. Administrations in *dictatorships* traditionally work according to a strict top-down approach.

As civil servants below the level of the political leadership are discouraged from making suggestions, they use to suffer from the lack of expertise which could be provided by the inferiors, which regularly leads to a breakdown of the system after an few decades. Modern communist states, which the People's Republic of Chinaforms an example of, therefore prefer to define a framework of permissible, or even encouraged, criticism and self-determination by inferiors, which would not affect the major state doctrine, but allows the use of professional and expertise-driven knowledge and the use of it for the decision-making persons in office.

SOFTWARE MEASUREMENT

The measurement information model is a structure linking information needs to the relevant entities and attributes of concern. Entities include processes, products, projects, and resources. The measurement information model describes how the relevant attributes are quantified and converted to indicators that provide a basis for decision-making.

The selection or definition of appropriate measures to address an information need begins with a measurable concept: an idea of which measurable attributes are related to an information need and how they are related. The measurement planner defines measurement constructs that link these attributes to a specifiedinformation need. Each construct may involve several types or levels of measures.

ENTITY

An entity is an object (for example, a process, product, project, or resource) that is to be characterized by measuring its attributes. Typical software engineering objects can be classified as products (*e.g.*, design document, source code, and test case), processes (*e.g.*, design process, testing process, requirements analysis process), projects, and resources (*e.g.*, the programmers and the testers). An entity may have one or more properties that are of interest to meet the information needs. In practice, an entity can be classified into more than one of the above categories.

MEASURABLE ATTRIBUTE

An attribute is a property or characteristic of an entity that can be distinguished quantitatively or qualitatively by human or automated means. An entity may have many attributes, only some of which may be of interest for measurement. The first step in defining a specific instantiation of the measurement information model is to select the attributes that are most relevant to the measurement user's information needs. A given attribute may be incorporated in multiple measurement constructs supporting different information needs.

BASE MEASURE

A base measure is an attribute and the method for quantifying it. A base measure is functionally independent of other measures. A base measure captures information about a single attribute. Data collection involves assigning values to base measures. Specifying the expected range and/or type of values of a base measure helps to verify the quality of the data collected.

Measurement Method

A measurement method is a logical sequence of operations, described generically, used in quantifying an attribute with respect to a specified scale. The operations may involve activities such as counting occurrences or observing the passage of time. The same measurement method may be applied to multiple attributes. However, each unique combination of an attribute and a method produces a different base measure. Some measure-ment methods may be implemented in multiple ways. A measurement procedure describes the specific implemen-tation of a measurement method within a given organizatio-nal context.

Type of Measurement Method

The type of measurement method depends on the nature of the operations used to quantify an attribute.

Two types of method may be distinguished:

1. *Subjective*: Quantification involving human judgment
2. *Objective*: Quantification based on numerical rules such as counting. These rules may be implemented via human or automated means.

Scale

A scale is an ordered set of values, continuous or discrete, or a set of categories to which the attribute is mapped. The measurement method maps the magnitude of the measured attribute to a value on a scale. A unit of measurement often is associated with a scale.

Type of Scale

The type of scale depends on the nature of the relationship between values on the scale.

Four types of scales are commonly defined:

1. *Nominal*: The measurement values are categorical. For example, the classification of defects by their type.
2. *Ordinal*: The measurement values are rankings. For example, the assignment of defects to a severity level.
3. *Interval*: The measurement values have equal distances corresponding to equal quantities of the *attribute*. For example, cyclomatic complexity has the minimum value of one, but each increment represents an additional path.
4. *Ratio:* The measurement values have equal distances corresponding to equal quantities of the *attribute* where the value of zero corresponds to none of the*attribute*. For example, the size of a software component in terms of LOC.

The method of measurement usually affects the type of *scale* that can be used reliably with a given *attribute*. For example, subjective methods of measurement usually only support ordinal or nominal scales.

Unit of Measurement

A unit of measurement is a particular quantity, defined and adopted by convention, with which other quantities of the same kind are compared in order to express their magnitude relative to that quantity. Only quantities expressed in the same units of measurement are directly comparable. Example of units include the hour and the meter.

DERIVED MEASURE

A derived measure is a measure that is defined as a

function of two or more base measures. Derived measures capture information about more than oneattribute. Simple transformations of base measures (for example, taking the square root of a base measure) do not add information, thus do not produce derived measures. Normalization of data often involves converting base measures into derived measures that can be used to compare different entities.

Measurement Function

A measurement function is an algorithm or calculation performed to combine two or more base measures. The scale and unit of the derived measure depend on the scales and units of the base measures from which it is composed as well as how they are combined by the function.

INDICATOR

An indicator is an estimate or evaluation of specified attributes derived from a model with respect to defined information needs. Indicators are the basis for analysis and decision-making. These are what should be presented to measurement users.

Measurement is always based on imperfect information, so quantifying the uncertainty, accuracy, or importance of indicators is an essential component of presenting the actual indicator value. Therefore, an interpretation of indicators is performed to provide the desired information product.

A measurement model is an algorithm or calculation combining one or more base and/or derived measures with associated decision criteria. It is based on an understanding of, or assumptions about, the expected relationship between the component measures and/or their behaviour over time. Models produce estimates or evaluations relevant to defined information needs. The scale and measurement method affect the choice of analysis techniques or models used to produceindicators. Decision criteria are numerical thresholds or targets used to determine the need for action or further investigation, or to describe the level of confidence in a given result. Decision criteria help to interpret the results of measurement. Decision criteria may be calculated or based on a conceptual understanding of expected behaviour. Decision criteria may be derived from historical data, plans, and heuristics, or computed as statistical control limits or statistical confidence limits.

MEASURABLE CONCEPT

A measurable concept is an abstract relationship between attributes of entities and information needs. For example, an Information need may be the need to compare the software development productivity of a project group against a target rate. The Measurable Concept in this case is "software development productivity rate". To evaluate the concept might require measuring the size of the software products and the amount of resource applied to create the products (depending on the chosen model of productivity). Additional examples of Measurable Concepts include quality, risk, performance, capability, maturity, and customer value.

SOFTWARE METRICS

Effective management of any process requires quantification, measurement, and modeling. Software metrics provide a quantitative basis for the development and validation of models of the software development process. Metrics can be used to improve software productivity and quality. This module introduces the most commonly used software metrics and reviews their use in constructing models of the software development process.

Although current metrics and models are certainly inadequate, a number of organizations are achieving promising results through their use. Results should improve further as we gain additional experience with various metrics and oftware metrics are numerical data related to software development. Metrics strongly support software project management activities.

A metric quantifies a characteristic of a process or product. Metrics can be directly observable quantities or can be derived from one or more directly observable quantities.

Examples of raw metrics include the number of source lines of code, number of documentation pages, number of staff-hours, number of tests, number of requirements, etc. Examples of derived metrics include source lines of code per staff-hour, defects per thousand lines of code, or a cost performance index. The term *indicator* is used to denote a representation of metric data that provides insight into an ongoing software development project or process improvement activity. Indicators are metrics in a form suitable for assessing project behaviour or process improvement. For example, an indicator may be the behaviour of a metric over time or the ratio of two metrics.

Indicators may include the comparison of actual values versus the plan, project stability metrics, or quality metrics. Examples of indicators used on a project include actual versus planned task completions, actual versus planned staffing, number of trouble reports written and resolved over time, and number of requirements changes over time. Indicators are used in conjunction with one another to provide a more complete picture of project or organization behaviour. For example, a progress indicator is related to requirements and size indicators. All three indicators should be used and interpreted together.

METRICS SET

The metrics to be collected provide indicators that track ongoing project progress, software products, and software development processes. Depending upon the nature of the project, specific contractual requirements, or management preference, a project may choose to collect additional metrics or to tailor the recommended set.

CHART CONSTRUCTION

Charts are prepared for the standard metrics. All charts require titles, legends, and labels for all axes. They should clearly and succinctly show the metrics of interest, with no excessive detail to detract the eye. Do not overuse different line types, patterns, or colour, or added dimensionality unless used specifically to differentiate items. Overlayed data is preferable to multiple charts when the different data are related to each other and can be meaningfully depicted without obscuring other details.

The most common type of chart is the tracking chart. This chart is used extensively for the Progress indicator, and is used in similar forms for many of the other indicators. For task progress, it depicts the cumulative number of planned and actual task completions (or milestones) against time. For other indicators, it may show actual versus planned staffing profiles, actual versus planned software size, actual versus planned resource utilization or other measures compared over time. There are many ways to modify the tracking chart. A horizontal planned line representing the cumulative goal can be drawn at the top, multiple types of tasks can be overlaid on a single tracking chart (such as design, code, and integration), or the chart can be overlaid with other types of data. It is recommended that tracked quantities be shown as a line chart, and that replanned task progress be shown as a separate planning line. The original planned baseline is kept on the chart, as well as all replanning data if there is more than a single replan.

PROGRESS

Progress indicators provide information on how well the project is performing with respect to planned task completions and keeping schedule commitments. Tasks are scheduled and then progress is tracked to the schedules. Metrics are collected for the activities and milestones identified in the project schedules. Metrics on actual completions are compared to those of planned completions to determine whether there are deviations to the plan. The difference between the actual and planned completions indicates the deviations from the plan.

Each project identifies tasks for which progress metrics will be collected. The completion criteria for each task must be well defined and measurable. The project should establish range limits (thresholds) on the planned task progress for the project. The thresholds are used for management of software development risk.

EFFORT

Effort indicators allow the software manager to track personnel resources. They provide visibility into the contribution of staffing to project costs, schedule adherence, product quality and the amount of effort required for each activity. Effort indicators include trends in actual staffing levels, staffing profile by activity or labour category, or a profile of unplanned staff loses.

Effort indicators may be used by all levels of project software management to measure the actual profile against the plan. Each level of management forms a profile for its area of control and monitors the actual profile against the plan. Determining the number of staff needed at any one time is an important function performed by software management. By summing the number of staff during each reporting period, the composite staffing profile for the project can be determined. These indicators are applied during all life-cycles phases, from project inception to project end. Effort metrics are to be collected and reported at least on a monthly basis.

The effort and cost metrics are related. By convention, effort metrics are non-cumulative expenditures of human resources, and cost metrics are cumulative levels of effort as tracked by earned value. Thus, cost metrics are a cumulative depiction of effort.

REVIEW RESULTS

Review Results indicators provide insight into the status of action items from life-cycle reviews. The term Action Item (AI) refers to inspection defects and customer comments. Reviews include the following:

- Formal inspections of software documents or code
- Formal customer milestones, *e.g.*, SSR, PDR, CDR, or TRR
- Informal peer evaluations of products, *e.g.*, walkthroughs, technical reviews, or internal PDRs
- Management reviews
- Process reviews, *e.g.*, SQA audits, SEI CMM assessments, or the causal analysis from formal inspections.

There are standards for some reviews, as well as procedures for conducting them. For example, formal inspections result in assertion logs that document the minor and major defects uncovered by the inspection process. A customer-conducted review such as a Preliminary Design Review (PDR) generates AIs that must be closed before approval of the Software Design Document. Therefore, standard review result indicators for a PDR are the number of comments written and their status (open, closed, and age).

Review metrics record the AIs identified in the review findings and track them until they are resolved. These metrics provide status on both products and processes. Review results are not to be used to evaluate the performance of individuals.

Review Results are collected and reported at least monthly at every stage of the software life cycle, but preferably weekly for key AIs.

TROUBLE REPORTS

TR indicators provide managers with insight into the quality of the product, software reliability, and the effectiveness of testing. They also provide information on the software development process. The terms defect and problem will be used interchangeably herein.

TR indicators are applicable only in the following life cycle stages (and each release of the software within these stages, and during the informal and formal test segments of these stages)

- Application test and integration,
- System test,
- Acceptance test.

Thus the TR indicators are applicable only to defects during the operation or execution of a computer programme. Due to the shortness of testing periods, and the dynamics involved between the test team and the implementation team that analyses the TRs and fixes the defects, the TR indicators are generally evaluated on a weekly basis.

The terms open *and* closed *are defined as follows:* Open The problem has been reported. Closed The investigation is complete and the action required to resolve the problem has been proposed, implemented, and verified to the satisfaction of all concerned. In some cases, a TR will be found to be invalid as part of the investigative process and closed immediately.

REQUIREMENTS STABILITY

Requirements Stability provides an indication of the completeness, stability, and understanding of the requirements. It indicates the number of changes to the requirements and the amount of information needed to complete the requirements definition. A lack of requirements stability can lead to poor product quality, increased cost, and schedule slippage.

Requirements stability indicators are in the form of trend charts that show the total number of requirements, cumulative changes to the requirements, and the number of TBDs over time. A TBD refers to an undefined requirement. Based on requirements stability trends, corrective action may be necessary.

Requirements stability is applicable during all life-cycles phases, from project inception to the end. The requirements stability indicators are most important during requirements and design phases. Requirements stability metrics are collected and reported on a monthly basis.

SIZE STABILITY

Software size is a critical input to project planning. The size estimate and other factors are used to derive effort and schedule before and during a project. The software manager tracks the actual versus planned software product size. Various indicators show trends in the estimated code size, trends by code type, the variation of actual software size from estimates or the size variation by release.

Size stability is derived from changes in the size estimate as time goes on. It provides an indication of the completeness and stability of the requirements, the understanding of the requirements, design thoroughness and stability, and the capability of the software development staff to meet the current budget and schedule. Size instability may indicate the need for corrective action. Size metrics are applicable during all life-cycle phases. Size metrics are collected and reported on a monthly basis, or more often as necessary.

COMPUTER RESOURCE UTILIZATION

Computer Resource Utilization indicators show whether the software is using the planned amount of system resources. The computer resources are normally CPU time, I/O, and memory. For some software, the constraints of computer resources significantly affect the design, implementation, and testing of the product. They can also be used to replan, re-estimate, and guide resource acquisition.

Computer resource utilization is planned during the requirements activity and reviewed during the design activity. Resources are monitored from the start of implementation activity to the end of the life cycle.

For memory utilization, the unit of data is the byte, word, or half-word. For CPU time, the unit of data is either MIPS (millions of instructions per second), or the percentage of CPU time used during a peak period. For I/O time, the unit of data is the percentage of I/O time used during a peak period.

Resource Utilization data is collected and reported at least monthly, with the period between collection and reporting becoming shorter as the software system nears completion and a better picture of software performance can be seen. Note that the resource utilization is normally an estimate until integration occurs, at which time the actual data is available.

TRAINING

Training indicators provide managers with information on the training programme and whether the staff has necessary skills. A trained staff is a commitment. The manager must ensure that the staff has the skills needed to perform their assigned tasks. The objective of the training indicator is to provide visibility into the training process, to ensure effective utilization of training, and to provide project software managers with an indication of their staff's skill mixture. The manager should investigate the deviations in the number of classes taught from the number of classes planned, and the deviation of the number of staff taught to the planned number. The quality of the training programme should also be determined from completed course evaluation sheets. The number of waivers requested and approved for training should also be tracked.

HALSTEAD'S SOFTWARE SCIENCE

Maurice Halstead's approach relied on his fundamental assumption that a programme should be viewed as an expression of language. His work was based on studying the complexities of languages — both programming and written languages. Halstead found what he believed were mathematically sound relationships among the number of variables, the type of programming language statements and the complexity of the code. He attacked part of the first and second reasons a programmer might find code complex.

The idea is that if you compute these variables and find that the programme level is not close to 1, the code may be too complex. You should look for ways to "tighten" the code. Halstead's work is sweeping, covering topics such as computing the optimal number of modules, predicting programme errors and computing the amount of time required for a programmer to implement an algorithm.

PROBLEMS

Halstead's groundbreaking work is criticized on several fronts. Some find fault with his methodology for deriving some mathematical relationships. Others find fault with some of his assumptions. For example, Halstead used a number called the Stroud number (ranging from five to 20), which represents how many elementary discriminations the human brain can perform in a "moment."

Another "fact" is that Halstead postulated the human brain can handle up to five chunks of material simultaneously. Many find equations derived on these assumptions represent very wishful thinking. Another difficulty with the Halstead metrics is that they are difficult to compute. How do you easily count the distinct and total operators and operands in a programme? Imagine counting these quantities every time you made a significant change to a programme. A metric is useless if you can't compute it quickly and easily.

Halstead stated that the lower the programme level, the more complex the programme. Unfortunately, he went no further. Is a programme with level.100 complex? How about one with level.005? All you can do is compare versions of the same programme and compare their programme levels. Recall that the McCabe metric gives an upper limit of 10 for complexity.

The computation of the Halstead metrics for the bubble sort suggest that the bubble sort, as implemented, is very complex. The problem is that the computation for the potential volume mandates the number of input and output parameters. For the bubble sort, only the array to be sorted is needed. The low number for the potential volume skews the programme and language levels.

STATE OF SOFTWARE

Code-level complexity measures have met with mixed success. Although their assumptions have an intuitively sound basis, they are not that good at predicting error rates or cost. Some studies have shown that both McCabe and Halstead do no better at predicting error rates and cost than simple lines-of-code measurements.

Some researchers use McCabe's and Halstead's work as a starting point. For example, Albrecht and Gafffney used some of Halstead's work to derive function points and code size based on operand count. Hansen suggests incorporating both cyclomatic complexity and software science. (Refer to "Measurement of Programme Complexity by the Pair-Cyclomatic Number, Operator Count," ACM SIGPLAN). Some researchers have incorporated several code complexity measurements into design complexity measurement schemes. There is no silver-bullet formula or methodology that yields exact results for software complexity. Studies that attempt to correlate error rates with computed complexity measures show mixed results. Some studies show that experienced programmers provide the best prediction of error rates and software complexity.

USING SOFTWARE

A popular use of the McCabe metric is for testing. McCabe himself cited software testing as a primary use for his metric. The cyclomatic complexity of code gives a lower limit for the number of test cases required for code coverage. Any shop serious about using complexity measurements must actively collect software metrics. With the change of century rapidly approaching, programmers must examine and change plenty of code. Many shops are looking at re-engineering some code because of the work mandated by the century change.

FUNCTION POINT

INTRODUCTION

Function Points and the Function Point Model are measurement tools to manage software. Function Points, with other business measures, become Software Metrics. Function Points measure Software size. Function Points measure functionality by objectively measuring functional requirements.

Function Points quantify and document assumptions in Estimating software development. Function Points and Function Point Analysis are objective; Function Points are consistent, and Function Points are auditable. Function Points are independent of technology.

Function Points even apply regardless of design. But Function Points do not measure people directly. Function Points is a macro tool, not a micro tool. Function Points are the foundation of a Software Metrics programme. Software Metrics include Function Points as a normalizing factor for comparison.Function Points in conjunction with time yield Productivity Software Metrics. Function Points in conjunction with defects yield Quality Software Metrics. Function Points with costs provide Unit Cost, Return on Investment, and Efficiency Software Metrics, never before available.

Function Points connect Software Metrics to measure Risk. Function Points can verify Staffing metrics. Function Points can evaluate Build, Buy and/or Outsource decisions. Function Points combine with SEI CMM measures, TQM measures, Baldrige measures, ISO and/or other software and business measures to prove overall status and value.

DOING THE RIGHT THINGS!

Function Points and Usage or Volume measures create Software Metrics that demonstrate an organization's ability to Leverage software's business impact. The Leverage of E Commerce is obvious, but until now unmeasured. Function Points support Customer Satisfaction measures to create Value Software Metrics.

Function Points and Skill measures provide Software Metrics for Employee Service Level Agreements to meet current and future company skill needs. Function Points can even measure the Corporate Vision and generate Software Metrics to report progress towards meeting it.

Function Points, Function Point Analysis, the Function Point Model, Supplemental Software Measures, and the Software Metrics they generate, are only the third measure that transcend every part of every organization. (The other two are time and money.) Without them your organization is only two thirds whole.

DEFINITION

A function point is a unit of measurement to express the amount of business functionality an information system provides to a user. Function points are the units of measure used by the IFPUG Functional Size Measurement Method. The IFPUG FSM Method is an ISO recognized software metric to size an information system based on the functionality that is perceived by the user of the information system, independent of the technology used to implement the information system. Function points were defined in 1979 in New Way of Looking at Tools by Allan Albrecht at IBM. The functional user requirements of the software are identified and each one is categorized into one of five types: outputs, inquiries, inputs, internal files, and external interfaces. Once the function is identified and categorized into a type, it is then assessed for complexity and assigned a number of function points. Each of these functional user requirements maps to an end-user business function, such as a data entry for an Input or a user query for an Inquiry. This distinction is important because it tends to make the functions measured in function points map easily into user-oriented requirements, but it also tends to hide internal functions (e.g. algorithms), which also require resources to implement. Over the years there have been different approaches proposed to deal with this perceived weakness, however there is no ISO recognized FSM Method that includes algorithmic complexity in the sizing result.

EXTERNAL INTERFACE FILES

The second Data Function a system provides an end user is also related to logical groupings of data. In this case the user is not responsible for maintaining the data. The data resides in another system and is maintained by another user or system. The user of the system being counted requires this data for reference purposes only. For example, it may be necessary for a pilot to reference position data from a satellite or ground-based facility during flight. The pilot does not have the responsibility for updating data at these sites but must reference it during the flight. Groupings of data from another system that are used only for reference purposes are defined as External Interface Files (EIF).

The remaining functions address the user's capability to access the data contained in ILFs and EIFs. This capability includes maintaining, inquiring and outputting of data. These are referred to as Transactional Functions.

EXTERNAL INPUT

The first Transactional Function allows a user to maintain

Internal Logical Files (ILFs) through the ability to add, change and delete the data. For example, a pilot can add, change and delete navigational information prior to and during the mission. In this case the pilot is utilizing a transaction referred to as an External Input (EI). An External Input gives the user the capability to maintain the data in ILF's through adding, changing and deleting its contents.

EXTERNAL OUTPUT

The next Transactional Function gives the user the ability to produce outputs. For example a pilot has the ability to separately display ground speed, true air speed and calibrated air speed. The results displayed are derived using data that is maintained and data that is referenced. In function point terminology the resulting display is called an External Output (EO).

EXTERNAL INQUIRIES

The final capability provided to users through a computerized system addresses the requirement to select and display specific data from files. To accomplish this a user inputs selection information that is used to retrieve data that meets the specific criteria. In this situation there is no manipulation of the data. It is a direct retrieval of information contained on the files. For example if a pilot displays terrain clearance data that was previously set, the resulting output is the direct retrieval of stored information. These transactions are referred to as External Inquiries (EQ).

In addition to the five functional components described above there are two adjustment factors that need to be considered in Function Point Analysis.

FUNCTIONAL COMPLEXITY

The first adjustment factor considers the Functional Complexity for each unique function. Functional Complexity is determined based on the combination of data groupings and data elements of a particular function. The number of data elements and unique groupings are counted and compared to a complexity matrix that will rate the function as low, average or high complexity. Each of the five functional components (ILF, EIF, EI, EO and EQ) has its own unique complexity matrix.

VALUE ADJUSTMENT FACTOR

The Unadjusted Function Point count is multiplied by the second adjustment factor called the Value Adjustment Factor. This factor considers the system's technical and operational characteristics and is calculated by answering 14 questions. The factors are:

Data Communications

The data and control information used in the application are sent or received over communication facilities.

Distributed Data Processing

Distributed data or processing functions are a characteristic of the application within the application boundary.

Performance

Application performance objectives, stated or approved by the user, in either response or throughput, influence (or will influence) the design, development, installation and support of the application.

Heavily Used Configuration

A heavily used operational configuration, requiring special design considerations, is a characteristic of the application.

Transaction Rate

The transaction rate is high and influences the design, development, installation and support.

On-line Data Entry

On-line data entry and control information functions are provided in the application.

End -User Efficiency

The on-line functions provided emphasize a design for end-user efficiency.

On-line Update

The application provides on-line update for the internal logical files.

Complex Processing

Complex processing is a characteristic of the application.

Reusability

The application and the code in the application have been specifically designed, developed and supported to be usable in other applications.

Installation Ease

Conversion and installation ease are characteristics of the application. A conversion and installation plan and/or conversion tools were provided and tested during the system test phase.

Operational Ease

Operational ease is a characteristic of the application. Effective start-up, backup and recovery procedures were provided and tested during the system test phase.

Multiple Sites

The application has been specifically designed, developed and supported to be installed at multiple sites for multiple organizations.

Facilitate Change

The application has been specifically designed, developed and supported to facilitate change. Each of these factors is scored based on their influence on the system being counted. The resulting score will increase or decrease the Unadjusted Function Point count by 35%. This calculation provides us with the Adjusted Function Point count.

APPROACH TO COUNTING FUNCTION POINTS

There are several approaches used to count function points. Q/P Management Group, Inc. has found that a structured workshop conducted with people who are knowledgeable of the functionality provided through the application is an efficient, accurate way of collecting the necessary data.

The workshop approach allows the counter to develop a representation of the application from a functional perspective and educate the participants about function points. Function point counting can be accomplished with minimal documentation. However, the accuracy and efficiency of the counting improves with appropriate documentation.

Benefits of Function Point Analysis

Organizations that adopt Function Point Analysis as a software metric realise many benefits including: improved project estimating; understanding project and maintenance productivity; managing changing project requirements; and gathering user requirements. Each of these is discussed below.

Estimating software projects is as much an art as a science. While there are several environmental factors that need to be considered in estimating projects, two key data points are essential. The first is the size of the deliverable. The second addresses how much of the deliverable can be produced within a defined period of time.

Size can be derived from Function Points, as described above. The second requirement for estimating is determining how long it takes to produce a function point. This delivery rate can be calculated based on past project performance or by using industry benchmarks.

The delivery rate is expressed in function points per hour (FP/Hr) and can be applied to similar proposed projects to estimate effort (*i.e.* Project Hours = estimated project function points FP/Hr). Productivity measurement is a natural output of Function Points Analysis. Since function points are technology independent they can be used as a vehicle to compare productivity across dissimilar tools and platforms. More importantly, they can be used to establish a productivity rate (i.e. FP/Hr) for a specific tool set and platform. Once productivity rates are established they can be used for project estimating as described above and tracked over time to determine the impact continuous process improvement initiatives have on productivity.

In addition to delivery productivity, function points can be used to evaluate the support requirements for maintaining systems. In this analysis, productivity is determined by calculating the number of function points one individual can support for a given system in a year (*i.e.* FP/FTE year). When compared with other systems, these rates help to identify which systems require the most support. The resulting analysis helps an organization develop a maintenance and replacement strategy for those systems that have high maintenance requirements.

Managing Change of Scope for an in-process project is another key benefit of Function Point Analysis. Once a project has been approved and the function point count has been established, it becomes a relatively easy task to identify, track and communicate new and changing requirements.

As requests come in from users for new displays or capabilities, function point counts are developed and applied against the rate. This result is then used to determine the impact on budget and effort. The user and the project team can then determine the importance of the request against its impact on budget and schedule.

At the conclusion of the project the final function point count can be evaluated against the initial estimate to determine the effectiveness of requirements gathering techniques. This analysis helps to identify opportunities to improve the requirements definition process.

Communicating Functional Requirements was the original objective behind the development of function points. Since it avoids technical terminology and focuses on user requirements it is an excellent vehicle to communicate with users. The techniques can be used to direct customer interviews and document the results of Joint Application Design (JAD) sessions. The resulting documentation provides a framework that describes user and technical requirements. In conclusion, Function Point Analysis has proven to be an accurate technique for sizing, documenting and communicating a system's capabilities. It has been successfully used to evaluate the functionality of real-time and embedded code systems, such as robot based warehouses and avionics, as well as traditional data processing.

CYCLOMATIC MEASURES

DESCRIPTION

Cyclomatic complexity measures the amount of decision logic in a single software module. It gives the number of recommended test for software.

Cyclomatic complexity is based entirely on the structure of software's control flow graph.

- *Control flow graph*: Control flow graphs describe the logic structure of software module.

Each flow consists of nodes and edges.

- *Nodes*: computation statements or expresions.
- *Edges*: represent transfer of control between nodes.

Each possible execution path of a software module has a corresponding path from the entry to the exit node of the module's control flow graph.

FROM LINEAR ALGEBRA

Rank of a matrix: number of linear independent rows. Each matrix has an unique rank that is less than or equal to the number of columns. The minimal set of vectors with maximum rank is known as a basis,and a basis can also be described as a linear independent set of vectors that generate all the vectors in the space by linear combination.

Considering any set of paths gives a matrix in which the columns correspond to edges and the rows correspond to paths. The maximum value of rank of this matrix is exactly the c.c. of the graph. This means that the c.c. is the number of paths in any independent set of paths that generate all possible paths by linear combination.

There are a few important points to note about the linear algebra of control flow graphs:

1. Each basis set has the same number of paths in it (c.c.), but there is no restriction on the number of different sets of basis paths,it means it is possible to have considerable freedom in selecting a basis set of paths to testing.
2. Although every path has corresponding vector, not every vector has a correcponding path.
3. Linear combination vectors of vectors that correspond to actual paths may be vectors that do not correspond to actual paths.

COMPLEXITY COMPUTATION Y

Initialization Analysis

The X server is the first application to run that is involved with direct rendering. After initializing its own resources, it starts the kernel device driver and waits for clients to connect. Then, when a direct rendering client connects, SAREA is created, the XFree86-GLX protocol is established, and other direct rendering resources are allocated. This section describes the operations necessary to bring the system to a steady state.

X Server Initialization

When the X server is started, several resources in both the X server and the kernel must be initialized if the GLX module is loaded.

Obviously, before the X server can do anything with the 3D graphics device, it will load the GLX module if it is specified in the XFree86 configuration file. When the GLX module (which contains the GLX protocol decoding and event handling routines) is loaded, the device-independent DRI module will also be loaded. The DRI module will then call the graphics device-dependent module (containing both the 2D code and the 3D initialization code) to handle the resource allocation outlined below.

X Resource Allocation Initialization

Several global X resources need to be allocated to handle the client's 3D rendering requests. These resources include the frame buffer, texture memory, other ancillary buffers, display list space, and the SAREA.

Frame Buffer

There are several approaches to allocating buffers in the frame buffer: static, static with dynamic reallocation of the unused space, and fully dynamic. Static buffer allocation is the approach we are adopting in the sample implementation for several reasons that will be outlined below.

Static allocation. During initialization, the resources supported by the graphics device are statically allocated. For example, if the device supports front, back and depth buffers in the frame buffer, then the frame buffer is divided into four areas. The first three are equal in size to the visible display area and are used for the three buffers (front, back and depth). The remaining frame buffer space remains unallocated and can be used for hardware cursor, font and pixmap caches, textures, pbuffers, etc.

Texture Memory

Texture memory is shared among all 3D rendering clients. On some types of graphics devices, it can be shared with other buffers, provided that these other buffers can be "kicked out" of the memory. On other devices, there is dedicated texture memory, which might or might not be sharable with other resources.

Since memory is a limited resource, it would be best if we could provide a mechanism to limit the memory reserved for textures. However, the format of texture memory on certain graphics devices is organized differently (banked, tiled, etc.) than the simple linear addressing used for most frame buffers. Therefore, the "size" of texture memory is device-dependent. This complicates the issue of using a single number for the size of texture memory. Another complication is that once the X server reports that a texture will fit in the graphics device memory, it must continue to fit for the life of the client (*i.e.*, the total texture memory for a client can never get smaller). Therefore, at initialization time, the maximum texture size and total texture memory available will need to be determined by the device-dependent driver. This driver will also provide a mechanism to determine if a set of textures will fit into texture memory.

Other Ancillary Buffers

All buffers associated with a window (*e.g.*, back, depth, and GID) are preallocated by the static frame-buffer allocation. Pixmap, pbuffers and other ancillary buffers are allocated out of the memory left after this static allocation. During X server initialization, the size off-screen memory available for these buffers will be calculated by the device-dependent driver.

Note that pbuffers can be "kicked out" (at least the old style could), and so they don't require virtualization like pixmaps and potentially the new style pbuffers.

Display Lists

For graphics devices that support display lists, the display list memory can be managed in the same way as texture memory. Otherwise, display lists will be held in the client virtual-address space.

SAREA

The SAREA is shared between the clients, the X server, and the kernel. It contains four segments that need to be shared: a per-device global hardware lock, per-context information, per-drawable information, and saved device state information.

Since OpenGL clients can create an arbitrary number of GLXDrawables, the size of this segment will need to grow. As with the per-context segment, the size of this segment can be limited to a fixed maximum. Again, the X server is the only process that writes to this segment, and it must maintain a list of available drawable slots that needs to be allocated and initialized.

- *Saved device state segment.* Each GLXContext needs to save the graphics hardware context when another GLXContext has ownership of the graphics device. This information is fixed in size for each graphics device, but will be allocated as needed because it can be quite large. In addition, if the graphics device can read/write its state information via DMA, this segment will need to be locked down during the request.

Kernel Initialization

When the X server opens the kernel device driver, the kernel loads and initializes the driver. See the next section for more details of the kernel device driver.

Double Buffer Optimizations

There are typically three approaches to hardware double buffering:

- If the hardware support Auxillary Per Pixel Control for the given mode, then that is the preferred method for double buffer support. However, if the hardware doesn't support Auxillary Per Pixel Control, then the following combined opproach to Video Page Flipping and Bitblt Double Buffering is a potential optimization.

Kernel Driver Initialization

When the kernel device driver is opened by the X server, the device driver might not be loaded. If not, the module is loaded by kerneld and the initialization routine is called. In either case, the open routine is then called and finishes initializing the driver.

Kernel DMA Initialization

Since the 3D graphics device drivers use DMA to communicate with the graphics device, we need to initialize the kernel device driver that will handle these requests. The kernel, in response to this request from the X server, allocates the DMA buffers that will be made available to direct rendering clients.

Kernel Interrupt Handling Initialization

Interrupts are generated in a number of situations including when a DMA buffer has been processed by the graphics device. To acknowledge the interrupt, the driver must know which register to set and to what value to set it. This information could be hard coded into the driver, or possibly a generic interface might be able to be written. If this is possible, the X server must provide information to the kernel as to how to respond to interrupts from the graphics device.

Hardware Context Switching

Since the kernel device driver must be able to handle multiple 3D clients each with a different GLXContext, there must be a way to save and restore the hardware graphics context for each GLXContext when switching between them. Space for these contexts will need to be allocated when they are created byglXCreateContext(). If the client can use this hardware context (*e.g.*, for software fallbacks or window moves), this information might be stored in the SAREA.

Client DMA wait Queues

Each direct rendering context will require a DMA wait queue from which its DMA buffers can be dispatched. These wait queues are allocated by the X server when a new GLXContext is created (glXCreateContext()).

Client Initialization

This section examines what happens before the client enters steady state behaviour. The basic sequence for direct-rendering client initialization is that the GL/GLX library is loaded, queries to the X server are made (*e.g.*, to determine the visuals/FBConfigs available and if direct rendering can be used), drawables and GLXContexts are created, and finally a GLXContext is associated with a drawable. This sequence assumes that the X server has already initialized the kernel device driver and has pre-allocated any static buffers requested by the user at server startup (as described above).

Library Loading

When a client is loaded, the GL/GLX library will automatically be loaded by the operating system, but the graphics device-specific module cannot be loaded until after the X server has informed the DRI module which driver to load (see below). The DRI module might not be loaded until after a direct rendering GLXContext has been requested.

Client Configuration Queries

During client initialization code, several configuration queries are commonly made. GLX has queries for its version number and a list of supported extensions. These requests are made through the standard GLX protocol stream. Since the set of supported extensions is device-dependent, similar queries in the device-dependent driver interface (in the X server) are provided that can be called by device-independent code in GLX.

One of the required GLX queries from the client is for the list of supported extended visuals (and FBConfigs in GLX 1.3). The visuals define the types of colour and ancillary buffers that are available and are device-dependent. The X server must provide the list of supported visuals (and FBConfigs) via the standard protocol transport layer (*e.g.*, Unix domain or TCP/IP sockets). Again, similar interfaces in the device-dependent driver are provided that can be called by the device-independent code in GLX. All of this information is known at server initialization time (above).

Drawable Creation

The client chooses the visual (or FBConfig) it needs and creates a drawable using the selected visual. If the drawable is a window, then, since we use a static resource allocation approach, the buffers are already allocated, and no additional frame buffer allocations are necessary at this time. However, if a dynamic resource allocation approach is added in the future, the buffers requested will need to be allocated.

Not all buffers need to be pre-allocated. For example, accumulation buffers can be emulated in software and might not be pre-allocated. If they are not, then, when the extended visual or FBConfig is associated with the drawable, the client library will need to allocate the accumulation buffer. In GLX 1.3, this can happen withglXCreateWindow(). For earlier versions of GLX, this will happen when a context is made current (below).

Pixmaps and Buffers

GLXPixmaps are created from an ordinary X11 pixmap, which is then passed to glXCreatePixmap(). GLXPbuffers are created directly by a GLX command. Since we are using a static allocation scheme, we know what ancillary buffers need to be created for these drawables. In the initial SI, these will be handled by indirect rendering or software fallbacks.

GLXContext Creation

The client must also create at least one GLXContext. The last flag to glXCreateContext() is a flag to request direct rendering. The first GLXContext created can trigger the library to initialize the direct rendering interface for this client. Several steps are required to setup the DRI.

First, the DRI library is loaded and initialized in the client and X server. The DRI library establishes the private communication mechanism between the client and X server (the XFree86-GLX protocol). The X server sends the SAREA shared memory segment ID to the client via this protocol and the client attaches to it. Next, the X server sends the device-dependent client side 3D graphics device driver module name to client via the XFree86-GLX protocol, which is loaded and initialized in the client.

The X server calls the kernel module to create a new WaitQueue and hardware graphics context corresponding to the new GLXContext. Finally, the client opens and initializes the kernel driver (including a request for DMA buffers).

Making a GLXContext current

The last stage before entering the steady state behaviour occurs when a GLXContext is associated with a GLXDrawable by making the context "current". This must occur before any 3D rendering can begin. The first time a GLXDrawable is bound to a direct rendering GLXContext it is registered with the X server and any buffers not already allocated are now allocated. If the GLXDrawable is a window that has not been mapped yet, then the buffers associated with the window are initialized to size zero. When a window is mapped, space in the pre-allocated static buffers are initialized, or in the case of dynamic allocation, buffers are allocated from the available offscreen area (if possible).

Steady-state Analysis

The initial steady-state analysis presented here assumes that the client(s) and X server have been started and have established all necessary communication channels (*e.g.*, the X, GLX and XFree86-GLX protocol streams and the SAREA segment). In the following analysis, we will impose simplifying assumptions to help direct the analysis towards the main line rendering case. We will then relax our initial assumptions and describe increasingly general cases.

Processing Rendering Requests

In the simplest case, rendering commands can be sent to the graphics device by putting them in a DMA buffer. Once a DMA buffer is full and needs to be dispatched to the graphics device, the buffer can be handed immediately to the kernel via an ioctl.

The kernel then schedules the DMA command buffer to be sent to the graphics device. If the graphics device is not busy (or the DMA input queue is not full), it can be immediately sent to the graphics device. Otherwise, it is put on the WaitQueue for the current context.

In hardware that can only process a single DMA buffer at a time, when the DMA buffer has finished processing, an IRQ is generated by the graphics device and handled by the kernel driver. In hardware that has a DMA input FIFO, IRQs can be generated after each buffer, after the input FIFO is empty or (in certain hardware) when a low-water mark has been reached. For both types of hardware, the kernel device driver resets the IRQ and schedules the next DMA buffer(s).

A further optimization for graphics devices that have input FIFOs for DMA requests is that if the FIFO is not full, the DMA request could be initiated directly from client space.

Synchronization

GLX has commands to synchronize direct rendering with indirect rendering or with ordinary X11 operations. These include glFlush(), glFinish(), glXWaitGL() and glXWaitX() synchronization primitives. The kernel driver provides several ioctls to handle each of the synchronization cases. In the simplest case (glFlush()), any partially filled DMA buffer will be sent to the kernel.

Since these will eventually be processed by the hardware, the function call can return. WithglFinish(), in addition to sending any partially filled DMA buffer to the kernel, the kernel will block the client process until all outstanding DMA requests have been completely processed by the graphics device. glXWaitGL() can be implemented using glFlush(), glXWaitX() can be implemented with XSync().

Buffer Swaps

Buffers swaps can be initiated by glXSwapBuffers(). When a client issues this request, any partially filled DMA buffers are sent to the kernel and all outstanding DMA buffers are processed before the buffer swap can take place. All subsequent rendering commands are blocked until the buffer has been swapped, but the client is not blocked and can continue to fill DMA buffers and send them to the kernel.

If multiple threads are rendering to a GLXDrawable, it is the client's responsibility to synchronize the threads. In addition, the idea of the *current* buffer (*e.g.*, front or back) must be shared by all GLXContexts bound to a given drawable. The X double buffer extension must also agree.

Many image transfer operations are required in the client-side direct rendering library. Initially these will be software routines that read directly from the memory mapped graphics device buffers (*e.g.*, frame buffer and texture buffer). These are device-dependent operations since the format of the transfer might be different, though certain abstractions should be possible (*e.g.*, linear buffers).

An optimization is to allow the client to perform DMA directly to/from the client's address space. Some hardware has support for page table translation and paging. Other hardware will require the ability to lock down pages and have them placed contiguously in physical memory.

The X server will need to manage how the frame and other buffers are allocated at the highest level. The layout of these buffers is determined at X server initialization time.

Texture Management

Each GLXContext appears to own the texture memory. In the present case, there is no contention. In subsequent cases, hardware context switching will take care of texture swapping as well (see below).

For a single context, the image transfer operations described above provides the necessary interfaces to transfer textures and subtextures to/from texture memory.

Display List Management

Display lists initially will be handled from within the client's virtual address space. For graphics devices that supports display lists, they can be stored and managed the same as texture memory.

If there is hardware support for selection and feedback, the rendering commands are sent to the graphics pipeline, which returns the requested data to the client. The amount of data can be quite large and are usually delivered to a collection of locked-down pages via DMA. The kernel should provide a mechanism for locking down pages in the client address space to hold the DMA buffer. Queries are handled similarly to selection and feedback, but the data returned are usually much smaller. When a query is made, the hardware graphics context state has to be read. If the GLXContext does not currently own the graphics device, the state can be read from the saved device state segment in SAREA. Otherwise, the graphics pipeline is temporarily stalled, so that the state can be read from the graphics device.

GLX has a "pbuffer clobbered" event. This can only be generated as a result of reconfiguring a drawable or creating a new one. Since pbuffers will initially be handled by the software, no clobbered events will be generated. However, when they are accelerated, the X server will have to wrap the appropriate routine to determine when the event needs to be generated.

X server can Draw

Assume: X server can draw (*e.g.*, 2D rendering) into other windows, but does not move the 3D window. This is a common case and should be optimized if possible. The only significant different between this case and the previous case, is that we must now lock the hardware before accessing the graphics device directly directly from the client, X server or kernel space.

The goal is to minimize state transitions and potentially avoid a full hardware graphics context switch by allowing the X server to save and restore 3D state around its access for GUI acceleration. Access to graphics device must be locked, either implicitly or explicitly. Each component of the system requires the hardware lock at some point. For the X server, the hardware lock is required when drawing or modifying any state. It is requested around blocks of 2D rendering, minimizing the potential graphics hardware context switches.

In the 3D client, the hardware lock is required during the software fallbacks (all other graphics device accesses are handled through DMA buffers). The kernel also must request the lock when it needs to send DMA requests to the graphics device. The hardware lock is contained in the *Hardware lock segment* of the SAREA which can be accessed by all system components.

A two-tiered locking scheme is used to minimize the process and kernel context switches necessary to grant the lock. The most common case, where a lock is requested by the last process to hold the lock, does not require any context switches. See the accompanying locks.txt file for more information on two-tiered locking (available late February 1999).

Graphics Hardware Context Switching

In addition to locking the graphics device, a graphics hardware context switch between the client and the X server is required. One possible solution is to perform a full context switch by the kernel (see the "multiple contexts" section below for a full explanation of how a full graphics hardware context switch is handled). However, the X server is a special case since it knows exactly when a context switch is required and what state needs to be saved and restored.

For the X server, the graphics hardware context switch is required only (a) when directly accessing the graphics device and (b) when the access changes the state of the graphics device. When this occurs, the X server can save the graphics device state (either via a DMA request or by reading the registers directly) before it performs its rendering commands and restore the graphics device state after it finishes.

Three examples will help clarify the situations where this type of optimization can be useful. First, using a cfb/mi routine to draw a line only accesses the frame buffer and does not alter any graphics device state. Second, on many vendor's cards changing the position of the hardware cursor does not affect the graphics device state. Third, certain graphics devices have two completely separate pipelines for 2D and 3D commands. If no 2D and 3D state is shared, then they can proceed independently (but usually not simultaneously, so the hardware lock is still required).

X server can move or resize the single 3D window. When the X server moves or resizes the 3D window, the client needs to stop drawing long enough for the X server to change the window, and it also needs to request the new window location, size and clipping information. Current 3D graphics devices can draw using window relative coordinates, though the window offset might not be able to be updated asynchronously (*i.e.*, it might only be possible to update this information between DMA buffers). Since this is an infrequent operation, it should be designed to have minimal impact on the other, higher priority cases.

X Server Operations

On the X server side, when a window move is performed, several operations must occur. First, the DMA buffers currently being processed by the graphics device must be completely processed before proceeding since they might associated with the old window position (unless the graphics device allows asynchronous window updates). Next, the X server grabs the hardware lock and waits for the graphics device to become quiescent. It then issues a bitblt to move the window and all of its associated buffers. It updates the window location in all of the contexts associated with the window, and increments the "Window information changed" ID in the SAREA to notify all clients rendering to the window of the change. It can then release the hardware lock.

Since the graphics hardware context has been updated with the new window offset, any outstanding DMA buffers for the context associated with the moved window will have the new window offset and thus will render at the correct screen location. The situation is slightly more complicated with window resizes or changes to the clipping information.

When a window is resized or when the clipping information changes due to another window popping up on top of the 3D window, outstanding DMA buffers might draw outside of the new window (if the window was made smaller). If the graphics device supports clipping planes, then this information can be updated in the graphics hardware context between DMA buffers. However, for devices that only support clipping rectangles, the outstanding DMA requests cannot be altered with the new clipping rects.

To minimize this effect, the X server can:

- Flush the DMA buffers in all contexts' WaitQueues associated with the window,
- Wait for these DMA buffers to be processed by the graphics device. However, this does not completely solve the problem as there could be a partially filled DMA buffer in the client(s) rendering to the window (see below).

3D Client Operations

On the client side, during each rendering operation, the client checks to see if it has the most current window information. If it does, then it can proceed as normal. However, if the X server has changed the window location, size or clipping information, the client issues a XFree86-DRI protocol request to get the new information. See the accompanying XFree86-DRI.txt file for more information on the XFree86-DRI protocol implementation. This information will be mainly used for software fallbacks. Since there could be several outstanding requests in the partially filled "current" DMA buffer, the rendering commands already in this buffer might draw outside of the window. The simplest solution to this problem is to send an expose event to the windows that are affected.

This could be accomplished as follows:

- Send the partially filled DMA buffer to the kernel,
- Wait for it to be processed,
- Generate a list of screen-relative rectangles for the affected region,
- Send a request to the X server to generate an expose event in the windows that overlap with that region.

On graphics devices that do not allow the window offset to be updated between DMA buffers, the situation described above will also occur for window moves. The "generate expose events" solution also will be used to solve the problem. It is not known at this time if any graphics devices of this type exist.

Assume: There are now multiple 3D clients, each of which has their own GLXContext(s). As with the previous case, multiple GLXContexts are actively used in rendering, and this case can be handled the same as the previous one. This section examines what happens after exiting steady state behaviour via destroying a rendering surface or context, or via process termination. Process suspension and switching virtual consoles are special cases and are dealt with in this section.

Destroying a Drawing Surface

If the drawing surface is a window, it can be destroyed by the window manager. When this occurs, the X server must notify the direct rendering client that the window was destroyed. However, before the window can be removed, the X server must wait until all outstanding DMA buffer requests associated with the window have been completely processed in order to avoid rendering to the destroyed window after it has been removed. When the client tries to draw to the window again, it recognizes that the window is no longer valid and cleans up its internal state associated with the window (*e.g.*, any local ancillary buffer), and returns an error. GLX 1.3 uses glXDestroyWindow() to explicitly notify the system that the window is no longer associated with GLX, and that its resources should be freed.

Since there are limited context slots available in the per-context segment of SAREA, a GLXContext's resources can be freed by calling glXDestroyContext()when it is no longer needed. If the GLXContext is current to any thread, the context cannot be destroyed until it is no longer current. When this happens, the X server marks the GLXContext's per-context slot as free, frees the saved device state, and notifies the kernel that the WaitQueue can be freed.

Texture objects and display lists can be shared by multiple GLXContexts. When a context is destroyed in the share list, the reference count should be decremented. If the reference count of the texture objects and/or display lists is zero, they can be freed as well.

Process Finalization

When a process exits, its direct rendering resources

should be freed and returned to the X server. If the termination is expected, the resources associated with the process are freed. The kernel reclaims its DMA buffers from the client. The X server frees the GLXDrawables and GLXContexts associated with the client. In the process of freeing the GLXContexts, the X server notifies the kernel that it should free any WaitQueues associated with the GLXContexts it is freeing. The saved device state is freed. The reference count to the SAREA is decremented. Finally, any additional resources used by the GLX and XFree86-GLX protocol streams are freed.

Detecting the client death is the hardest part of unexpected process termination. Once detected, the resources are freed as in the graceful termination case outlined above. The kernel detects when a direct rendering client process dies since it has registered itself with the kernel exit procedure.

If the client does not hold the hardware lock, then it can proceed as in the graceful termination case. If the hardware lock is held, the lock is broken. The graphics device might be in an unusable state (*e.g.*, waiting for data during a texture upload), and might need to be reset. After reset, the graceful termination case can proceed.

Processes can suspend themselves via a signal that cannot be blocked, SIGSTOP. If the process holds the hardware lock during this time, the SIGSTOP signal must be delayed until the lock is freed. This can be handled in the kernel. As an initial approximation, the kernel can turn off SIGSTOP for all direct rendering clients.

XFree86 has the ability to switch to a different virtual console when the X server is running. This action causes the X server to draw to a copy of the frame buffer in the X server virtual address space. For direct rendering clients, this solution is not possible. A simple solution to use in the initial SI is to halt all direct access to the graphics device by grabbing the hardware lock.

In addition to switching virtual consoles, XFree86 can be started on multiple consoles (with different displays). Initially, only the first display will support direct rendering.

Future Enhancements

MMIO

This architecture has been designed with MMIO based 3D solution in mind, but the initial SI will be optimized for DMA based solutions. A more complete MMIO driven implementation can be added later.

Base support in the initial SI that will be useful for an MMIO-only solution is unprivileged mapping of MMIO regions and a fast two-tier lock. Additional optimizations that will be useful are virtualizing the hardware via a page fault mechanism and a mechanism for updating shared library pointers directly.

Device-specific Kernel Driver

Several optimizations (mentioned above) can be added by allowing a device-specific kernel driver to hook out certain functions in the generic kernel driver.

Other Enhancements

We should consider additional enhancements including:

- Multiple displays and multiple screens
- More complex buffer swapping (cushion buffering, swap every N retraces, synchronous window swapping)

Glossary

MMIO

Memory-Mapped Input-Output. In this document, we use the term MMIO to refer to operations that access a region of graphics card memory that has been memory-mapped into the virtual address space, or to operations that access graphics hardware registers via a memory-mapping of the registers into the virtual address space (in contrast to PIO).

Note that graphics hardware "registers" may actually be pseudo-registers that provide access to the hardware FIFO command queue.

PIO

Programmed Input-Output. In this document, we use the term PIO to refer specifically to operations that *must* use the Intel in and out instructions (or equivalent non-Intel instructions) to access the graphics hardware (in contrast to using memory-mapped graphics hardware registers, which allow for the use ofmov instructions).

MODULARIZATION

MODULAR SOFTWARE DESIGN

In order to produce programmes that are readable, reliable, and can be easily maintained or modified, one must use modular software design. This means that, instead of having a large collection of statements strung together in one partition of in-line code, we segment or divide the statements into logical groups called modules. Each module performs one or two tasks, then passes control to another module. By breaking up the code into "bite-sized chunks", so to speak, we are able to better control the flow of data and control. This is especially true in large software systems.

OVERVIEW OF MODULAR SOFTWARE DESIGN

We begin with several definitions (*Hint:* These may be useful to learn for a future exam) in support of a brief discussion of software design goals. We then progress to examples of code segmentation.

In the early days of computer programming, when people coded programmes in *machine code* (ones and zeroes), it was quite difficult to determine programme function and structure from looking at the code. Humans tend to look at problems solved on a computer in a linguistic sort of way, *i.e.*, expect some flow of control or data to be expressed in the programming language. Ones and zeros don't tell us much, and they certainly give little indication of programme structure or data/control flow.

Bibliography

Alan, C.: *Mobile Software Security*, London: Free Press, 1992.

Anderson, R.: *Security Engineering: A Guide to Building Dependable Distributed Systems, New York*, NY: John Wiley and Sons, 2001.

Barry, W.: *Software Security Economics*, London: Prentice Hall, 2003.

Bock, J.: *NET Security*, Berkeley, CA: Apress LP, 2002.

Brown, K.: *Programming Windows Security*, New York, NY: Addison Wesley Longman, 2000.

Curtin, M.: *Developing Trust: Online Privacy and Security*, Berkeley, CA: Apress LP, 2001.

Fogie, S.: *Windows .Net Server Security Handbook*, New York, NY: Prentice Hall PTR, 2002.

Gasser, M.: *Building a Secure Computer System*, New York, NY: Van Nostrand Reinhold, 1988.

Gollmann, D.: *Computer Security*, New York, NY: John Wiley & Sons, 2006.

Howard, M.: *Deadly Sins of Software Security*, New York, NY: McGraw-Hill Osborne Media, 2005.

Macchia, B.: *NET Framework Security*, New York, NY: Addison Wesley Longman, 2002.

Mouratidis, H.: *Integrating Security and Software Engineering: Advances and Future Vison. Hershey*, PA: Idea Group Publishing 2005.

Rubin, A. *The Whitehat Security Arsenal: Tackling the Threats. Reading*, MA: Addison-Wesley, 1999.

Schneier, B.: *Applied Cryptography: Protocols, Algorithms, and Source Code in C, Second Edition*, New York, NY: Wiley, John & Sons, 1995.

Seven, D.: *ASP.NET Security*, Birmingham, UK: Wrox Press, 2002.

Tom, D.: *Structured Analysis and System Security*, US: Yourdon Press, 2000.

Viega, J.: *Software Security*, New York, NY: McGraw-Hill Osborne Media, 2005.

William, A.: *Compilers and Computer Security*, New York: John Wiley & Sons Publication, 2001.

Index